Shino Centric Vision of Asia

Shino Centric Vision of Asia

Dr. Sanjay Singh
Ashutosh Kumar

PRASHANT PUBLISHING HOUSE
DELHI-110094

Published by :
Prashant Publishing House
C-34, 28 Foota Road, Gali-3,
West Karwal Nagar, Delhi-110094
Phone : 011-22963970, Mob. : 9810396373
e-mail.: prashantpublishinghouse@gmail.com

Shino Centric Vision of Asia

First Published 2018

ISBN 978-81-938012-5-3

PRINTED IN INDIA
Published by Mr. R.K. Jha M/s Prashant Publishing House and Published at H.S. Offset House Press, Delhi.

Contents

Preface

Sinocentrism refers to the ideology that China is the cultural center of the world. The Sinocentric model was not seriously challenged until contact with the European powers in the 18th and 19th century, in particular the First Opium War. This was partly due to the fact that sustained contact between the Chinese Empire and other empires of the pre-modern period was limited. By the mid 19th century, imperial China was well past its peak and was on the verge of collapse. In the late 19th century, the Sinocentric tributary state system in East Asia was superseded by the Westphalian multi-state system.

The Sinocentric model of political relations and Sinocentric belief in cultural superiority (especially against the West) came to an end in the 19th century. The Sinocentric ideology suffered a further blow when Imperial Japan, having undergone the Meiji Restoration, defeated China in the First Sino-Japanese War. As a result, China adopted the Westphalian system of equal independent states. In modern Chinese foreign policy, the People's Republic of China has stated repeatedly that it will never seek hegemony. However, some believe there are Chinese who still hold Sinocentric beliefs.

The Sinocentric system was a hierarchical model of international relations, dominated by China, that prevailed in East Asia until the weakening of the Qing Dynasty and the encroachment of European and Japanese imperialists in the second half of the nineteenth century. At the center of the system stood China, ruled by the dynasty that had presumably gained the Mandate of Heaven. This Celestial Empire (ShénzhM´u), distinguished by its Confucian codes of morality and propriety, regarded itself as the only civilization in the world; the emperor of China (huangdi) was regarded as the only legitimate emperor of the entire world (lands all under heaven or tianxia).

Surrounding countries such as Japan, Korea, and Vietnam were regarded as vassals of China, and relations between the Chinese Empire and these peoples were interpreted as tributary relationships under which these countries offered tribute to the emperor of China and received titles and privileges in return. Only China had an emperor, or huangdi , who was the "Son of Heaven" and had divine qualities; rulers of other countries were given lesser titles such as king or Wang . Peoples from states outside of China were regarded as "barbarians."

The cultural and economic centrality of China was recognized throughout Asia, and most countries submitted to the Sinocentric model, in order to enjoy the benefits of political recognition and trade with China. However, the attitudes of the various tributary nations towards China varied according to their political strength and physical distance from China. While they received many elements of culture—such as the Chinese written language, Confucianism, and Buddhism—from China, at various times tributary nations asserted their autonomy and attempted to deliberately exclude Chinese influence. Some people in countries such as South Korea, Japan, Indonesia and Vietnamstill harbor a historical resentment towards China.

Sinocentrism is also not synonymous with Chinese nationalism. The successive dynasties in China's history were Sinocentric in the sense that they regarded Chinese civilization to be universal in its reach and application. Chinese nationalism, in contrast, is a more modern concept focused primarily on the idea of a unified, cohesive, and powerful Chinese nation, as one of the nations of the world.

This is a reference book. All the matter is just compiled and edited in nature, taken from the various sources which are in public domain.

As the book addresses this crucial issue quite deftly, it is hoped that it would prove to be a source of great information for the reader.

—Editor

1

Introduction

Sinocentrism refers to the ideology that China is the cultural center of the world.

Overview and context

Depending on the historical context, sinocentrism can refer to either the ethnocentrism of the Han society and culture, or the modern concept of zhonghua minzu. The concept was popular among the Chinese elites up to the final demisme of Qing dynasty. The concept came to an end in 19th century and suffered several more blows in 20th century, and as a result is not as widely popular among Chinese people in the present day. In pre-modern times, it often took the form of viewing China as the most advanced civilization in the world, and external ethnic groups or foreign nations as being uncivilized to various degrees, a distinction known in Chinese as the Hua–Yi distinction.

SINOCENTRIC SYSTEM

The Sinocentric system was a hierarchical system of international relations that prevailed in East Asia before the adoption of the Westphalian system in modern times. Surrounding countries such as Japan (which cut off its vassal relationship with China during the Heian period, because it regarded itself as the superior culture), Korea, the Ryukyu Kingdom, and Vietnam were regarded as vassals of China and relations between the Chinese Empire and these peoples were interpreted as tributary relationships under which these countries offered tribute to the Emperor of China. Areas outside the Sinocentric influence were called *Huawaizhidi* , meaning *uncivilized lands.*

At the center of the system stood China, ruled by the dynasty that had gained the Mandate of Heaven . This *Celestial Dynasty* , distinguished by its Confucian codes of morality and propriety, regarded itself as the most prominent civilization in the world; the emperor of China (*Huangdi*) was regarded as the only legitimate Emperor of the entire world.

Under this scheme of international relations, only China had an emperor or *Huangdi* , who was the Son of Heaven ; other countries only had Kings or *Wang* . The Japanese use of the term Heavenly Emperor for the ruler of Japan was a subversion of this principle. Throughout history, the Koreans sometimes refer to their hierarchy as King, conforming with traditional Korean belief of Posterity of Heaven.

Identification of the heartland and the legitimacy of dynastic succession were both essential aspects of the system. Originally the center was synonymous with the Zhongyuan, an area that was expanded through invasion and conquest over many centuries. The dynastic succession was at times subject to radical changes in interpretation, such as the period of the Southern Song when the ruling dynasty lost the traditional heartland to the northern barbarians. Outside the center were several concentric circles. Local ethnic minorities were not regarded as 'foreign countries'. However, they were governed by their own leaders called *Local Commanders* , subject to recognition by the Emperor, and were exempt from the Chinese bureaucratic system.

Outside this circle were the tributary states which offered tribute to the emperor of China and over which China exercised suzerainty. Under the Ming Dynasty, when the tribute system entered its peak, these states were classified into a number of groups. The southeastern barbarians (category one) included some of the major states of East Asia and Southeast Asia, such as Korea, Japan, the Ryukyu Kingdom, Annam, Thailand, Champa, and Java. A second group of southeastern barbarians covered countries like Sulu, Malacca, and Sri Lanka. Many of these are independent states in modern times.

In addition, there were northern barbarians, northeastern barbarians, and two large categories of western barbarians (from Shanxi, west of Lanzhou, and modern-day Xinjiang), none of which have survived into modern times as separate or independent states.

The situation was complicated by the fact that some tributary states had their own tributaries. Laos was a tributary of Vietnam and the Ryûkyû Kingdom paid tribute to both China and Japan. Tsushima Island was also a tributary of Goryeo and Joseon dynasties of Korea.

Beyond the circle of tributary states were countries in a trading relationship with China. The Portuguese, for instance, were allowed to trade with China from leased territory in Macau but did not officially enter the tributary system. During the Qing dynasty's rule of Taiwan, some Qing officials have used the term *Huawaizhidi* to refer to Taiwan (Formosa), specifically to areas in Taiwan that have yet to be fully cultivated, developed and under the control of the Qing government.

While Sinocentrism tends to be identified as a politically inspired system of international relations, in fact it possessed an important economic aspect. The Sinocentric tribute and trade system provided Northeast and Southeast Asia with a political and economic framework for international trade. Countries wishing to trade with China were required to submit to a suzerain-vassal relationship with the Chinese sovereign. After investiture of the ruler in question, the missions were allowed to come to China to pay tribute to the Chinese emperor. In exchange, tributary missions were presented with return bestowals. Special licences were issued to merchants accompanying these missions to carry out trade. Trade was also permitted at land frontiers and specified ports. This sinocentric trade zone was based on the use of silver as a currency with prices set by reference to Chinese prices. The Sinocentric model was not seriously challenged until contact with the European powers in the 18th and 19th century, in particular the First Opium War. This was partly due to the fact that sustained contact between the Chinese Empire and other empires of the pre-modern period was limited. By the mid 19th century, imperial China was well past its peak and was on the verge of collapse.

In the late 19th century, the Sinocentric tributary state system in East Asia was superseded by the Westphalian multi-state system.

RESPONSES OF OTHER COUNTRIES

Within Asia, the cultural and economic centrality of China was recognized and most countries submitted to the Sinocentric model, if only to enjoy the benefits of a trading relationship. However, clear differences of nuance can be discerned in the responses of different countries.

Korea

The Korean peninsula was greatly influenced by its geographic and historic proximity to China. Until the era of the Three Kingdoms of Korea, Southern Korean states had been protected from Chinese invasions by militarily powerful Northern Korean states such as Goguryeo which ruled the northern region of Korean peninsula and Manchu. Goguryeo considered herself as an equally supreme state as China and adopted her own centric system to adjacent countries. Refusing to pay any tributes and continuing to conquer eastern territories of China altogether incurred a series of massive Chinese invasions of Goguryeo from 598 to 614, which ended disastrously and they mainly contributed to the fall of Chinese Sui dynasty in 618. Such numerous defeats of the Chinese raised the sense of ethnic superiority in Goguryeo and further expansions into the Chinese territories continued.

After Goguryeo finally collapsed by allied forces of Silla, one of the Three Kingdoms of Korea, and Tang dynasty in 668,

Silla, now being the sole ruler of Korean peninsula, more readily started the tribute system between Silla and Tang. However, such ties between two countries were greatly weakened after Silla's submission to Goryeo who claimed to succeed Goguryeo.

Goryeo's relationship with Chinese Song dynasty remained equal but close and very profitable bilateral trade propspered without the tribute system as Goryeo's ginseng and porcelain were highly priced in China whereas Chinese silks were somewhat popular in Goryeo. This peaceful relationship ended when Mongol invasions of Korea, as a part of a general campaign to conquer China and rest of Asia, occurred in 1231. After 30 years of fierce resistance, both Goryeo and Mongols finally sued for peace and became a dependency of the Mongol Yuan dynasty under Mongol influences of the Goryeo royal courts. Soon after the weakening of Yuan dynasty, Goryeo retook their lost territories from the Mongol Empire by military campaigns and regained her sovereign rights.

During the Joseon dynasty (1392–1910) period, however, they encouraged the entrenchment of Korean Confucian ideals and doctrines in Korean society and voluntarily entered herself into the Sinocentric system. After the Ming dynasty, which regarded itself as huá, cultured civilization was considered to have collapsed under the invasion of the Qing from Manchuria, who were considered barbarian in 1644. The Ming was thought of as the last true Sino culture.

The Sinocentrism in Joseon came to an end in the 19th century when the Korean Empire was proclaimed by Emperor Gojong. Ever since, Sinocentrism, known as Junghwa-sasang in Korea, has been regarded as an example of the imprudent and disdainful delusions of the Joseon dynasty.

This started with the simultaneous influx of European culture and the decline of the Qing dynasty in the early 19th century. It had been claimed by many historians and philosophers in Korea that the acceptance of Confucianism as a state ideology was the main contribution to military weakness and resultant external aggressions in the Joseon dynasty.

Vietnam

Vietnam (Annam) had an intimate but not always peaceful relationship with China. Vietnam was part of various Chinese dynasties and kingdoms for approximately 900 years before gaining independence in the 10th century. In subsequent centuries the Vietnamese drove out Chinese invaders on a number of occasions, to the extent that conflict with China may be seen as one of the main themes of Vietnamese history.

However, Vietnam was also heavily Sinicized, using Classical Chinese as its official literary language and adopting most aspects of Chinese culture, including the administrative system, architecture, philosophy, religion, literature of China, and even a general cultural outlook. Vietnam persistently identified itself in relation to China, regarding itself as the kingdom of the south as against China in the north, as seen in this line from a poem (in Classical Chinese) by General Lý Thý ng Ki t (1019–1105): *Nam Qu c sõn hà Nam Đ cý.* which means "Over mountains and rivers of the South reigns the Emperor of the South".

In adopting Chinese customs, the Vietnamese court also began to adopt Sinocentric world view during the expanding Le and Nguyen dynasties. "Trung Qu c" was used as a name for Vietnam by Emperor Gia Long in 1805. It was said "Hán di h u h n" ("*the Vietnamese and the barbarians must have clear borders*") by the Gia Long Emperor (Nguy n Phúc Ánh) when differentiating between Khmer and Vietnamese. Minh Mang implemented an acculturation integration policy directed at minority non-Vietnamese peoples. Thanh nhân was used to refer to ethnic Chinese by the Vietnamese while Vietnamese called themselves as Hán nhân in Vietnam during the 1800s under Nguy n rule. Cambodia was regularly called *Cao Man Qu c* , the country of "upper barbarians". In 1815, Gia Long claimed 13 countries as Vietnamese vassals, including Luang Prabang, Vientiane, Burma, Tran Ninh in eastern Laos, and two countries called "Th y Xá Qu c" and "H a Xá Qu c", which were actually Malayo-Polynesian Jarai tribes living between Vietnam and Cambodia. Mirroring the Chinese model, the Vietnamese court attempted to regulate the presentation of tribute to the Vietnamese court, participation in New Year and emperor's birthday ceremonies, as well as the travel routes and size of tributary missions.

Vietnamese Nguyen Emperor Minh M ng sinicized ethnic minorities such as Cambodians, claimed the legacy of Confucianism and China's Han dynasty for Vietnam, and used the term Han people (Hán nhân) to refer to the Vietnamese. Minh Mang declared that "We must hope that their barbarian habits will be subconsciously dissipated, and that they will daily become more infected by Han [Sino-Vietnamese] customs." These policies were directed at the Khmer and hill tribes. The Nguyen lord Nguyen Phuc Chu had referred to Vietnamese as "Han people" in 1712 when differentiating between Vietnamese and Chams. The Nguyen Lords established after 1790. It was said "Hán di h u h n" ("*the Vietnamese and the barbarians must have clear borders*") by the Gia Long Emperor (Nguy n Phúc Ánh) when differentiating between Khmer and Vietnamese. Minh Mang implemented an acculturation integration policy directed at minority non-Vietnamese peoples. Thanh nhân or Đý ng nhân were used to refer to ethnic Chinese by the Vietnamese while Vietnamese called themselves as Hán dân and Hán nhân in Vietnam during the 1800s under Nguy n rule. Chinese style clothing was forced on Vietnamese people by the Nguy n. Trousers have been adopted by White H'mong. The trousers replaced the traditional skirts of the females of the White Hmong. The tunics and trouser clothing of the Han Chinese on the Ming tradition was worn by the Vietnamese. The Ao Dai was created when tucks which were close fitting and compact were added in the 1920s to this Chinese style. Trousers and tunics on the Chinese pattern in 1774 were ordered by the Nguy n Phúc Khoát to replace the sarong type Vietnamese clothing. The Chinese clothing in the form of trousers and tunic were mandated by the Vietnamese Nguyen government. It was up to the 1920s in Vietnam's north area in isolated hamlets wear skirts were worn. The Chinese Ming dynasty, Tang dynasty, and Han dynasty clothing was ordered to be adopted by Vietnamese military and bureaucrats by the Nguyen Lord Nguy n Phúc Khoát (Nguyen The Tong).

Chinese influence waned as French influence rose in the 19th century, and Vietnam eventually abolished the Imperial examinations and stopped using Chinese characters and the related Ch Nôm script in the 20th century.

Japan

In Japan, an ambivalent tone was set early in its relationship with China. Shôtoku Taishi (574–622), Prince Regent of Japan, is famous for having sent a letter to the Emperor of China starting with the words: "The Emperor of the land where the sun rises sends a letter to the Emperor of the land where the sun sets to ask if you are healthy". This is commonly believed as the origin of the name Nihon (source of the sun), although the actual characters for Nihon were not used.

Not long after this, however, Japan remodeled its entire state and administrative apparatus on the Chinese system under the Taika Reform (645), the beginning of a period of Chinese influence on many aspects of Japanese culture until Imperial Japanese embassies to China were abolished in 894.

In 1401, during the Muromachi period, the *shôgun* Yoshimitsu restarted the lapsed tribute system (1401), describing himself in a letter to the Chinese Emperor as "Your subject, the King of Japan" while also a subject of the Japanese Emperor. The benefit of the tribute system was a profitable trade. The trade was called *Kangô* trade (means tally trade) and Japanese products were traded for Chinese goods. This relationship ended with the last envoy of Japanese monk Sakugen Shûryô in 1551, which was Ashikaga Yoshiteru's era, including a 20 years suspension by Ashikaga Yoshimochi. These embassies were sent to China on 19 occasions.

In the years 1592–1593 Toyotomi Hideyoshi, having unified Japan, tried to conquer Korea as a prelude to conquering Ming China. The attempt to conquer "all under heaven" (itself a sinocentric concept identifying China as "the world") ended in failure.

Japanese responses to Sinocentric concepts have not always been so straightforward. The Mongol invasions in 1274 and 1281 evoked a national consciousness of the role of the kamikaze in defeating the enemy. Less than fifty years later (1339–43), Kitabatake Chikafusa wrote the Jinnô Shôtôki ('Chronicle of the Direct Descent of the Divine Sovereigns') emphasizing the divine descent of the imperial line. The Jinnô Shôtôki provided a Shinto view of history stressing the divine nature of Japan and its spiritual supremacy over China and India.

In the Tokugawa era, the study of Kokugaku arose as an attempt to reconstruct and recover the authentic native roots of Japanese culture, particularly Shintoism, excluding later elements borrowed from China. In 1657, Tokugawa Mitsukuni established the Mito School, which was charged with writing a history of Japan as a perfect exemplar of a "nation" under Confucian thought, with the emphasis on unified rule by the emperors and respect for the imperial court and Shinto deities.

In an ironic affirmation of the spirit of Sinocentrism, claims were even heard that the Japanese, not the Chinese, were the legitimate heirs of Chinese culture. In the early Edo period, neo-Confucianist Yamaga Sokô asserted that Japan was superior to China in Confucian terms and more deserving of the name "*Chûgoku*". Other scholars picked this up, notably Aizawa Seishisai, an adherent of the Mito School, in his political tract *Shinron* (New Theses) in 1825.

As a country that had much to gain by eclipsing Chinese power in East Asia, Japan in more recent times has perhaps been most ardent in identifying and demolishing what it dismissively calls *Chûka shisô*, loosely meaning 'Zhonghua ideology'. One manifestation of Japanese resistance to Sinocentrism was the insistence for many years in the early 20th century on using the name *Shina* for China, based on the Western word 'China', in preference to *Chûgoku* (Central Country) advocated by the Chinese themselves.

Another example is the claim, heard among some commentators on China, that general depopulation and the incursion of races from the north during the period of the Three Kingdoms led to the virtual replacement of the original Chinese race by non-Chinese. The general thrust of this kind of claim is to deny the continuity of a "pure" Chinese civilization and discredit modern Chinese claims and appeals to their ancient history.

Burma

Unlike East Asian states, which communicated in written Chinese, Burma used a different written language in its communications with China. While China consistently regarded Burma as a vassal, Burma records indicate that Burma considered itself as China's equal. Under the Burmese interpretation, Burma was the "younger brother" and China was the "elder brother".

Thailand

Thailand was always subordinate to China as a vassal or a tributary state from the Sui dynasty until the Taiping Rebellion of the late Qing dynasty in the mid-19th century. The Sukhothai Kingdom established official relations with the Yuan dynasty during the reign of King Ram Khamhaeng. Wei Yuan, the 19th century Chinese scholar, considered Thailand to be the strongest and most loyal of China's Southeast Asian tributaries, citing the time when Thailand offered to directly attack Japan to divert the Japanese in their planned invasions of Korea and the Asian mainland, as well as other acts of loyalty to the Ming dynasty. Thailand was welcoming and open to Chinese immigrants, who dominated commerce and trade, and achieved high positions in the government.

Sri Lanka

Sri Lanka was a tributary state of the Ming dynasty for many years. It was during this period that Chinese hegemony was most impactful on Sri Lankan politics and commerce. Sri

Lankan kings provided tribute to Chinese emperors in the form of pearls, Filigreed gold, gems, ivory and valances. Notably, Parakramabahu VI of Kotte established relations with China in 1416 to appease the Yongle Emperor and to win his support and integrate himself with the Chinese emperor following the Ming–Kotte War. Sri Lanka, like Japan, was considered *yuanyi* (remote foreigners) in *jueyu* (remote territories) under the Imperial Chinese Tributary System.

Europe

The best-known official encounter between Sinocentrism and Europeans was the celebrated Macartney Embassy of 1792-93, which sought to establish a permanent British presence in Peking and open up trade relations. The rebuff of the Chinese Emperor to the British overtures and the British refusal to kowtow to the Emperor of China has passed into legend in Chinese folk culture. In response to the British request to recognise Macartney as ambassador, the Emperor wrote:

The Celestial Empire, ruling all within the four seas, simply concentrates on carrying out the affairs of Government properly... We have never valued ingenious articles, nor do we have the slightest need of your country's manufactures, therefore O King, as regards to your request to send someone to remain at the capital, which it is not in harmony with the regulations of the Celestial Empire - we also feel very much that it is of no advantage to your country. Half a century later, Western Europe forced their way in via the Opium War. Led by the British, one western power after another imposed unequal treaties on China, including provisions of extraterritoriality that excluded Europeans from the application of local laws.

CULTURAL SINOCENTRISM

In a cultural sense, Sinocentrism refers to the tendency to regard Chinese culture as more ancient than or superior to other cultures. This often involves regarding neighboring countries as mere cultural offshoots of China. The geographical dimension of traditional Sinocentrism was highlighted by Chinese reactions to the publication of the first world map by the Jesuit Matteo Ricci (1552–1610):

Lately Matteo Ricci utilized some false teachings to fool people, and scholars unanimously believed him...take for example the position of China on the map. He puts it not in the center but slightly to the West and inclined to the north. This is altogether far from the truth, for China should be in the center of the world, which we can prove by the single fact that we can see the North Star resting at the zenith of the heaven at midnight. How can China be treated like a small unimportant country, and placed slightly to the north as in this map?

In the late Ming and Qing periods, there was a belief in Chinese cultural circles that knowledge entering China from the West had already existed in China in the past. This trend of thought was known in Chinese as *xi xue zhong yuan* (literally 'Western knowledge has Chinese origins'). *Xi xue zhong yuan* was a way to not only enhance the prestige of ancient Chinese learning, but also that of Western learning and make it more acceptable to the Chinese at that time. One notable example was *Chouren Zhuan* ("Biographies of Astronomers and Mathematicians"), a book by the Qing dynasty scholar Ruan Yuan which adopted the point of view that some Western sciences had an ancient Chinese origin. Scholars such as Ruan saw astronomy and mathematics as a key to deciphering the ancient classics. Until the Sino-Japanese War, some intellectuals believed that some of the sciences and technologies coming from Europe were actually lost ancient Chinese knowledge. The Chinese have abandoned the idea of *xi xue zhong yuan* since the early 20th century.

Indigenous criticism

Followers of Chinese Buddhism were some of the fiercest critics of Sinocentrism, since they followed a religion that originated in India, rather than China. The monk Zhiyi (538–597 CE) referred to China as "Zhendan", rather than by any epithet that emphasized China's centrality, such as Zhongguo or Zhonghua. "Zhendan" originated in a transcription of the Sanskrit word for China, "Cinisthana". Another anti-Sinocentric name for China used by Buddhists was "country of the Han" or "region of the Han". Reacting to an insecurity against China's indigenous religions of Confucianism and Daoism, Buddhists in China asserted that Confucius and Yan Hui were avatars of the Buddha, and that Confucianism was merely an offshoot of Buddhism. When Buddhists had influence in the court, such as in the minority-led Tang and Yuan dynasties, they successfully persuaded the imperial governments to censor and destroy Daoist texts. They especially hated the *Huahujing*, which made the opposite argument to that of the Buddhists; that Buddhism was an offshoot of Daoism.

Liu Ji, one of the key advisors of Zhu Yuanzhang (the founder of the Ming dynasty) generally supported the idea that while the Chinese and the non-Chinese are different, they are actually equal. Liu was therefore arguing against the idea that the Chinese were and are superior to other people.

Culturally, one of the most famous attacks on Sinocentrism and its associated beliefs was made by the author Lu Xun in *The True Story of Ah Q*, satirizing the ridiculous way in which the protagonist claimed "spiritual victories" despite being humiliated and defeated.

Today

The Sinocentric model of political relations and Sinocentric belief in cultural superiority (especially against the West) came to an end in the 19th century. The Sinocentric ideology suffered a further blow when Imperial Japan, having undergone the Meiji Restoration, defeated China in the First Sino-Japanese War. As a result, China adopted the Westphalian system of equal independent states. In modern Chinese foreign policy, the People's Republic of China has stated repeatedly that it will never seek hegemony. However, some believe there are Chinese who still hold Sinocentric beliefs.

Related concepts

Successive peoples from the north, such as the Xianbei, Jurchens, Mongols, or Manchus, were quite ready to place themselves at the center of the model, although they were not always successful. The Xianbei empires during the Southern and Northern dynasties, for example, regarded the Han Chinese regimes of southern China as "barbarians" because they refused to submit to Xianbei rule. Similarly, the Manchu Qing dynasty regarded the initial wave of European incursions during the mid-19th century as "barbarians".

Sinocentrism is also not synonymous with Chinese nationalism. The successive dynasties in China's history were Sinocentric in the sense that they regarded Chinese civilization to be universal in its reach and application. Chinese nationalism, in contrast, is a more modern concept focused primarily on the idea of a unified, cohesive, and powerful Chinese nation, as one of the nations of the world.

2

The Sinocentric System

The Sinocentric system was a hierarchical model of international relations, dominated by China, that prevailed in East Asia until the weakening of the Qing Dynasty and the encroachment of European and Japanese imperialists in the second half of the nineteenth century. At the center of the system stood China, ruled by the dynasty that had presumably gained the Mandate of Heaven. This *Celestial Empire* (*ShénzhM´u*), distinguished by its Confucian codes of morality and propriety, regarded itself as the only civilization in the world; the emperor of China *(huangdi)* was regarded as the only legitimate emperor of the entire world (lands *all under heaven* or *tianxia*).

Surrounding countries such as Japan, Korea, and Vietnam were regarded as vassals of China, and relations between the Chinese Empire and these peoples were interpreted as tributary relationships under which these countries offered tribute to the emperor of China and received titles and privileges in return. Only China had an emperor, or *huangdi* , who was the "Son of Heaven" and had divine qualities; rulers of other countries were given lesser titles such as king or *Wang* . Peoples from states outside of China were regarded as "barbarians."

Identification of the heartland and the legitimacy of dynastic succession were both essential aspects of Sinocentrism. Originally the center was synonymous with the North China Plain, an area that was expanded through invasion and conquest over many centuries. Sinocentrism, unlike Han chauvinism, did not necessarily have a racial basis in Han Chinese ethnicity. Successive peoples from the north, such as the Xianbei, Jurchens, and Manchus, took their place at the center with varying degrees of success. The Xianbei empires during the Southern and Northern Dynasties, for example, regarded the Han Chinese regimes of southern China as "barbarians" because they refused to submit to Xianbei rule. Similarly, the Manchu Qing Dynasty regarded the initial wave of European incursions during the mid-nineteenth century as "barbarians."

Outside the center were several concentric circles. Local ethnic minorities were not regarded as foreign countries, but were governed by their own leaders, subject to recognition by the emperor, and were exempt from the Chinese bureaucratic system. Outside this circle were the tributary states, which offered tribute to the emperor of China and over which China exercised suzerainty.

Under the Ming Dynasty, when the tribute system entered its peak, these states were classified into a number of groups. The southeastern barbarians included some of the major states of East Asia and Southeast Asia, such as Korea, Japan, the Ryk´kyk´ Kingdom, Annam, Cambodia, Vietnam, Siam, Champa, and Java. A second group of southeastern barbarians was made up of countries such as Sulu, Malacca, and Sri Lanka, many of which are modern independent states. In addition, there were northern barbarians, northeastern barbarians, and two large categories of western barbarians (from Shanxi, west of Lanzhou, and modern-day Xinjiang), none of which have survived into modern times as separate states. The system was complicated by the fact that some tributary states had their own tributaries. Laos was a tributary of Vietnam and the Ryk´kyk´ Kingdom paid tribute to both China and Japan.

Beyond the circle of tributary states were countries which were involved in a trading relationship with China. The Portuguese, for instance, were allowed to trade with China from leased territory in Macau but did not officially enter the tributary system.

While Sinocentrism is usually identified as a political structure of international relationships, it possessed an important economic aspect. The Sinocentric tribute system provided Northeast and Southeast Asia with a political and economic framework for international trade. Countries wishing to trade with China were required to submit to a suzerain-vassal relationship with the Chinese sovereign. After official investiture of a national ruler, missions from that country were allowed to come to China to pay tribute to the Chinese emperor. In exchange, tributary missions were presented with return bestowals, such as gifts, titles and official tokens of recognition. Special trading licenses were issued to merchants accompanying these missions to China, and trade was also permitted at land frontiers and specified ports. This Sinocentric trade was based on the use of silver as a currency, with prices set by reference to Chinese prices.

ATTITUDES OF TRIBUTARY COUNTRIES

The cultural and economic centrality of China was recognized throughout Asia, and most countries submitted to the Sinocentric model, in order to enjoy the benefits of political recognition and trade with China. However, the attitudes of the various tributary nations towards China varied according to their political strength and physical distance from China. While they received many elements of culture—such as the Chinese written language, Confucianism, and Buddhism—from China, at various times tributary nations asserted their autonomy and attempted to deliberately exclude Chinese influence. Some people in countries such as South Korea, Japan, Indonesia and Vietnamstill harbor a historical resentment towards China.

Japan

The Japanese are described in China's Book of Han, completed in 111 C.E. and covering the period of Chinese history from 206 B.C.E. to 25 C.E., as "the people of Wo, who are divided into more than one hundred states, and who bring tribute at fixed intervals." The Book of Later Han, composed in the fifth century by Fan Ye and covering the Eastern Han period from 25 to 220 C.E., relates that in 57 C.E. the "state of Nu in Wo" sent emissaries to the Later Han court, and received a gold seal from the emperor.

In the seventh century, however, Shotoku Taishi (574-622), prince regent of Japan, antagonized the emperor of China by sending him a letter starting with the words: "The emperor of the land where the sun rises sends a letter to the emperor of the land where the sun sets to ask if you are healthy?". Soon after this, under the Taika Reforms, the Japanese court reformed its administrative apparatus and system of land distribution to resemble the Chinese system, initiating a prolonged period of Chinese influence on all aspects of Japanese culture.

Japan experienced alternating periods of interaction with China, during which Chinese influence on Japanese culture was strong, and periods of isolation during which a heightened sense of Japanese cultural superiority developed. In the late thirteenth century, when two attempted Mongol invasions were thwarted with the help of typhoons, called "*kamikaze*" (divine wind), Japan acquired a strong national identity.

The *JinnM′shM′tM′ki* ("Chronicle of the Direct Descent of the Divine Sovereigns"), written between 1339 and 1343 by Kitabatake Chikafusa, emphasized the divine descent of the imperial line and Japan's spiritual supremacy over China and India. In 1401, during the Muromachi period, the shogun Yoshimitsu, desiring trade with China, restarted the lapsed tribute system, and Japan again received cultural influences from China, such as Zen Buddhism.

During the Tokugawa era, centering on the study of *kokugaku* ("native studies"), a movement emerged to reconstruct and recover the authentic native roots of Japanese culture, particularly Shinto, and exclude later elements borrowed from China. During the early Edo period, neo-Confucianist Yamaga

Soko asserted that Japan was superior to China in its application of Confucianism and more deserving of the name "*Chk´goku.* Later scholars picked up this theme, notably Aizawa Seishisai in his political tract *Shinron* ("New Theses") in 1825.

As a rival of China for political and economic dominance of East Asia, Japan has remained critical of Sinocentrism, and more recently, of Chinese nationalism (*zhonghua minzu*). Japanese scholars have been active crticis of what they term *Chk´ka shisM´*, loosely meaning "*zhonghua* ideology." After Japan defeated China in the First (1894-1895) and Second Sino-Japanese Wars (1937-1945), the Japanese insisted for several decades on using the name *Shina* for China, based on the Western word "China," in preference to the name *Chk´goku* ("Central Country") advocated by the Chinese themselves. One of the enduring perceptions among Sinologists in Japan is that general depopulation and the incursion of races from the north during the period of the Three Kingdoms led to the virtual replacement of the original Chinese race by non-Chinese.

Vietnam

Vietnam was under Chinese rule for approximately one thousand years before gaining independence in the tenth century. In subsequent centuries the Vietnamese drove out Chinese invaders on a number of occasions, and conflict with China may be seen as one of the major themes of Vietnamese history. However, Vietnam was heavily Sinicized, using Classical Chinese as its official literary language and adopting most aspects of Chinese culture, including the administrative system, architecture, philosophy, religion, and literature of China.

Vietnam persistently identified itself as the "Kingdom of the South" in relation to China in the north, as represented in this line from a poem (in Chinese) by General Lý Th ng Ki t (1019–1105): "*Over mountains and rivers of the South reigns the Emperor of the South.* "

The name "Vi t" itself is cognate with Yue, referring to peoples of Southern China who were largely conquered by the North under the Qin Dynasty. The Vietnamese are considered as belonging to the Yue. The current name of the country, Vietnam, is derived from Nam Vi t, meaning *Southern Yue,* the name of a post-Qin kingdom covering southern China and northern Vietnam. The Chinese, who were unwilling to recognize Vietnam as a successor to the Southern Yue state, altered this to Vi t Nam.

Myanmar

Unlike East Asian states, which communicated in written Chinese, Myanmar (Burma) used a different written language in communicationwith China. While China consistently regarded Myanmar as a vassal, Myanma records indicate that Myanmar considered itself as China's equal. The Burmese interpreted Myanmar as the "younger brother" and China as the "elder brother."

Europe

The most famous official encounter between Sinocentrism and the self-assertion of Europeans was the celebrated Macartney Embassy(the Macartney Mission) of 1792–1793, which sought to establish a permanent British presence in Peking and open up trade relations. The account of the Chinese emperor's rejection of British overtures and the British refusal to *kowtow* to the emperor of China became legend. In response to the British request that the Chinese recognize Macartney as ambassador, the emperor wrote:

The Celestial Empire, ruling all within the four seas, simply concentrates on carrying out the affairs of Government properly...We have never valued ingenious articles, nor do we have the slightest need of your country's manufactures, therefore O King, as regards to your request to send someone to remain at the capital, which it is not in harmony with the regulations of the Celestial Empire—we also feel very much that it is of no advantage to your country.

In 1842 the British defeated Chinese forces in the First Opium War, and the Qing authorities signed the Treaty of Nanjing, agreeing to open several low-tariff trade ports to

Britain, yielding Hong Kong to Britain, and allowing British missionaries to work in China.

Following the British, one Western power after another imposed "unequal treaties" on China, including provisions of extraterritoriality that excluded Europeans from the jurisdiction of local laws. The defeat of the Imperial army by a small Anglo-French military force during the Second Opium War, coupled with the flight (and subsequent death) of the emperor and the burning of the Summer Palace was a shocking blow to the once powerful Qing Dynasty. The Treaty of Tianjin (1858), ratified in October 1860, guaranteed freedom of religionin China, legalized the opium trade and granted England additional territory in Kowloon.

These two treaties marked the end of Sinocentrism as a system of international relations in Asia, and the adoption of the Westphaliansystem in which every state was regarded as a sovereign nation on an equal legal standing with all other states.

CULTURAL SINOCENTRISM

A traditional Sinocentric attitude was evident in the Chinese reaction when the Jesuit Matteo Ricci published the first map of the world in Chinese in 1584, at the request of the governor of Chao-k'ing, who printed copies for his friends:

Lately Matteo Ricci utilized some false teachings to fool people, and scholars unanimously believed him...take for example the position of China on the map. He puts it not in the center but slightly to the West and inclined to the north. This is altogether far from the truth, for China should be in the center of the world, which we can prove by the single fact that we can see the North Star resting at the zenith of the heaven at midnight. How can China be treated like a small unimportant country, and placed slightly to the north as in this map?

In a cultural sense, Sinocentrism refers to a tendency to regard neighboring countries as mere cultural offshoots of China.

A Sinocentric view of East Asia is justified to some extent by the fact that China has a far longer history than neighboring countries, and that these countries borrowed heavily from the Chinese model at an early stage in their historical development. However, cultural Sinocentrism often goes beyond this to deny the uniqueness or validity of surrounding countries as separate cultures. Some Sinocentrists claim that aspects of Chinese culture which were borrowed from the West actually go back to Chinese antecedents, or that some aspects of Western culture were originally borrowed from China.

In a famous attack on Sinocentrism and its associated beliefs, *The True Story of Ah Q* (1921) by Lu Xun, the character Ah Q is a satirized representation of the national character, believing that everyone different from himself is inferior and a barbarian, and interpreting humiliations and defeats as "spiritual victories."

Chinese nationalism

Sinocentrism is not synonymous with Chinese nationalism (*zhonghua minzu*). The successive dynasties of China were Sinocentric in the sense that they regarded Chinese civilization to be universal in its reach and application. Chinese nationalism, in contrast, is a more modern concept focused primarily on the idea of a unified, cohesive, and powerful Chinese nation, as one of the nations of the world.

The period between the end of the First Opium War and the founding of the People's Republic of China in 1949 was known as the "century of humiliation" (*bainian guochi*). The capitulation of the Qin government to foreign powers, the unequal treaties, and the Treaty of Versailles, which gave Chinese territory taken by the Germans during World War I to the Japanese, roused public sentiment against the government and led eventually to the rise of the Nationalist Party and then the Chinese Communist Party.

Faced with the challenge of uniting an ethnically diverse population, whose citizens traditionally identified themselves with local kinship associations, into a strong independent nation, the Chinese Communist Party began to promote the concept of "Chinese nationalism" (*zhonghua minzu*). China was represented as a nation which had originated in a "cradle of civilization" in the Yellow River Basin and had interacted with various ethnic groups over the centuries, yet retained its cultural character.

Archeological evidence of the multiple origins of the Chinese people was suppressed. The concept was reinforced by appeals to anti-imperialist sentiments in the context of the Cold War, political rivalry with the Soviet Union during the 1960s, and the involvement of the United States and its European allies in wars in Vietnam and Korea.

A SINO-CENTRIC ASIA UNLIKELY

How Asia's geopolitical landscape will evolve over the next couple of decades is not easy to foresee. But it is apparent that an increasingly assertive China is unwittingly reinforcing America's role in Asia as the implicit guarantor of security and stability.

There are at least four possible Asian security scenarios. The first is the rise of a Sino-centric Asia, as desired by Beijing. China seeks a multipolar world but a unipolar Asia. By contrast, the United States desires a unipolar world but a multipolar Asia. A second scenario is of the U.S. remaining Asia's principal security anchor.

A third possibility is the emergence of a constellation of Asian states with common interests working together to ensure both power equilibrium and an Asia that is not unipolar. A fourth scenario is of an Asia characterized by several resurgent powers, including Japan, India, Vietnam, Indonesia and a reunified Korea.

Of the four scenarios, the least unlikely is the first one. China's neighbors increasingly are uneasy about its growing power and assertiveness. While Beijing aspires to shape a Sino-centric Asia, its actions hardly make it a credible candidate for

Asian leadership. Brute power cannot buy leadership. After all, leadership can come not from untrammeled power, but from other states' consent or tacit acceptance. If leadership could be built on brute force, schoolyard bullies would be class presidents.

In any event, China's power may be vast and rapidly growing, yet it lacks the power of compulsion. In other words, China does not have the capability to militarily rout or compel any rival, let alone enforce its will on Asia.

As China seeks to translate its economic clout into major geopolitical advantage in Asia, a nation that once boasted of "having friends everywhere" finds that its accumulating power might inspire awe, but its actions are spurring new concerns and fears.

Which states will accept China as Asia's leader? Six decades of ruthless repression has failed to win China acceptance even in Tibet and Xinjiang, as the Tibetan and Uighur revolts of 2008 and 2009 attested.

Leadership involves much more than the possession of enormous economic and military power. It demands the power of ideas that can galvanize others. Such power also serves as the moral veneer to the assertiveness often involved in the pursuit of any particular cause.

The Cold War, for example, was won by the U.S. and its allies not so much by military means as by spreading the ideas of political freedom and market capitalism to other regions that, in the words of strategic thinker Stanley A. Weiss, "helped suck the lifeblood out of communism's global appeal," making it incapable of meeting the widespread yearning for a better and more-open life.

China has shown itself good at assertive promotion of national interests and in playing classical balance-of-power geopolitics. But to assume the mantle of leadership in Asia by displacing the U.S., it must do more than just pursue its own interests or contain potential peer rivals. The overly assertive policies and actions of a next-door rising power make Asian states look to a distant protector. With its defense spending having grown almost twice as fast as its GDP, China is now beginning to take the gloves off, confident that it has acquired the necessary muscle.

This has been exemplified by several developments — from China's inclusion of the South China Sea in its "core" national interests on a par with Taiwan and Tibet to its efforts to present the Yellow Sea as its virtually exclusive military-operation zone.

Add to the picture large-scale naval exercises in recent months first off Japan's Ryukyu Islands, then in the South China Sea and most recently in the Yellow Sea.

China also has increasingly questioned India's sovereignty over Arunachal Pradesh, the northeastern Indian state that Beijing calls "Southern Tibet" and claims largely as its own. Indian defense officials have reported a rising number of Chinese military incursions across the 4,057-km Himalayan border.

Through its actions, China indeed has proven a diplomatic boon for Washington in strengthening and expanding U.S. security arrangements in Asia. South Korea has tightened its military alliance with the U.S., Japan has backing away from an effort to get the U.S. to move its marine air base out of Okinawa, and India, Vietnam, Indonesia and the Philippines, among others, have drawn closer to the U.S.

In terms of power-projection force capabilities or the range of military bases and security allies in Asia, no power or combination of powers is likely to match the U.S. in the next quarter of a century.

While America's continued central role in Asia is safe, the long-term viability of its security arrangements boils down to one word: Credibility. The credibility of America's security assurances to allies and partners, and its readiness to stand by them when it comes to the crunch, will determine the strength and size of its security-alliance system in Asia in the years ahead. The third and fourth scenarios can unfold even if the U.S. remains the principal security anchor for Asia. A number of Asian countries have already started building mutually beneficial security cooperation on a bilateral basis, thereby laying the groundwork for a potential web of interlocking strategic partnerships.

A combination of the second and third scenarios is a plausible prospect, but it demands forward-looking policies in Washington, Tokyo, New Delhi, Seoul, Hanoi, Jakarta, Canberra and elsewhere. A constellation of Asian states linked by strategic cooperation and with close ties to the U.S. has become critical to help institute power stability in Asia. America's continued role as a credible guarantor of Asian security, however, is a function not of its military strength but political will in Washington.

3

AIIB and Beijing's Vision for a Sinocentric World Order

Across Asia and beyond, the weight of China's rise is being increasingly felt, shifting the orbits of regional actors and placing the global economy on an increasingly eastern tilt. At the moment, China is the largest economy in the world by purchasing power parity (PPP), the second largest in overall measurements of gross domestic product (GDP), and is soon to become home to the world's largest population centre. Despite this enormous economic footprint, it is only in recent years that China has sought to become a stakeholder in global governance. This process received a renewed sense of impetus with the arrival of Xi Jinping.

Since he rose to power in November 2012, President Xi's policy initiatives have revealed a grand vision of what China should be. In the last few years he has wasted little time in seeking to transform Beijing into a key hub within the international system. This can be seen as China's response to the threat posed by climate change, increased commitments to United Nations peacekeeping forces and in hosting international sports competitions. China under Xi is a nation increasingly engaged with the world, while also seeking to advance its own interests. This is also evident in the sphere of international finance and institutions, where China has launched a wave of initiatives, which are both challenging and complementing the post-1945 Bretton Woods system. Perhaps the best example of this is the creation of the Asian Infrastructure Investment Bank (AIIB).

China as an institutional founder?

There are few areas where China has been more dissatisfied with its position globally than in the world of international finance. In spite of its attempts to reform, the International Monetary Fund and World Bank remain dominated by the United States and Europe, much to the chagrin of developing states, and especially China. Within the Asia-Pacific, the Asian Development Bank (ADB), which has a similar structure to the World Bank and has been in existence since 1966, has been the leading financial institution. There, the majority stakes are controlled by Japan and the United States, with the ABD president always being from Japan. The AIIB is the first international institution in which China is the principal state and major stakeholder. It represents a step forward for Beijing to secure a new position for itself within the international order but outside the contemporary post-1945 system.

According to current estimates, Beijing will be the dominant state in the institution with a 30.34% shareholding in the AIIB, whose initial capital worth is estimated at $50 billion, but is expected to increase to $100 billion by year's end. As a founding member, China has the largest share of the vote for the institution at 26.06%, and the AIIB will be headquartered not in New York or Geneva but in Beijing.

The president of the World Bank, Jim Yong Kim, along with leading figures within the ABD, has welcomed the creation of a China-led financial institution. However, behind the diplomatic discourse, there exist real concerns in Washington and Tokyo surrounding the dilution of Bretton Woods institutions such as the World Bank. Further to this point, there are concerns regarding the overall transparency of the AIIB vis-à-vis environmental and corruption standards. These concerns play into wider fears relating to the increased economic influence of China and the relative decline of US influence in the Asia-Pacific region.

These concerns in Tokyo and Washington have been exacerbated by the international reaction to the AIIB. On the diplomatic front, the AIIB represents a major endorsement of China as an institutional founder and a major strategic misstep by the United States. Over twenty-one Asian nations, including India, a nascent US partner in Asia, have signed up to become founding members. Even in the face of diplomatic opposition from the United States, key regional and international allies such as the United Kingdom, South Korea and Australia have signed up to join the AIIB, bringing the total number of states to 57.

ONE BELT, ONE ROAD

The AIIB represents an individual component of a far larger strategy that would see China at the heart of a network of economic institutions and initiatives, returning Beijing to its historic role as the Middle Kingdom. Announced in October 2013, during President Xi's trip to Central Asia, the One Belt, One Road program represents the grand strategic initiative under which Chinese foreign policy is operating. The AIIB, as part of this program, is designed to fund the infrastructure investment that will allow the two components of One Belt, One road to come to fruition.

The land-based Silk Road Economic Belt will seek to reconnect China with the markets of Europe, the Middle East and Central Asia. Particularly within Central Asia, Beijing is investing heavily in dilapidated Soviet infrastructure, and in spite of cordial ties on the surface, One Belt, One Road has the potential to undermine Russia's traditional influence in the region.

Meanwhile, the oceangoing Maritime Silk Road will connect Chinese trade with the nations of South East Asia and the Indian Ocean. Within India, the strategic inroads made by China in Sri Lanka have not gone unnoticed. The 4, 000 acre Hambantota Port would service rising Chinese naval ambitions while also becoming a nexus for Chinese exports into the Indian sub-continent and the lucrative Persian Gulf.

Above all else the Maritime Silk Road would build upon the growing strategic relationship with African states. Even as the United States is boosting its counter-terrorism cooperation with Kenya and Ethiopia to combat Al-Shabaab, the new African Union headquarters in Addis Ababa was financed entirely by Beijing, symbolizing China's growing presence on the continent.

CHINA AS THE MIDDLE KINGDOM

If successful, Beijing estimates the One Belt, One Road initiative will add an additional USD $2.5 trillion to China's trade in the next decade. In context that is more than the total value of China's exports in 2013, thereby cementing its status as the world's largest trading nation. This gives China unprecedented financial influence that has not been seen internationally for over two hundred years.

Through One Belt, One Road, Beijing is seeking to re-establish an identity that first emerged during the Han Dynasty of China as the Middle Kingdom; the centre of international trade, commerce and civilization. Thus, it is no small coincidence that states in Central Asia, the Indian subcontinent and the Middle East are the subject of such focus from Beijing. Under the Ming and Qing Dynasties, China was a major trading partner and a sought-after destination for all these regions. The attempt by Beijing to create a contemporary successor to the Silk Road of antiquity draws heavily on China's trading past.

The Asian Infrastructure Investment Bank, designed to mirror western institutions, is indicative of China's increasing financial influence in the Asia-Pacific and beyond. The question now is whether China will seek to capitalize on this economic power and turn it into political leverage.

JAPAN, CHINA AND THE US SPAR IN THE EAST AND SOUTH CHINA SEAS

In China's international relations, 2010 has been the Year of Zero Sum. On a series of issues, the Western and Asian democracies have demanded that China accept policies that advance their agendas while sacrificing Chinese interests.

On one level this is the inevitable outcome of the Obama administration's repositioning of its foreign policy away from the amoral, Westphalian-style horse-trading of national interests of the Bush administration. The United States has now established global adherence to norms championed by the U.S. and its allies—non-proliferation, global warming, democracy, freedom of information, freedom of navigation, open currency markets, and human rights—as the cornerstone of its foreign policy. This does not necessarily mean, of course, that the U.S. holds itself or its allies to such high standards in these realms, notably global warming, but even human rights and freedom of navigation. By accident or design, the insistence on these norms as the driver behind global policy leaves nations, particularly an authoritarian government like the PRC, which is outside of the U.S.-defined mainstream on virtually all of these issues, little scope to define and advance its competing national interests as legitimate.

It also has the effect of isolating China from Western and some Asian democracies—a useful geopolitical windfall for nations anxious about China's rising economic, military, and geopolitical clout and the global gains Beijing made in the first decade of the 20th century while the Bush administration was asleep at the Asian switch.

In 2010, China was called upon to sacrifice its own interests on virtually all of the Obama administration's key initiatives. On global warming, China was asked to abandon the highly favourable terms of the Kyoto Protocol for an economically costly cap on its greenhouse gas emissions even as the U.S. failed to commit to any significant controls. On the issue of Google, the Obama administration (which counts a significant number of Google insiders in its tech-policy brain trust) called on China to tear down that Great Firewall, something that China considers an unacceptable political risk.

On Iran, China was pressed to put its energy security and alliance with Iran at risk in order to join the U.S.-led crusade against Iran's nuclear ambitions. On North Korea, China was told to abandon its useful buffer, the DPRK, and join a chorus of condemnation over the sinking of the Cheonan that would shift the focus toward the reunification of the peninsula under the aegis of the United States and the ROK. On currency, the U.S. has demanded that China substantially appreciate its currency with the anticipated result of reducing its exports so the United States can try to find a way out of its economic difficulties.

Not only did the PRC resist American pressures on each of these fronts, but it also summoned up the energy to protest the awarding of the Nobel Peace Prize to Liu Xiaobo, the imprisoned activist, whose organization receives funding from the U.S. government's National Endowment for Democracy, whose candidacy was championed by the PRC's arch-foe, the Dalai Lama, and whose platform calls for replacing the PRC's political monopoly with a multi-party democracy.

And then there is the issue of the island groups. The East and South China Seas are home to dozens of contested islands, atolls, and sandbars, virtually all of them uninhabited. China has asserted sovereignty over virtually the entire area, including two potential flashpoints: the Paracels, which it seized from South Vietnam in 1974, and the Diaoyutai/Senkaku Islands, which have been firmly under Japanese sovereignty (with an interlude of American occupation) since 1895.

The situation in the Paracels—and China's patent unwillingness to negotiate on the question of the islands while asserting effective sovereignty through measures like organizing Paracels tourism—has provoked the strong resentment of the Vietnamese government. For several years, Vietnam has attempted to cultivate a relationship with the United States and involve Washington on its side in the dispute. This was a temptation the U.S. resisted until this year, when Secretary of State Hillary Clinton declared that the United States had "a national interest" in freedom of navigation in the South China Sea.

This statement was understood as an overt attempt to multilateralize the issue. It was also, therefore, a direct challenge to China, which was asked once again to sacrifice its interests, specifically the advantages of its preferred negotiation strategy: fully leveraging its regional clout by negotiating bilaterally with its smaller Asian neighbours without the complication of placating the ASEAN group as a whole or coping with the intrusive presence of the United States.

The most recent event in China's *annus horribilus* is the dust-up over the Diaoyutai/Senkaku Islands. In this case, the United States may have actually been trying to chart a middle way, but saw its policy blown out of the water by strident Japanese and Chinese nationalism.

A standoff between a Chinese fishing trawler and two Japanese Coast Guard vessels on September 7 off the Diaoyutai/Senkaku Islands led to the Japanese detention of Captain Zhan Qixiong and the provocative assertion that his case would be adjudicated under Japanese domestic law, rather than resolved through quiet diplomacy between Tokyo and Beijing.

On any given day, hundreds of Chinese boats fish within Japan's proclaimed Economic Exclusion Zone (EEZ); a few boats, including apparently Captain Zhan's, don't scruple to cross the line demarcating Japan's territorial waters to fish close to the uninhabited islands.

News reports suggest that Zhan was something of a hothead. All it took was a Japanese over-reaction to make him a national hero. Japan's hawkish minister Maehara Seiji can take a lion's share of the credit or blame for blowing up the incident. The Asahi newspaper reported the timeline as follows: Maehara was still Minister of Land, Infrastructure, Transport and Tourism – in charge of the Coast Guard – at the time of the incident.

Immediately after the trawler collided with Japan Coast Guard vessels on Sept 7, Maehara called Coast Guard Commandant Suzuki Hisayasu and told him, "The captain of the Chinese fishing boat must be arrested."

Maehara also called Chief Cabinet Secretary Sengoku Yoshito and told him, "It is better to persist resolutely against China."

At first, China responded calmly.

Reflecting back on that time, a Chinese government source said, "By sticking to a calm response, China was trying to encourage Japan to release the captain on its own accord."

But Maehara refused to back down.

He told close aides: "The prime minister's office was hesitant so I had to make the decision to arrest the captain. There was no mistake in the handling of the matter."

Maehara was appointed foreign minister on September 21, days after his aggressive intervention in the incident.

It is rather ironic that Japan would demand diplomatic engagement of China in the South China Sea while simultaneously foreswearing it over the Daioyutai/Senkaku Islands. More important, the Diaoyutai/Senkaku story is not simply a matter of Japan standing up to the big Chinese bully.

By distance, geography, and history Taiwan has the best claim on the Diaoyutai Islands (which are a mere 170 km from Taiwan and separated from Okinawa by 410 km and a deep undersea trench), which Japan acquired during the course of imperial skullduggery involving the seizure of Okinawa in 1872.

With its display of undersea terrain, Google Earth provides an interesting perspective on these tiny islands just north of Taiwan, at 25°44'30.48" N 123°28'21.39"E, and separated from Japan's Ryukyu Islands by the Okinawa Trough which, Wikipedia tells us, "marks the edge of the continental shelf of the East China Sea".

Taipei responded to the incident by vociferously advancing its interest. President Ma Ying-jeou, who has played the Diaoyutai card throughout his entire political career, dispatched 12 Coast Guard vessels to shield a boat of Taiwanese activists that made a symbolic approach within 19 miles of the island on September 15. The Japanese Coast Guard warned them off. Taiwanese media reported:

On several occasions the Kan En No. 99," which means "Showing Grace" in the Chinese language, was just two meters from being rammed by Japan's patrol ships.

Taking into consideration the aggressiveness of the Japanese Coast Guard, it is easy to understand how frustration, fear, and anger might have combined with poor seamanship and bullheadedness to produce Captain Zhan's collision. After Captain Zhan's detention was extended, with indictment in a Japanese court apparently imminent, China moved aggressively both in the public and official spheres. Cancelling scheduled negotiations with Japan over undersea oil and gas deposits in the vicinity of Diaoyutai, it also canceled bilateral talks on airline flights and told Chinese travel agencies not to accept applications for tour groups to visit Japan – scuppering two initiatives that Maehara had championed as tourism minister.

China also allegedly cut off exports of rare earth oxides to Japan and the government detained four Japanese employees of Fujita in Shijiazhuang, capital of North China's Hebei province, on charges of espionage-related activity, apparently in retaliation. Three of the men were subsequently released, and the fourth was returned after a period of detention that roughly matched Captain Zhan's. Judging from the Asahi article, Prime Minister Kan was not pleased that his term had begun with a major diplomatic dust-up courtesy of Maehara and his patron, Democratic Party of Japan (DPJ) secretary general Okada Katsuya. Okada and Maehara are the two most powerful proponents of a strong US alliance within the DPJ, whose platform has emphasized accommodation with Japan's Asian neighbours. As exchanges with China became more heated, Maehara recklessly upped the ante by pulling in the United States.

At the time of the crisis, it was well-known to Japan that the Obama administration had little interest in supporting Japanese assertions of sovereignty over the Senkaku Islands.

In August 2010, *The Japan Times* reported:

The Obama administration has decided not to state explicitly that the Senkaku Islands, which are under Japan's control but claimed by China, are subject to the Japan-U.S. security treaty, in a shift from the position of George W. Bush, sources said Monday.

Although the U.S. government has not officially changed its stance that the Japan-U.S. pact applies to the uninhabited East China Sea islets, known in China as the Diaoyu isles, the shift from making a direct reference to them could become a source of concern for Tokyo as it addresses moves by Beijing, the sources said. Taiwan also claims the islets.

The administration of Barack Obama has already notified Japan of the change in policy, but Tokyo may have to take countermeasures in light of China's increasing activities in the East China Sea, according to the sources.

Whether Foreign Minister Maehara's hard line one month later in September was provoked by the perceived need for Japan to stand up to China—or whether it was an affront calculated to force an unenthusiastic Obama administration to side with Japan on the Senkakus—remains to be determined.

After Maehara met with Secretary of State Hillary Clinton in New York, AFP reported:

"According to the Japanese minister, Clinton said that the Senkakus ... are subject to Article 5 of the bilateral security treaty, which authorizes the US to protect Japan in the event of an armed attack 'in the territories under the administration of Japan'," the report said.

Whatever was said in private, publicly the State Department did not inject itself in the controversy by explicitly extending the US security umbrella over the Senkakus. According to the AFP report, State Department spokesperson Philip Crowley limited himself to the observation that the Senkaku issue was "complicated".

It appears that Maehara abused the secretary of state's confidence by making public her sensitive and probably strongly caveated assurances of US support for Japan, in order to secure U.S. military backing for Japan's claim to Diaoyutai/Senkakus, and for his aggressive move in ordering the arrest and prosecution of the Chinese captain.

Hopeful overreach continued with the Japanese press reporting that Defence Secretary Robert Gates and Admiral Mike Mullen, chairman of the U.S. joint chiefs of staff, had, in the words of the Japanese public-service broadcaster NHK, "indicated that the US security agreement with Japan covers the Senkaku Islands."

"Indicated" is much too strong a word.

The actual transcript of the Department of Defence briefing was long on waffling and offered no explicit commitment:

Q Chinese Premier Wen in New York on Tuesday threatened action against Japan if it didn't return the captain of the ship. I'm wondering, does the US security umbrella extend to the Senkakus – the Senkaku islands?

ADM MULLEN: I think we're watching those – that tension very, very carefully, and certainly our commitment to the region remains. And, you know, we're hopeful that the political and diplomatic efforts would reduce that tension specifically, and haven't seen anything that would, I guess, raise the alarm levels higher than that. And obviously we're very, very strongly in support of, you know, our ally in that region, Japan.

Q And second -

SEC GATES: And we'll – and we would fulfil our alliance responsibilities.

In follow-on questions at the September 24 press briefing, the US State Department cited remarks by Jeffrey Bader, chairman of the National Security Council that the dispute was a matter between China and Japan.

Further awkward parsing was pre-empted as Prime Minister Kan cut the legs out from under Maehara and Okada in the best circular firing squad tradition of the hapless DPJ by agreeing to Zhan's release. The two hawks are striving to disguise their embarrassment with escalating anti-Chinese bluster.

At a time that China was saying that the case of Captain Zhan was "basically over ", Maehara told the Japanese media that China's demand for an apology demonstrated its "undemocratic nature". He also made the provocative statement that China might be preparing to violate an agreement with Japan not to drill unilaterally for oil and gas in contested portions of the East China Sea.

Despite Japan's humiliating retreat from its initial aggressive posture, the U.S. nevertheless received a propaganda windfall. Any threat, real or imputed, that China will deploy its military, economic, and financial clout to advance its interests in the East and South China Seas, strengthens the desire of China's neighbours for a closer US alliance, or so U.S. Asia strategists believe.

Doyle McManus, the Washington correspondent of the Los Angeles Times, delivered the conventional US wisdom:

Because of China's truculence, US relations with Japan, Korea and Vietnam have almost never been better.

Actually, the root cause of friction in East Asia in 2010 is the Obama administration's determination to "return to Asia", most evident in the planned series of U.S.-ROK and U.S.-Japan joint military exercises in China's backyard, and the encouragement this has given to anxious nations to pursue confrontations with China they might otherwise avoid. Certainly this has emboldened Japan, Korea, and Vietnam to confront the Chinese dragon.

It was Japanese, not Chinese, truculence that dictated the decision made at the cabinet level to arrest and try Zhan after the collision near Diaoyutai/Senkaku. This comes at a time of Vietnamese efforts to engage the United States as a counterweight to China, particularly over the nagging question of the Hoang Sa/Paracel/Xisha Islands in the South China Seas, which China seized from South Vietnam after a bloody encounter in 1974.

The issue gained heightened visibility with the report that China "formally declared to the United States that the South China Sea is a core interest", implying to Western observers that China regarded the fate of the uninhabited islands and their associated oil and gas deposits as an existential issue presumably worthy of the attention of the People's Liberation Army. In keeping with the theme of dubious, thinly sourced news reports with a Japanese link, however, this news item derived, virtually in its entirety, from a brief report filed by Kyodo News Service's Washington Bureau on July 3, that the Chinese had stated this position to James Steinberg and Jeffrey Bader when they were in Beijing in March 2010.

The report is anonymously sourced from somebody who was apparently not directly involved in the meetings — it states that the Chinese position was "presumably" conveyed by State Councilor Dai Bingguo. It is also interesting that this scoop was leaked to a Japanese news office in Washington; none of the plugged-in American news organizations got the story at that time (the only apparent corroboration is a statement in a July 2010 story by John Pomfret that Dai Bingguo had made the South China Sea a core interest in representation to Hillary Clinton during a "tense exchange" in May; and, as far as can be seen, Steinberg and Bader have not been asked to confirm the report.

It would appear noteworthy that the Chinese saw fit to announce this position to the only party they are attempting to exclude from the South China Sea dispute, the United States, while not conveying it to Vietnam, the Philippines, Malaysia, Brunei, or Indonesia, the interlocutors with whom it is trying to impose a series of bilateral negotiations. The United States is now apparently happy to spread the "core interests" meme, at least in private conversations between U.S. government officials and American reporters, although its accuracy and context have yet to be made part of the public record.

China has never officially confirmed or denied the story. Within China, there is skepticism that the Chinese government made any statement claiming South China Sea core interest. As far as the public record goes, China remains committed to freedom of navigation in the South China Sea, the Declaration on the Conduct of Parties in the South China Sea (a standstill agreement negotiated with ASEAN in 2002), and negotiated settlements over disputed islands. Yet the fact remains that such statements remain exclusively in the realm of US journalism.

It is possible, of course, that the phrase "core interest" came up in the context of the continual criss-crossing of the South China Sea by the two US Navy surveillance vessels *Impeccable* and *Victory*.

The US Navy exploits a loophole in the Law of the Sea Convention allowing free transit through a nation's exclusive economic zone in order to monitor and map the area near China's strategic submarine base on Hainan Island. As such, U.S. efforts to undercut China's nuclear deterrent—and improve U.S. prospects of intercepting and destroying China's southern submarine fleet in case of a confrontation over Taiwan—could be construed as a matter of China's "core interest" that the Chinese government might want to raise with American diplomats.

In any case, as publicly defined by the United States, China's "core interest" in the South China Sea is a matter of sandbars, not submarines, and this has prompted the U.S. to inject itself in the South China Sea disputes as the champion of the Association of Southeast Asian Nations members, especially Vietnam, against Chinese territorial overreach. The "core interest" story has been a public relations gold mine for the United States as China has watched in dismay and frustration as several ASEAN nations led by Vietnam and Singapore lined up with the United States to push for internationalizing the dispute. However, the welter of islets and rocks presents a nearly intractable problem even if all the concerned parties desire a friendly solution. Even in the unlikely event that the ASEAN countries were to maintain a united front against

China with US encouragement, it is unlikely that China will surrender its claims in an adversarial venue.

Benign neglect—in PRC terms, a policy of postponing thorny territorial issues while negotiating joint development of resources in disputed areas—has served the South China Sea pretty well over the last three decades and would probably be the best way to handle the problem in the future. A universal commitment to free passage through the vital waterways of the archipelago – a principle already accepted by all parties to the myriad territorial, fishing, and undersea resource disputes – is probably worth the price of tacit acknowledgement of the less than ideal status quo.

U.S. pressure on China in the South China Sea was quickly joined by Japan. In July, Okada was already pressing the South China Sea issue at the ASEAN Regional Forum. In a deliberate echo of Clinton's July 23 statement injecting the US "national interest" into the South China Sea matter, Okada involved Japan:

Foreign Minister Katsuya Okada on Tuesday expressed his concern over territorial disputes in the South China Sea mainly between China and Southeast Asian nations, saying the instability in the area could hamper Japan's trade and pose a threat to regional peace. "The instability deriving from differing views on territorial issues between China and ASEAN nations could undermine peace in Asia," Okada told a press conference. "We should get rid of such a destabilizing factor as soon as possible."

Given the realities of the situation, the eagerness of the U.S. and Japan to work through the Western press to turn the South China Sea issue into a regional crisis is worth noting.

A September 22 Wall Street Journal piece, entitled "US, ASEAN to Push Back Against China," offered what it sold as a privileged preview of the ASEAN-US joint statement blockbuster:

On Friday, Mr. Obama and the Asean leaders will issue a joint statement in which Washington has proposed text reaffirming the importance of freedom of navigation in the South China Sea, according to the Associated Press.

It said the statement would oppose the "use or threat of force by any claimant attempting to enforce disputed claims in the South China Sea."

The wording is significant – and provocative for China – because it mirrors that of a speech by US Secretary of State Hillary Clinton at another Asean meeting in Hanoi in July.

Japan's NHK obtained a copy of the same draft (bear in mind that Japan was not party to the agreement and not the most likely conduit for a leak). Headline writers throughout the world ran leads like "US backs ASEAN stand against use of force in Spratlys. "

However, the actual text of the joint statement said nothing about disputes in the South China Sea. Apparently, the edifice of US-ASEAN solidarity was not strong enough to withstand a strong, disapproving shove administered publicly by China's Foreign Ministry on September 21 and undoubtedly through numerous private channels.

Having missed the boat on the joint announcement, the *Wall Street Journal*compounded its problems in an untimely encomium celebrating collective Japanese and ASEAN backbone vis-à-vis China:

Japan – the main US ally in the region – is leading the way in confronting China, taking an unusually firm line in a dispute over a collision between a Chinese fishing trawler and two Japanese Coast Guard ships near disputed islands in the East China Sea two weeks ago.

Evidence of the backlash – and its effect on China – is apparent in the current dispute between Beijing and Tokyo over the ship collision near the disputed islands called Diaoyu in China and Senkaku in Japan. Japan has released the trawler and the 14 crew, but continues to detain the ship's captain.

China has summoned Japan's ambassador six times and suspended high-level government exchanges. Mr. Wen, China's premier, personally demanded the captain's release on Tuesday. Yet Tokyo has stood firm, apparently gambling that Beijing doesn't want to damage commercial relations or provoke the kind of anti-Japanese violence that almost spiraled out of control during a similar row in 2005.

"Clinton's stand in Hanoi may have contributed to Japan's demonstration of more backbone than most of us give it credit for having in its current territorial confrontation with China," said Mark Borthwick, director of the United States Asia Pacific Council at the East-West Centre in Washington.

Four days later, Japan folded and returned Captain Zhan.

The unambiguous victory for China makes it hard to give credence to assertions that China's foreign policy is out of control and driven by weakness, arrogance, runaway PLA hotheads, or cadet Politburo members recklessly burnishing their nationalistic credentials in the run-up to China's generational leadership change, due in 2012. Nevertheless, John Pomfret did his best to spin a clear-cut diplomatic victory for Beijing as evidence of China's foreign policy dysfunction and Japanese determination:

The increasingly bitter dispute between China and Japan over a small group of islands in the Pacific is heightening concerns in capitals across the globe over who controls China's foreign policy.

A new generation of officials in the military, key government ministries and state-owned companies has begun to define how China deals with the rest of the world. Emboldened by China's economic expansion, these officials are taking advantage of a weakened leadership at the top of the Communist Party to assert their interests in ways that would have been impossible even a decade ago.

It used to be that Chinese officials complained about the Byzantine decision-making process in the United States. Today, from Washington to Tokyo, the talk is about how difficult it is to contend with the explosion of special interests shaping China's worldview.

The fine lines between spin, self-delusion, and lazy disregard for geopolitical realities seem to be blurring, at least in the foreign affairs quadrant of the Western media.

USA Today pitched in, graciously ignoring Maehara's role in intentionally escalating the confrontation, with a story under the headline, "China's Aggressive Posture Stuns Japan, Experts". McClatchy, at least, indulged in honest sour grapes resentment: "Is a rising China getting too big for its britches?"

The simplest explanation of China's response was that China's elites and public were largely united in their anger at Japan's deliberate high-handedness over the issue of Captain Zhan and fishing rights in the vicinity of Diaoyutai; and the Chinese leadership recognized that any sign of weakness on Diaoyutai might encourage Vietnamese moves on the Paracels with U.S. and Japanese backing.

In Japan, the DPJ government, attempting to deal with the political fallout stemming from its retreat, continues to emphasize its absolute sovereignty over the islands and is reportedly mulling the stationing of a permanent garrison "near" Diaoyutai/Senkaku, presumably on Ishigaki Island, about one hundred miles from Diaoyutai, the nearest major inhabited island and the place where Captain Zhan was detained.

At the September 29 press conference of China's Ministry of Foreign Affairs, Japan was called on to "adopt concrete actions to eliminate the negative effect on China-Japan relations brought by the incident and make practical efforts to mend bilateral relations."

It is not clear what practical efforts China expects, or what Japan can be realistically expected to do in order to reassure Beijing that Tokyo is no longer interested in filling the role of one of America's front-line assets on China's borders.

Asia Times reported in early October that China, which sees no sign that Japan genuinely regrets inflaming the Diaoyutai/Senkaku situation, indicated at an ASEAN get-together in Hanoi that it is not quite ready to consider the issue resolved after all:

Chinese Defence Minister Liang Guanglie's decision to lecture Japan's Defence Minister Kitazawa Toshimi about how the incident near the disputed Diaoyu Islands between the Chinese fishing trawler and the Japanese Coast Guard demonstrated that Japan still does a poor job of handling sensitive issues affecting both countries, and is proof of a lasting chill. Liang wanted to remind Japan that Japan needs to resolve these and other matters in a way that ensures that China's approval will be forthcoming.... This lecture was taking place just as China was issuing a terse announcement about its new maritime enforcement policies. Sun Zhihui, director of the State Oceanic Administration revealed that China intends "to strengthen patrols and supervision in order to protect the country's maritime rights and interests".

At the same time, Chinese Premier Wen Jiabao at a meeting in Brussels informed Japanese Prime Minister Kan Naoto that China had no plans to relinquish its claim to the Diaoyu Islands (called Senkaku by Japan) which the Chinese have always depicted as "an inherent part of the Chinese territory".

"The Diaoyu Islands have been Chinese territory since ancient times," Wen told Kan.

At the same meeting, China rather slyly implied to the United States that its beef was with Tokyo, not Washington (and perhaps rewarded the Obama administration for its equivocal support of Maehara on the issue of Senkaku sovereignty).

The PRC extended to Defence Secretary Gates a longed-for invitation to visit Beijing and printed a picture in state media of Gates and Liang solemnly clasping hands in Hanoi under the heading *Gates to visit China, defence ties normalize.*

Recently, Beijing has been ramping up the rhetoric on the Diaoyutai/Senkaku Islands, seemingly in order to highlight Tokyo's discomfiture and sense of abandonment on the issue—"beating a dog in the water", in Chinese parlance.

Japan has responded in kind. Geopolitical considerations aside, both sides see domestic political advantage in escalating the war of words. Chinese nationalist hotheads were given relatively free reign to stage abusive, anti-Japanese demonstrations in several cities on October 16.

Foreign Minister Maehara responded by calling China's reaction "extremely hysterical"; China's Foreign Ministry, not to be outdone, stated that it was "shocked" at Maehara's statement.

Former Prime Minister Abe emerged from obscurity to toss Hitler into the mix, accusing China of yearning for "Lebensraum" (for some reason, he decided not to run with a more apt World War II analogy and accuse China of harboring ambitions to establish a Greater East Asia Co-Prosperity Sphere).

It appears that the Diaoyutai/Senkaku Islands will remain a low-level and—at least to hardliners in China, Japan, and the U.S.– not completely unwelcome irritant in China's foreign affairs rather than the foundation for a meaningful diplomatic breakthrough in China's relationship with its smaller and anxious neighbours.

There is a remarkable but virtually unnoted parallel between the Diaoyutai/Senkaku case and another confrontation during which the U.S. and its ally pushed, China pushed back, and the U.S. team folded: the Cheonan affair. Faced with U.S. and ROK efforts to use the sinking of the Cheonan as a justification for ostracizing the DPRK and making the fate of the peninsula a matter for the UN Security Council (and not the China-mediated Six Party Talks), China issued a high-level public endorsement of the Kim Jong Il regime and successfully pressured the Lee Myung-bak government to accept a return to the Six Party Talks.

The true lesson of the Diaoyutai/Senkaku crisis is that on regional matters China will ferociously oppose would-be US proxies like Japan—and South Korea and Vietnam–if they presume to advance US interests at Chinese expense. The other lesson that China would like its neighbours and enemies to extract from the situation is that the United States is happy to have its allies foment politically useful confrontations with

China, but unwilling to alienate China by backing its proxies with determined diplomatic and military escalation when things get tough.

It appears that Beijing can and will deploy its preferred weapons— diplomatic pressure, economic coercion, legal jeopardy for foreign nationals and their interests —with far more speed and determination than the US and its allies can bring to bear despite their overwhelming military superiority. The United States and its Asian partners have done a good job of irritating China and provoking a dangerous crisis; they have yet to prove they can do as good a job of dealing with the consequences.

THE UNITED STATES BE AFRAID OF CHINA'S "STRING OF PEARLS"?

With Donald Trump's recent official visit to China, the question of whether this emerging power is a threat to American hegemony has been brought back to the table. This menace of a new powerful Middle Empire expresses itself mainly through the tensions emerging around the so-called "String of Pearls". According to Lt. Col. Christopher Pehrson, researcher at the Strategic Studies Institute, the "String of Pearls" describes the manifestation of China's rising geopolitical influence through efforts to increase access to ports and airfields, develop special diplomatic relationships, and modernize military forces that extend from the South China Sea through the Strait of Malacca, across the Indian Ocean, and onto the Arabian Gulf. This concept was introduced during a study by Booz Allen Hamilton, an American management consulting firm, and is thus a Western concept not recognized by Beijing's government. Nonetheless, the String of Pearls is of geopolitical importance for China and represents a strategic threat for the US.

For the last decade, China has shown an increasing interest in expanding its sea power and more specifically its projection power in order to develop its capabilities to intervene across the world. This interest resulted in the acquisition by the

People's Liberation Army Navy (PLAN) of modern Russian destroyers (cf. *Guanghzou class destroyers)* and other warships, as well as through the acquisition of an aircraft carrier in 2012, the *Liaoning*, and the planned construction of two new ones, as reported by Dave Majumdar, defense editor for the National Interest. While doing so, China also developed a network of "pearls" where each pearl represents a port or an island state in which China has launched some development program or has concluded some agreement in order to be able to use these ports. This network enables China's navy to have some refueling stations alongside the commercial routes going through the Indian Ocean in order for the PLAN to ensure the security in the area.

However, this function is usually undertaken by the U.S. Navy and its 5th Fleet. With China's emerging interest in imposing itself as a regional power and taking an active part in the protection of the region, the United States faces rising opposition. While this new actor should be seen in a positive way to ensure international peace and the fight against piracy in the Indian Ocean, recent events have led to rising tensions. In fact, on July 11 of this year, China inaugurated its first foreign military base in Djibouti. This new naval base is considered as a message of China's willingness to assert itself on the international scene and compete with U.S. military hegemony in the Indian Ocean.

Even though Donald Trump is not a fierce defender of the role often attributed to the United States of the "world's policeman", he and U.S. generals have sent a warning message to China about its intentions during the regular Malabar exercises in 2017. These annual joint naval exercises between the United States, Japan, and India were brought to a new level this year with the participation of no less than 16 warships, two submarines and over 95 aircraft from the three countries, emphasizing the rising tension in the region around the question of naval power.

Nonetheless, if the United States is concerned by the development of the String of Pearls initiative it is due to the heavy pressure this project imposes on India, one of America's strongest allies in the region. With the development of the String of Pearls, India fears a strategy of encirclement from China as can be seen on the provided map. The heavy investments of China in neighboring countries and plans to open another military base in Gwadar, the third port of Pakistan, the sworn enemy of India, is another threat to the geopolitical interests of India. Confronted with the development of possible military bases alongside its coasts and with the rapid modernization of the Chinese navy, India is calling on the United States to contain Chinese ambitions. However, with the difficult relationship between Donald Trump and Xi Jinping it is legitimate to wonder if the United States will be able to do such a thing.

In any case, the development of the String of Pearls has led to an increase in tensions in South and Southeast Asia and also to a new maritime arms race between regional powers, whether it be India, Japan, China, or to some lesser extent Vietnam. The Trump administration's foreign policies have also brought forward the question of whether the United States has the capacity and the willingness to maintain peace in the area and to ensure goodwill between these countries.

4

Chinese Imperialism and Strategy

Historically, ancient China has been one of the world's oldest empires. In ancient Chinese political theory, relations between foreign states were governed by the tributary system. Since the Emperor of China held the Mandate of Heaven, his rule was universal and extended to All under heaven. Sometimes neighboring states were actual protectorates or vassal states over which China exerted large amounts of influence, while in other cases foreign states merely acknowledged China's nominal suzerainty in order to gain access to Chinese trade, which took place through the tributary system.

EARLY CHINESE EXPANSIONS

The king of the ancient state of Qin first unified the Chinese empire in 221 BC by conquering all of the other states in what was then considered China and proclaimed himself the "First Emperor" and became known as Qin Shi Huangdi.

The ancient Han Dynasty (202 BC-220 AD) established control over northern Vietnam, northern Korea, and the Tarim Basin of Central Asia. The short-lived Sui Dynasty (581–618 AD) reinvaded Annam (northern Vietnam) and attacked Champa (southern Vietnam), while they also attempted to conquer Korea, which failed. The later Tang Dynasty (618–907) aided the Korean Silla Kingdom in defeating their two Korean rivals, yet became shortchanged when they discovered Silla was not about to allow the Tang to claim much of Goguryeo's territory (as it had been under the Chinese Han Dynasty's control a few centuries before, the Han having wrested it from native kingdoms at that time). The Tang Dynasty established control over the Tarim Basin region as well, fighting wars with the new Tibetan Empire and stripping them of their colonies in Central Asia (which was abandoned after the An Lushan Rebellion). The Song Dynasty (960–1279), in securing maritime trade routes that ran from South East Asia into the Indian Ocean, had established fortified trade bases in the Philippines. The Mongol-led Yuan Dynasty(1279–1368) made attempts to invade Japan after securing the Korean peninsula through the vassaldom of the Korean Goryeo dynasty, yet both of these military ventures failed.

Qing territorial expansion

By the late 19th century, in response to competition with other states, the Qing government of China attempted to exert direct control of its frontier areas by conquest or, if already under military control, conversion into provinces.

Ming dynasty loyalists from China invaded Taiwan and expelled Dutch colonialists from the island during the Siege of Fort Zeelandia and founded the Chinese Kingdom of Tungning. The Ming loyalists quickly moved to replace the institutions and culture of Dutch colonial rule with Han Chinese colonial rule. Language and religious institutions left by the Dutch were closed and replaced with Confucian temples and Chinese language schools for both Han Chinese and aboriginals. Officials encouraged new immigration of Han Chinese from China into territory further inland, turning aboriginal lands into new farmland. After fighting between the Ming loyalists and the Qing during the Revolt of the Three Feudatories, the Qing attacked the Kingdom of Tungning. the Qing won the Battle of Penghu and the Ming loyalists submitted to Qing rule. Tungning was annexed as part of Fujian province. The Qing were "reluctant colonizers" but became convinced of Taiwan's value to their empire due to the threat the island posed if used as a base by rival powers, and by its abundant resources. The Qing turned Taiwan into its own province in 1885, after Japanese interest and a defeated French invasion attempt.

After British troops invaded Tibet in the waning days of the Qing Dynasty, the Qing responded by sending Zhao Erfeng to further integrate Tibet into China. He succeeded in abolishing the powers of the Tibetan local leaders in Kham and appointing Chinese magistrates in their places by 1909–10. Qing forces were also sent to Ü-Tsang in 1910 to establish a direct control over Tibet proper, though a province was never established in this area.

Process of expansion

The ability of Qing China to project power into Central Asia came about because of two changes, one social and one technological. The social change was that under the Qing dynasty, from 1642, China came under the control of the Manchus who organised their military forces around cavalry which was more suited for power projection than traditional Chinese infantry. The technological change was advances in the cannon and artillery which negated the military advantage that the people of the Steppe had with their cavalry (although cannons and firearms were used in China centuries beforehand to combat similar threats). Zunghar Khanate was the last great independent nomadic power on the steppe in Central Asia. The Dzungars were deliberately exterminated in a brutal campaign during the Zunghar Genocide by Manchu Bannermen and Khalkha Mongols. It has been estimated that more than a million people were slaughtered, and it took generations for it to recover. The Manchu ruling family (Aisin Gioro) was a supporter of Tibetan Buddhism and so many of the ruling groups were linked by religion.

CHINA'S STRATEGIC PERSPECTIVE

China's interests in Afghanistan and Pakistan are complex and multi-dimensional, and are primarily driven by internal considerations. Currently, China's leaders are concerned that a significant drop in economic growth – a result of the global economic crisis – will lead to increased levels of unemployment and destabilizing levels of popular unrest. China's need to maintain economic growth and domestic stability significantly inform its approach to Afghanistan and Pakistan. China certainly does not want to see nuclear-armed Pakistan be overrun by Islamic extremists. Nor does it want to see a degree of instability in either country that could complicate China's access to their resources and transit routes. Additionally, of particular concern to Chinese authorities is the possibly that extremists could migrate from Afghanistan or Pakistan into China, or that their activities could catalyze extremists groups in its interior provinces.

Regionally, China sees Afghanistan and Pakistan as components of a broader struggle for dominance over South and Central Asia. China's close relationship with Pakistan is largely a check against India's rise as a dominant power in South Asia. From this point of view, a stable and friendly Afghanistan gives Pakistan an important degree of "strategic depth" against India's nuclear capabilities and conventional military superiority. According to this logic, China benefits from an Afghanistan that is stable and friendly to Pakistan, because it allows Islamabad to focus on India. Thus, India's forays into Afghanistan are seen by some in China as "designed to achieve four objectives: contain Pakistan, enhance energy security, combat terrorism, and pin down China's development."

Another key dimension of China's approach to Afghanistan and Pakistan is Beijing's perception of the United States. Since 2001, the United States has been profoundly focused on the "Arc of Instability" from the Middle East to South Asia, and the ongoing shift of military resources from Iraq to Afghanistan. In addition to requiring significant amounts of policymaker attention, this focus directly impacts the ability of U.S. leaders to engage in the Asia-Pacific region. This focus, combined with a difficult economic picture constraining future defense and international aid budgets, has necessarily diverted resources and high-level attention away from China and the Asia-Pacific, forcing the U.S. to essentially operate in the region with one hand tied behind its back. Washington's focus elsewhere, and a relatively stable strategic environment with no military threats, reinforces Chinese perceptions of the current period as a "window of opportunity" allowing China to focus on its own economic growth and development.

To date, China's leaders have not commented directly on the implications of the U.S. involvement in extended occupations in Iraq and Afghanistan. Beijing continues to view the United States as the world's most powerful nation and China's most important relationship, and does not want to jeopardize US-Sino relations with unvarnished criticism or harping about the ongoing wars. However, since the U.S. invasion of Afghanistan in 2001, official Chinese media has not hesitated to emphasize indications of instability, reports of civilian deaths, and questions about U.S. will to preserve stability in Afghanistan and Pakistan.

China highlights problems in Afghanistan and Pakistan for several reasons. First, China perceives itself as the leader of the developing world and is therefore charged with highlighting what they see as victims of U.S. hegemony. Second, China seeks to cultivate positive relations with Muslim-majority countries for their natural resources and their votes in multilateral fora.

Another key driver of China's perspective on Afghanistan and Pakistan is concern about ties between Islamic militants in Afghanistan and Pakistan and the the Uyghur Muslim minority population in Xinjiang province. China is concerned that the militant Islamist ideology in Afghanistan could bleed into China's Uyghur population and feed what many in Beijing see as a terrorist problem. The difficulty for U.S. policymakers is distinguishing between terrorist groups and legitimate resistors against the Chinese Communist Party. China claims that a Uyghur separatist group called the East Turkestan Islamic Movement (ETIM) has had contacts with Al Qaeda, and the U.S. has designated ETIM as a terrorist organization. That being said, ETIM's true size and the accuracy of its reported connections with Al Qaeda remain unclear. However, Beijing's concerns about its Uyghur population and possible connections with extremists in Afghanistan and Pakistan raise questions about China's willingness to tolerate U.S. military forces in these countries as a tool to keep extremist forces pinned down and focused away from China. Chinese strategists are uncomfortable with a large U.S. military presence along China's border, and some analysts have expressed concern that U.S. bases in the region supporting operations in Afghanistan are part of a plot to perpetuate U.S. domination of the region. At the same time, however, the U.S. presence in Afghanistan prevents Al Qaeda from focusing on China and helps suppress Islamist groups along China's periphery.

China's Approach to Afghanistan

China's interests in Afghanistan are both economic and strategic. China was largely disengaged from Afghanistan until President Hamid Karzai's government opened up its energy, mineral, and raw materials to foreign investors. In 2007, China was Afghanistan's fifth-largest trading partner, behind Pakistan, the EU, the U.S., and India. China has developed significant portions of Afghanistan's infrastructure, including telephone networks, irrigation projects, public hospitals, and several other construction projects. The crown in jewel in China's investments is the $3.5 billion stake in Afghanistan's Aynak copper field, one of the world's largest with the potential for $88 billion worth of ore. This investment was coupled with the construction of a $500 million electrical plant and the development of a railway from Tajikistan to Pakistan for distribution. Equally important for Kabul is the project's potential need to employ 10,000 Afghans and the $400 million of projected royalties it would accrue yearly, representing more than half of its current annual state budget.

Also important to China is Afghanistan's potential as a source for raw materials. China's booming economy is fueled by foreign natural resources like oil, natural gas, and other minerals. China's iron-ore demand increased close to 15 percent in the first 8 months of 2007, while copper demand surged by almost 35 percent in the same period. This is driving an approach to the region focused on maintaining access to foreign resources and markets. Afghan oil reserves were recently upgraded 18 times by a U.S. geological survey, estimates standing at an average of 1,596 million barrels, while Afghanistan's natural gas reserves were upgraded by a factor of three, standing at a mean of 15,687 trillion cubic feet. Afghanistan also has large iron ore deposits between Herat and the Panjsher Valley, and gold reserves in the northern provinces of Badakshan, Takhar, and Ghazni. Major copper fields also exist in Jawkhar, Darband, and in abovementioned Aynak, located around 30 km southeast of Kabul.

Also of great important to Beijing is Afghanistan's geographic location, which sets it at the triangular cross-roads between China, energy suppliers in the Middle East, and key Indian Ocean transit points from Pakistan. As the easiest transportation route for the exploitation of the estimated 23 billion tons of oil and 3 trillion cubic meters of gas in the Central Asian Republics, Afghanistan plays a central role in China's attempts to diversify its access to foreign resources.

PAKISTAN'S STRATEGIES OF CHINA

After the emergence of the CARs, Pakistan moved actively into Central Asia, but policy makers were clearly divided as to what Pakistan would gain out of Central Asia. While some wanted an Islamic revolution in Central Asia, others wanted open trade links through Afghanistan. The dichotomy of views revealed the limits of Pakistan's Central Asia Policy. Moreover, during this period, the Central Asian leaders were extremely wary of Pakistan because of its involvement in the Afghan war and its support to the mujahideen. During the Pakistan-backed Taliban era in Afghanistan, bilateral relations between Pakistan and the Central Asian states touched rock bottom.

After Pakistan joined the global war against terrorism as a frontline state, bilateral relations began to be revisited. During the past few years, frequent visits by Central Asian and

Pakistani officials to each other's states reflect the changing nature of their bilateral relations. A number of agreements have been signed covering such areas as trade and tourism, cultural and economic cooperation during these visits. Pakistan has developed institutionalised arrangements for this purpose. Joint Economic Commissions (JECs) have been established with all the Central Asian states. Under a Special Technical Assistance Programme (STAP) initiated in 1992-93, Pakistan provides training facilities, which are fully funded by Islamabad. The programme includes courses ranging from English language, banking and accountancy to diplomacy.

In this context President General Pervez Musharraf's visit to Uzbekistan and Kyrgyzstan in March 2005 was significant. Earlier, the two-day official visit of President Nursultan Nazarbayev of Kazakhstan in December 2003 to Islamabad was a step towards strengthening bilateral ties between the two countries. During this visit, both the leaders decided to hold annual foreign ministerial consultations. While speaking at the Pakistan-Kazakhstan Business Forum, President Nazarbayev identified three zones of technological parks of information and biotechnology where Pakistani companies could invest significantly.

It is important to note that during the Tajik Foreign Minister's visit to Islamabad in January 2004, he assured President Musharraf that Tajikistan would not allow Indian military bases on its soil. This was followed by the visit of Tajik President Emomali Rahmanov to Islamabad in May 2004. During this visit, eight agreements were inked covering abolition of visas for holders of diplomatic passports, avoidance of double taxation, cooperation between the education ministers and justice ministers, combating drug trafficking, and cooperation between official news agencies and promotion and protection of investment. Pakistan-Uzbekistan relations have also been improving over the past few years given the changed security paradigm. During Uzbek President Karimov's recent visit to Islamabad in May 2006, both sides agreed to expand trade and economic ties and coordinate anti-terrorism activities. It was also planned to extend road and rail links that would enable the CARs, particularly Uzbekistan, to make use of Pakistan's seaports to develop commerce with other regions. A joint fight against extremism and terrorism has, of late, been on top of the list for both the countries. During his March 2005 visit President Musharraf assured the Uzbek leader of his determination to wipe out terrorists, including a substantial number of Uzbek nationals, from the tribal areas. How far these promises will be fulfilled is yet to be seen.

In an attempt to build strong ties with Central Asia, Pakistan has sought to use its cultural links with this region. It is perceived that Pakistan is the cultural extension of the Central Asian region that in turn is seen to be in fusion with the South Asian social milieu. In this context, a Pakistani scholar opined, "Pakistan's political existence and emergence on the world map would not have materialised but for the primordial relationship that glues us together. The roots of our faith, undoubtedly, lie in the Arabian soil but our cultural linkages are with Central Asian civilisation, which in itself is an amalgam of diverse influence and cross-cultural fertilisation"

Cooperation in the fields of education and culture is an important aspect of Pakistan-Central Asia relations. There are number of Central Asian students studying in Pakistan and similarly Pakistani students in the CARs. The lack of information makes it difficult to provide the total number of Pakistani students studying in all CARs. However, the example of Kyrgyzstan can be cited. Kyrgyz students have been pursuing studies in Pakistani educational institutions in various fields such as engineering, business administration, information technology and the English language. Kyrgyz civil servants also attend training programmes in Pakistan. Conversely, over 350 Pakistani students are currently pursuing studies, mainly in medical colleges, in Kyrgyzstan.

Quest for "Strategic Depth"

The emergence of Central Asia was viewed as an opportunity for Pakistan to spread its sphere of influence beyond Afghanistan thus providing "strategic depth" against India. As mentioned earlier, Pakistan's desire to expand its influence in Afghanistan has been very central to Islamabad's strategic thinking. In the view of Gen. Mirza Aslam Beg, "...Afghanistan will be a great source of strength to Pakistan to face any crisis and danger that it may encounter. In fact, the security of Pakistan, Iran and Afghanistan is interlinked and is indivisible..." While examining Pakistan's Afghan policy, it has been argued that its defence planning has been handicapped by the lack of territorial depth to absorb an attack by India and then to retaliate. This elusive quest for strategic depth has guided Pakistan in its ambitious involvement in Afghanistan in spite of the multiple implications for its social fabric and political culture. Thus, Pakistan's Afghan policy was constructed with an objective to create a subservient government in Afghanistan that would be friendly to Pakistan, militarily too weak to question the Durand line and unstable to raise the Pushtunistan issue. In addition to this, the military strategists argued that a friendly Afghanistan would give Kashmiri militants a base from where they could be trained, funded and armed. The Central Asian region was seen as an extension of Pakistan's strategic space.

The end of the Taliban regime in Afghanistan has not brought any fundamental change in Pakistan's Afghan policy. Afghanistan is still very central to Pakistan's strategic thinking, and is akin to being Pakistan's backwaters. Wary about how the current situation would unfold in Afghanistan, Islamabad is trying to cement its ties with the current regime in Kabul while supporting Taliban elements and has not given up its grand strategy of establishing a friendly government in Kabul. It is believed that Pakistan's new proxy war in Afghanistan is slowly unravelling itself. There is the resurgence of Taliban in Afghanistan. The Taliban are supported by the Pakistani establishment itself – from low-level military officers and some ministers to religious parties and their jihadi infrastructure. The ISI too has been proactively working to bring the Taliban back to its life. There has been constant accusation by Afghanistan of Pakistan's interference and its support to the

Taliban and Al Qaida elements to create trouble for Kabul. Afghan President Hamid Karzai during his visit in February 2006 provided evidence to President Musharraf implicating Pakistan in the recruitment, training and equipping of Islamic radical suicide bombers. The senior Afghan official who accompanied President Karzai said, "In places like Karachi, Pakistani extremist groups working on behalf of the Taliban for a fee, carry out the recruitment and then bring them to safe houses in Balochistan for training and equipping with vests." In a recent visit to Islamabad, Gen. Johan Abizaid, the head of the US Central Command reportedly showed the Pakistanis, intelligence photographs of Taliban training camps at an undisclosed location and asked for them to be shut down.

Three years ago, Dr. Timothy D. Hoyt, Associate Professor of Strategy and policy at the US Naval War College, in a hearing before the House Committee on International relations in October 2003 accused Pakistan of providing sanctuary to terrorist groups, that enjoy strong support among active and retired Army officers and intelligence officials. He said: "So long as Pakistan relies on terrorism to achieve its political objectives, it will be impossible to eliminate terrorism and the Al Qaeda presence in the region."

Geo-Economic

Transport Corridors and Access to Warm Waters: Many Pakistani leaders refer to their country as the gateway to Central Asia and strongly believe that good relations with the region would not only enhance its security but also provide enormous economic opportunities. In the post-Cold War period, Islamabad tried to revive its fortunes with the West by selling its new geo-strategic importance.

This brings us to the question, is Pakistan the gateway to Central Asia? Geographically, Pakistan provides a gateway to Central Asia from south/southeast; but it is not the only gateway to the seas of the south. This is the impression that Pakistani leaders have tried to create in an attempt to identify themselves with Central Asia, further their co-operation with the region and make Pakistan more relevant not only to the CARs and its neighbouring states but also to the West. In fact, Iran provides another gateway to Central Asia and has done a great deal to develop good communication systems with the region. Yet another gateway is via Turkey in the southwest.

Pakistan has been trying to make itself more relevant to Central Asia by offering the states several proposals for creating trade and transport corridors and access to ports. President General Pervez Musharraf has emphasised this time and again.

He said, "...our geo-strategic significance can't be reduced. We need to realise that we have understood that and therefore we have constructed a new port at Gwadar which is at the mouth of the Gulf almost." In March 2005, he stated again: "we are fully focused on making use of our central location and constructing ports and putting in place a network of infrastructure." Recently, he has approved a railways reconstruction programme, which would link Gwadar with the other countries via rail. It is believed that this could make Pakistan the economic and trade hub for the CARs, Gulf, Western China and South Asia.

Pakistan's geo-strategic location admittedly makes it difficult for Central Asia to ignore it. For Turkmenistan and southern Uzbekistan, the shortest route to the sea lies through Iran, but for all other states, the shortest route is through Afghanistan and Pakistan. Karachi is the nearest port city for Central Asia and by air Islamabad is closer to Tashkent than it is to Karachi.

Dushanbe is only an hour's flight from Islamabad, and by road through Afghanistan the distance from Dushanbe to Karachi is 2,720 km. In contrast, the port of Bandar Abbas is 3,400 km, Vladivostok 9,500 km and Rostov on the Don 4,200 km away. This makes Pakistan important for the CARs. Despite little success so far, Pakistan is trying to improve its connectivity to the CARs through Afghanistan and China.

In this respect, the ADB has offered $2 billion to the Pakistan railway network, which will enable Pakistan to become one of the most attractive international trade routes to the CARs, Iran and China. Pakistan and Afghanistan have already agreed to lay a 103-km railway track between Chaman and Kandahar, which would be extended to Turkmenistan and other CARs. The feasibility study of the Quetta-Kandahar railway track has been completed and Pakistan would construct the 10-12 km railway track to the Afghan border. The track from the Afghan border to Kandahar would be the responsibility of the Afghan government. The World Bank has agreed to provide $1.8 billion to Pakistan for its $6 billion National Trade Corridor (NTC) improvement programme to meet domestic transportation requirements and provide transit facilities to Central Asia, Western China, Afghanistan and Iran.

Pakistan has also proposed to construct a $90-million road through the Boroghil Pass in the Yarkhun valley to link it with the CARs. Of the 13 passes, which lead to Afghanistan from Chitral district, the Boroghil Pass is the easiest and lowest in altitude. This pass remains closed for a very short period late in winter. The road will extend to Wakhan, 13-65 km wide strategic strip in northeast Afghanistan. The area links Afghanistan with Pakistan in the south, Tajikistan in the north and China in the east.

The Wakhan-Boroghil route has been preferred against the one passing through the central parts of Afghanistan due to the security situation. This road will connect the 12,484-foot-high Boroghil pass at the northwest of the Yarkhum valley in Chitral with Sarhad-i-Langar in Wakhan at a distance of about 95 km and move on to Iskashim in Tajikistan leading to the Tajik capital Dushanbe via the Korung-Kalai Chumb and Kulob areas. From the Boroghil Pass, the road will traverse over 300 km long valley and reach Peshawar. The distance from Tajikistan to Peshawar via the Wakhan-Chitral route is estimated to be 700 km. This road will also branch off to the northern areas via the 10,500-foot-high Shandur Pass and merge into the Karakoram Highway. The Pakistan government has already sanctioned a number of road projects to interlink the northern areas and Chitral.

The quadrilateral agreement signed by Pakistan, China, Kyrgyzstan, and Kazakhstan is expected to give a boost to trading activities among member-nations through the Karakoram Highway. On October 10, 2006 a road connection along the Karakorum route, Islamabad-Kashgar-Bishkek-Almaty, was opened by Pakistan. Pakistan has also offered use of the Gwadar deep-sea port to the CARs. This port would serve as a mother port at the strategic location opposite to the Strait of Hormuz and at the mouth of the Persian Gulf. The first phase of this project is already over. The completion of the Gwadar Port would be a milestone for Pakistan in this context. When it comes online alongside Karachi, it will provide the shortest access to the Arabian Sea for large parts of Central Asia. On December 31, 2005, a meeting of Pakistan-Uzbekistan Joint Ministerial Commission was held in Tashkent, where the two sides agreed to enter into a trilateral transit trade agreement with Afghanistan to benefit from land routes and the Gwadar port facility.

During Kyrgyz President Askar Akaev's two-day visit to Pakistan on January 17-18, 2005, it was agreed that Pakistan would import electricity from Kyrgyzstan and both countries would build roads to improve trade. It was decided to strengthen links through Kashgar in China and on to Bishkek and also through the Karakoram Highway. The road being constructed on the Karakoram Highway to link the two countries completed by 2006, promoting Pak-Kyrgzy trade. Establishment of a railway link from Gwadar to Taftan in Iran via Saindak is also being planned. A road from Gwadar to Sandak, running parallel to the Iran-Pakistan border, will make it the shortest route to reach Central Asia from the warm waters of the Arabian Sea. Another 515-km long highway connecting Gwadar via Pangur, Khaan, Chaghi and Rabat up to the heart of Western Afghanistan is being planned. This would link Pakistan by road directly with the CARs.

Pakistan is also giving priority to road and rail links and related facilities for more effective and mutually beneficial access to Central Asia. Air services to Tashkent and Almaty have already been resumed. Similar services to other parts of the region are under active consideration. The laying of railway tracks from Turkmenistan to Pakistan via Afghanistan is an important part of this programme. Pakistan's Ministry of Railways has completed a feasibility study for a Chaman-Kandahar rail project.

The quadrilateral agreement is also gradually being implemented. The completion of the Murghab-Kulma road from Tajikistan to China linking the Karakoram Highway to Pakistan is also a significant development. Once operational, it will boost transit trade between Pakistan and Central Asia.

Energy and Pipeline Politics: Pakistan is also looking at the huge energy resources of Central Asia. It wants to make Pakistan the energy-transit corridor in South Asia and the Asia-Pacific region, which will bring huge economic gains for the country. Pakistan is most likely to face a energy crisis in natural gas, power and oil in the next 3-4 that could choke its economic growth for many years to come. It is estimated that Pakistan's total energy requirement would increase by about 48 per cent to 80 million tonnes of oil equivalent (MTOE) in 2010 from about 54 MTOE currently.

According to official energy demand forecast, the demand for natural gas, having about 50 per cent share in the country's energy consumption would increase by 44 per cent to the 39 MTOE currently. The power shortage is expected to be little over 5,250 MW by 2010. Oil demand would also increase by over 23 per cent to about 21 million tonnes in 2010 from the current demand of 16.8 million tonnes. Therefore, Central Asia could be a future source of energy for Pakistan.

Pakistan's importance for Central Asian countries needs to be viewed in the context of the entire pipeline politics in the region. As a transit country, Pakistan provides these states with an outlet of their energy resources. In view of the instability in Afghanistan and Balochistan, the success of these pipelines from Central Asia however remains a big question mark. Despite these uncertainties Pakistan wants to keep the Central Asian states engaged with the hope of providing a transit route for their energy resources. In pursuit of its strategy to control the pipelines and gain greater influence, it is trying to sign various agreements with these Republics. Pakistan has signed 21 agreements and MoUs in oil, gas, energy, trade, science and culture with Turkmenistan. In the energy sector, Turkmenistan, Afghanistan and Pakistan (TAP) signed an agreement in December 2002 for a gas pipeline from Turkmenistan via Afghanistan to Pakistan, whose estimated cost is $2.5 billion. The ADB is the lead coordinating partner. It has, in addition to financial and technical assistance, played an important role in integrating efforts to realise the project. Several sessions of the Steering Committee on the TAP Gas Pipeline Project have been held so far. During a ministerial level TAP meeting on February 16, 2006, in Ashkabad, Turkmenistan agreed to provide sovereign guarantees to Pakistan to supply 3.2 billion cubic feet gas per day for 30 years. This assurance was restated during Pakistan Foreign Minister Khursheed Kasuri's visit to Turkmenistan in May 2006. However, a major hurdle to the project remains the volatile situation in Afghanistan.

While Turkmenistan can provide gas to Pakistan, Tajikistan and Kyrgyzstan have the potential to be substantial producers of hydroelectric power. Being geographically closest to Tajikistan, Pakistan stands to benefit from its hydroelectric potential. An inter-governmental agreement to that effect has already been signed. Pakistan's Water and Power Minister Liaquat Ali Jatoi has recently said, "the government is considering importing electricity from CARs via Afghanistan as an option to meet its demand and has signed an MoU with Tajikstan to import 1000 MW as well as initiated transmission routing assessment to bring such power to Pakistan." An advisor to Kyrgyz Prime Minister Omarov said that his government was also considering a transmission line from China to Pakistan with an estimated cost of $1.4 billion. Pakistan has also signed an agreement to import electricity from Kyrgyzstan through Tajikistan and Afghanistan. Indubitably, terrain and weather conditions are clear impediments to this project, yet both states appear determined to pursue it.

Trade

With the emergence of the newly independent Central Asian States, the business elite group in Pakistan viewed this region as offering immense economic opportunities. Central Asia was seen not only as a source of needed raw materials but also as a potential export market. Some estimates even suggested that the region had a potential market of $80 billion and if Pakistan secures even 5 per cent of this market, it could earn up to $4 billion a year. In December 1991, a 23-member delegation was send to Central Asia headed by the then Minister of Commerce Sardar Asif Ahmed Ali. A $30-million credit facility was given to Uzbekistan and $10 million to all other Central Asian Republics. These credit lines were not utilised by the Central Asian countries and Pakistan was unable to keep its commitment to provide the credit lines in future. The effort to open a fullfledged National Bank of Pakistan (NBP) met with complete failure. The NBP representative office was set up in 1995 in Tashkent but it could not facilitate the opening of a branch till 2002.

Despite high hopes, the trade between Pakistan and Central Asia remains limited. During 1992-93 Pakistani exports to the region amounted to $5.6 m and imports were $0.51 m. The figures for 1993-1995 indicate an increase as compared to 1992-93. During 1997-98 Pakistan's total trade with Kazakhstan accounted for $19.9 m.; for Kyrgyzstan 07.91m; Tajikistan $10.29m; Turkmenistan $07.75m; and Uzbekistan $35.34m. However, in subsequent years the trade figures do not indicate any major increase.

Pakistan's recent initiatives in Central Asia involve strengthening economic ties with the CARs. As mentioned earlier, Pakistan has established JECs with all the CARs. In its trade policy for 2006-07, Pakistan seeked to focus on export growth in regional Muslim countries, particularly Iran, Afghanistan and the CARs. It has been decided to establish export centres and warehouses at Peshawar and Quetta and an export centre in Islamabad. In this context the visit of

Kyrgyzstan President Askar Akaev on January 17, 2005 is of significance. Both countries signed a MoU on cooperation between the foreign ministries of the two countries on different regional and international issues. Two agreements were signed on cooperation and mutual assistance in customs related matters and avoidance of double taxation. President Akaev also offered to provide electricity to Pakistan. This was his third visit, earlier ones being in 1994 and 1995. Kyrgyzstan and Pakistan are signatories to the Quadrilateral Agreement along with China and Kazakhstan, effective since May 2004, which aims at promoting regional trade through Pakistan's Karakoram Highway. During the first meeting of the Pakistan-Kyrgyz Joint Ministerial Commission (JMC) in Islamabad, both sides negotiated on issues of taxation, culture, and visa restrictions for enhancing the volume of bilateral ties. Pakistan is also exploring the possibility of investing in the pharmaceutical sector in Turkmenistan.

As mentioned earlier the ECO provides another common platform to generate economic activity in the region. Within the framework of the ECO the volume of trade has not increased significantly. In fact, the ECO has failed to bring about great economic or commercial results. Competition among the member-states has been the major limitation for the success of this organisation. As Pakistan's Prime Minister Shaukat Aziz recently emphasised, the organisation needs to be used for making result-oriented policies instead of offering mere lip service. ECO can be an effective organisation if the ECO Trade Agreement, Transit Transport Agreement and the Trade and Development Bank become operational. So far, Pakistan has not been able to achieve much in terms of building economic and trade ties with the CARs. Their efforts to set up banks and hotels have received severe setbacks in Central Asia.

Regional Organisations

Apart from using its Islamic card to tie the CARs in its strategic fold against India, Islamabad also sought to use multilateral bodies in the region. Its desire to balance India through regional organisations got manifested in their wooing neighbouring Iran, Turkey, Afghanistan, and the CARs into the Economic Co-operation Organisation (ECO). Under this forum, states are expected to develop closer economic interaction.

In November 1992, Pakistan, Iran, Turkey, Afghanistan and the five former Soviet republics of Kazakhstan, Azerbaijan, Kyrgyzstan, Turkmenistan, and Uzbekistan created an extended Muslim economic bloc linking Asia and Europe.

Former Prime Minister Nawaz Sharif noted in a speech marking the occasion that the ECO "now corresponds to the boundaries of the ancient area, which brought prosperity and civilisation through fruitful exchanges along the historic silk route. The people of these lands have a shared history and common spiritual and cultural values."

Nawaz Sharif added his belief that extensive investment in infrastructure and encouragement of the private sector were the most important immediate objectives. He noted that Pakistan was building a major highway network to link Central Asia to the Arabian Sea and that its railroads were "poised to link not only member-states but also ECO with Europe, Russia, and South Asia." He added: "peace in Afghanistan is essential for political harmony and fruitful cooperation in our entire region."

Speaking about the achievements of ECO, Pakistani foreign minister Khursheed Mahmood Kasuri stated that it had made considerable progress in the trade, transport and energy sectors. The second ECO Commerce Ministers' Meeting held in Islamabad in July 2003 approved the ECO Trade Agreement (ECOTA). The agreement envisages reduction of tariffs up to 15 per cent over a period of eight years (15 years in case of Afghanistan) on at least 80 per cent of goods on tariff lines. Para-tariff and non-tariff barriers would be eliminated within a period of two years. He further stated that the implementation of ECOTA would pave the way for economic integration of the region. New strategies and plans are expected to be adopted to make the organisation more effective.

Despite claims made by Pakistan's ministers about ECO's progress, it has so far been a non-starter. The establishment of a free trade zone is difficult when basic infrastructure necessary in this regard is lacking. Moreover, the competing interests of Iran, Pakistan and Turkey limit the role ECO can play in the region. Instability in Afghanistan remains a major obstruction for expanding the area of cooperation.

Islamabad also sponsored the membership of the newly independent Central Asian countries in the Organisation of Islamic Countries (OIC). This was yet another drive to bring the CARs into the Ummah. Pakistan has also been keen to join the SCO. In early 2001, Pakistan applied for observer status but the Central Asian members of the organisation blocked its entry. A major stumbling block was Pakistan's support for the Taliban government in Afghanistan.

Though China supported Pakistan's membership, Russia wanted India to simultaneously join SCO. It was only in June 2005 that the applications of Pakistan, Iran and India were simultaneously considered and approved with consensus for granting observer status in the SCO at the Council of Heads of States Meeting in Astana on July 5, 2005. Pakistan is also a member of Conference on Interaction and Confidence-Building Measures in Asia (CICA). Much to the chagrin of Pakistan, India is included in both these organisations.

POSSIBLE MOTIVATIONAL FACTORS BEHIND THIS STRATEGY

China's development during the past decade, from its expanding economy and increased global influence to its growing military might and demand for energy, presented tremendous challenges to their leaders as they managed the turmoil of massive structural, technological, and social changes. The governing three key worries of the Chinese government have been:-elites of China had three overarching concerns:-

a. Regime survival.

b. Territorial integrity.

c. Domestic stability.

In the succeeding paragraphs these three concerns and their impact on the economy have been highlighted. The relation between the economy and the string of pearls strategy has also been shown.

Regime Survival

Regime survival was has always been and will shall remain the foremost concern of the ruling Chinese Communist Party (CCP). The party leadership is It is aware that their survival depends upon the satisfaction of the Chinese people and their ability how well they are able to protect Chinese national interests. The collapse of the When Soviet Union collapsed and the end of the Cold War ended, Communism was exposed deduced as a communism as a "bankrupt ideology with a flawed economic system". To avoid the same fate as had befallen the erstwhile USSR, the Chinese adopted a "socialist market economy". Although a lot of economic and social reforms have taken place but , in the middle of it the CCP has maintained a strict authoritarian control. The CCP is aware of the fact that as long as the economy is thriving the populace willl be satisfied and hence there would not be a serious threat to the current regime.

Territorial Integrity

China has in the recent past adopted a strategy of befriending its neighbours with the notable exceptions being India and Taiwan and in the process has met with considerable success too. Although certain contentious issues still remain with the countries such as Japan over some disputed islands but more or less China has successfully demilitarized its land borders in the nNorthern and the cCentral aAsia.

On the central Central asian Asian front, China has become more influential under the support of the Shanghai Cooperation Organization (SCO), whose member states consist of China, Russia, Kazakhstan, Uzbekistan, Kyrgyzstan, and Tajikistan, along with the observer members of India, Pakistan, Iran, and

Mongolia. It is slowly but surely laying to rest the dispute over Tibet although in a more subtle way.

The only spanner in the wheel that remains is its relations and territorial disputes with India which are not showing any signs of fast progress. However, the relations with India have been more of a sine curve with statements against one another coming from both sides.

India has more or less recognized China's claims to Tibet and China has reciprocated by recognizing India's claim to the Himalayan state of Sikkim. Even with respect to Taiwan, Chinese policy attempts to balance the "stick" of diplomatic and military pressure with the "carrot" of mutually beneficial cross-strait economic ties. With the last elections in Taiwan throwing some startling results in favour of cChina, the day is not far off when it will come into some sort of agreement with Taiwan also. What has made China want to have good relations with its immediate neighbours . neighbours. The one thing that comes to mind is 'economy'. It seems that the ever increasing demands of increased economic development are the driving forces behind China's improved relations with her neighbors.

Domestic Stability

Again successful economic development is perceived as key to China's third area of strategic concern, domestic stability. CCP is focused inward, and primarily domestic politics drive China's foreign and economic policies. Changes to the economic system and the decision to embrace globalization are causing major shifts in Chinese society. The Chinese government is aware that although it is moving towards becoming an economically prosperous nation but everything is not in order inside their house. ThHere are large disparities between the economy of the people who are living in the coastal cities such as Shanghai and the people who are living in the interior less developed regions which have not seen the effects of the information revolution. Due to this class distinction due as a result of theto economic stratification, the government is wary and knows that if there are anti government demonstrations they cannot be repressed as was done earlier, the famous example being of the Tiananmen Square crackdown of June 1989. Thus to address this issue the regime is aware that it needs to bring economic parity to its provinces such as Yunnan and Xinjiang. In meeting this challenge, the government must foster economic prosperity to satisfy the demands and expectations of the Chinese people.

Link with Energy

All these three abovementioned factors, as have been shown in the preceding paragraphs, are inescapably linked with the economic prosperity of China. The government iof China is aware that the greatest strength of cChina as also its greatest vulnerability is the its economy and hence it has based its national policy and strategy on economyaround this key factor.

For its economy to continue thriving, as is with the case of all nations, China knows that it has to rely upon continued and sustained import of energy. Since energy provides the foundation of the economy, China's economic policy depends on the success of its energy policy. As the energy resources available within the country are quite limited and cannot ascribe to the full economy; hence it China, therefore, has to rely in a big way on the external sources of energy and raw materials. To import these energy resources and raw materials, it has to have a good and effective transportation system both on land and at sea is required. The three major problems that were faced by China in importing energy via land based routes were that firstly, most of the energy rich nations are either not connected by land; secondly, it would take a major effort and would not be cost effective to connect them with land and thirdly, even if these nations were connected, their links pass through other nations which may be a risk keeping in mind the fluid world order and changing equations. Hence, it was important that the 'Sea Lines Of Communications' , which were importing the major chunk of energy be secured . Securing Sea Lines of Communications for energy and raw materials supports China's energy policy and is the principal motivation behind the "String of Pearls." This is how and why the "String of Pearls" relates to China's Grand National Strategy.

Protection of SLOCs

The question that arises here is that from whowhom is the protection is required, if at all.? Whom does China fear? Over 70 percent of the total oil imports of China come from either the Middle East or the African countries majority of which is transported through sea and this will remain so for the foreseeable future. Hence, China has a long-term commitment to these supply sources due to which it has been trying to build up better relations with these countries whether that comes as monetary help or in some other form. For eg, Saudi Arabia is China's largest crude oil supplier, and the Saudi national oil company, Aramco, is a 25 percent investor in China's biggest refinery and petrochemical complex. China recently signed a 25-year oil and natural gas deal with Iran, its biggest ever, worth over $70 billion. In Africa, China has invested $3 billion to develop Sudan's unexploited oil resources, including a 930-mile pipeline, a refinery, and a sea port.

As already brought out, the infrastructure required to develop an overland link is massive and the cost quite high which does not justify the construction of these overland links. The regional instability in and around these regions is also a major worry for China and ; which further adds to the uncertainty of future development and long-term reliability.

The current means available to China for the protection of these sea lines of communication were very limited. Moreover, seen with the fact that these communication lines pass through the Sstrait of Hormuz and the Malacca straits, which are considered to be a haven for sea pirates. 37 incidents occurred in the Malacca Strait in 2004, many of which "involved the crew being kidnapped for ransom" or "attacked by machine guns and rocket launchers." This increase in the piracy was also a major factor which prompted china to go in for development of some pearls to protect its sea assets. Also, China is aware that in case of a conflict, as brought out earlier, it will be very easy to choke its energy lines and if proper protection is not provided to them, then it wcould become a major weakness for China.

Thus, it is very clear that the motivation behind the string of pearls is as given above in the preceding paragraphs. However, if given a closer look not all the 'pearls' will be safeguarding the sea lines of communication. In the succeeding chapters it will be brought out that China is now engaged in a major way to establish bases all around the world where it thinks that its energy requirements can be met. These bases although may not threaten India directly but the way china is going around the world to garner maximum energy sourcessources; they may prove to be detrimental to the interest of India and other powers in future.

5

China's Silk Road Fund: Towards a Sinocentric Asia

An often overlooked commonality between BRICS countries is their contested claim for regional leadership. However, the regional ambitions articulated at differing degree of specificity and coherence in Brasília, Moscow, Beijing and Delhi, are generally received with indifference, skepticism or outright fear in neighboring capitals. It is no coincidence that countries such as Argentina and Pakistan are the most vocal critics of their respective bigger neighbor's quest to become a permanent member of the UN Security Council. In the same way, China's and Russia's regional leadership claims generate apprehension by neighbors such as Japan and Kazakhstan, respectively.

Each BRICS country's difficulty is three-fold. First, they need to develop a cohesive and compelling vision of what they want their region to look like - how to improve transport links, how to promote democracy or political stability, which regional institutions to establish, and how the region should relate to the rest of the world. Second, they need to convince neighbors that the implementation of such a project generates positive results for the entire region, and that fears of regional bullying are unwarranted. Finally, they need to muster the diplomatic and financial muscle to turn their vision into reality - after all, infrastructure projects (roads, ports, etc.) to connect the region tend to be costly and complex. Over the past decades, none of the BRICS has been particularly successful in addressing the three concerns, largely due to internal development challenges.

Yet more recently, China has arguably been the most active and capable backing up its leadership claim with an actual vision.

After Xi Jinping articulated a vision for China's ties with Central Asia last year during a visit to Kazakhstan, he now announced an initial $40 billion for a "Silk Road fund" to invest in infrastructure and industrial and financial cooperation, seeking to "break the connectivity bottleneck" in Asia. Xi made the pledge when he met with leaders of Bangladesh, Cambodia, Laos, Mongolia, Myanmar, Pakistan and Tajikistan. The Fund is nothing less than the first step towards a regional system of mutually beneficial political and economic relations with China at the center: As the President argued, linking Asian countries is

not merely about building roads and bridges or making linear connection of different places. More importantly, it should be a three-way combination of infrastructure, institutions and people-to-people exchanges and a five-way progress in policy communication, infrastructure connectivity, trade link, capital flow and understanding among peoples.

Of course, China's dream of a sinocentric Asia predates Xi. A direct train to Duisburg in Germany left Chongqing in 2011. A map of the envisioned Silk Road published by Xinhua depicts two routes: one through Kazakhstan, Kyrgyzstan and Iran en route to Austria; and a maritime route from Chinese to Antwerp in Belgium. While the latter is set to benefit China's eastern coastal regions, the landroutes are also seen as a tool to enhance economic development in the poorer, landlocked western provinces of China.

Shannon Tiezzi shows how the Chinese media is meticulously covering China's regional project. She writes that

Xinhua's recently unveiled an updated, interactive map depicting the extent of two Silk Road projects. A quick comparison to Xinhua's earlier version of the map reveals a number of new

"stops" that have been added in the past six months, including Moscow, Russia; Dushanbe, Tajikistan; Jakarta, Indonesia; and Colombo, Sri Lanka. And Beijing is still expanding its list of potential partners: in his recent visit to China, Afghan President Ashraf Ghani indicated his country's willingness to be part of the project.

Given how expensive and durable the construction of train and road links is, Xi's large-scale investments in the region may tie neighbors into a sinocentric Asia for decades, significantly reducing their governments' capacity or incentives to oppose China. As Kerry Brown, Director of the China Studies Centre at the University of Sydney, has recently argued,

There are obligations being created here, dependencies and commitments, that many who are included in the Silk Road idea might need to seriously consider.

China's Silk Road Fund can be seen as part of a larger effort to establish a series of complementary or parallel structures in the region that may at some point challenge existing institutions such as the World Bank or the Asian Development Bank.

It may also be seen as a threat by Russia and India, who will rightly interpret China's efforts as a challenge to their own attempts to assume regional leadership. Still, while China's economic power provides it with far more room for maneuver in the region, the other BRICS countries should certainly keep the case of China's Silk Road project in mind as they articulate their own regional strategies.

SILK ROAD

The Silk Road or Silk Route was an old system of exchange courses that for quite a long time were vital to social collaboration through locales of the Asian landmass interfacing the West and East from China to the Mediterranean Sea.

The Silk Road gets its name from the lucrative exchange Chinese silkcarried out along its length, starting amid the Han administration (207 BCE – 220 CE). The Han line extended

Central Asian segments of the exchange courses around 114 BCE by the Han administration, to a great extent through the missions and investigations of the Chinese majestic emissary, Zhang Qian.

The Chinese appreciated the wellbeing of their exchange items and expanded the Great Wall of China to guarantee the assurance of the exchange course.

Exchange on the Silk Road assumed a noteworthy part in the improvement of the human advancements of China, the Indian subcontinent, Persia, Europe, the Horn of Africa and Arabia, opening long-separate, political and financial relations between the civic establishments. In spite of the fact that silk was positively the real exchange thing sent out from China, numerous different merchandise were exchanged, and religions,syncretic theories, and different advances, and additionally ailments, likewise spread along the Silk Routes. Notwithstanding monetary exchange, the Silk Road served as a method for doing social exchange among the human advancements along its system.

The main traders during antiquity included the Chinese, Arabs, Turks,Indians, Persians, Somalis, Greeks, Syrians, Romans, Armenians, Bactrians, and (from the 5th to the 8th century) the Sogdians.

In June 2014 UNESCO designated the Chang'an-Tianshan corridor of the Silk Road as a World Heritage Site.

Name

The Silk Road derives its name from the lucrative Chinese silk trade, a major reason for the connection of trade routes into an extensive transcontinental network.The German terms *Seidenstraße* and *Seidenstraßen* ("the Silk Road/Route") were coined by Ferdinand von Richthofen, who made seven expeditions to China from 1868 to 1872. Some scholars prefer the term "Silk Routes" because the road included an extensive network of routes, though few were more than rough caravan tracks.

History

Precursors—Cross-continental Journeys

As the domestication of pack animals and the development of shipping technology highly increased the capacity for prehistoric people to carry heavier loads over greater distances, cultural exchanges and trade developed rapidly. In addition, the vast grassland steppes of Asia provided fertile grazing, water, and easy passage forcaravans, enabling merchants to travel immense distances, from the shores of the Pacific to Africa and deep into Europe, without trespassing on agricultural lands and arousing hostility.

Chinese and Central Asian contacts

From the 2nd millennium BCE, nephrite jade was being traded from mines in the region of Yarkand and Khotan to China. Significantly, these mines were not very far from the lapis lazuli and spinel ("Balas Ruby") mines in Badakhshan, and, although separated by the formidable Pamir Mountains, routes across them were apparently in use from very early times. Some remnants of what was probably Chinese silk have been found in Ancient Egyptfrom 1070 BCE. The Great Oasis cities of central Asia played a crucial role in the effective functioning of the silk road trades. The originating source seems sufficiently reliable, but silk unfortunately degrades very rapidly. It is therefore impossible to verify whether it was actually cultivated silk (which would almost certainly have come from China) or a type of "wild silk", which might have come from the Mediterranean region or the Middle East.

Following contacts between metropolitan China and nomadic western border territories in the 8th century BCE, gold was introduced from Central Asia, and Chinese jade carvers began to make imitation designs of the steppes, adopting theScythian-style animal art of the steppes (depictions of animals locked in combat). This style is particularly reflected in the rectangular belt plaques made of gold and bronze with alternate versions in jade and steatite.

The expansion of Scythian cultures, stretching from the Hungarian plain and theCarpathians to the Chinese Kansu Corridor, and linking the Middle East with Northern India and the Punjab, undoubtedly played an important role in the development of the Silk Road. Scythians accompanied the Assyrian Esarhaddon on his invasion of Egypt, and their distinctive triangular arrowheads have been found as far south as Aswan. These nomadic peoples were dependent upon neighbouring settled populations for a number of important technologies, and in addition to raiding vulnerable settlements for these commodities, they also encouraged long-distance merchants as a source of income through the enforced payment of tariffs. Soghdian Scythian merchants played a vital role in later periods in the development of the Silk Road.

Persian Royal Road

By the time of Herodotus (c. 475 BCE), the Royal Road of the Persian Empireran some 2,857 km (1,775 mi) from the city of Susa on the Karun (250 km (155 mi) east of the Tigris) to the port of Smyrna (modern Ýzmir in Turkey) on the Aegean Sea. It was maintained and protected by the Achaemenid Empire(c. 500–330 BCE) and had postal stations and relays at regular intervals. By having fresh horses and riders ready at each relay, royal couriers could carry messages the entire distance in nine days, while normal travellers took about three months.

Hellenistic era

The next major step in the development of the Silk Road was the expansion of the Greekempire of Alexander the Great into Central Asia. In August 329 BCE, at the mouth of theFergana Valley in Tajikistan across the mountain pass from the modern Chinese province ofXinjiang, Alexander founded the city of Alexandria Eschate or “Alexandria The Furthest”.This later became a major staging point on the northern Silk Route.

The Greeks remained in Central Asia for the next three centuries, first through the administration of the Seleucid

Empire, and then with the establishment of the Greco-Bactrian Kingdom (250 BCE-125 BCE) in Bactria (modern Afghanistan, Tajikistan, and Pakistan) and the later Indo-Greek Kingdom (180 BCE - 10 CE) in modern northern Pakistan and Afghanistan. They continued to expand eastward, especially during the reign of Euthydemus(230–200 BCE), who extended his control beyond Alexandria Eschate to Sogdiana. There are indications that he may have led expeditions as far as Kashgar in Chinese Turkestan, leading to the first known contacts between China and the West around 200 BCE. The Greek historian Strabo writes, *"they extended their empire even as far as the Seres (China) and the Phryni."*

The Hellenistic world and Classical Greek philosophy mixed with Eastern philosophies,leading to syncretisms such as Greco-Buddhism.

Chinese exploration of Central Asia

With the Mediterranean linked to the Fergana Valley, the next step was to open a route across the Tarim Basin and the Hexi Corridor to China Proper. This extension came around 130 BCE, with the embassies of the Han dynasty to Central Asia following the reports of the ambassadorZhang Qian (who was originally sent to obtain an alliance with theYuezhi against the Xiongnu).Zhang Qian visited directly the kingdom ofDayuan in Ferghana, the territories of the Yuezhi in Transoxiana, theBactrian country of Daxia with its remnants of Greco-Bactrian rule, andKangju.

He also made reports on neighbouring countries that he did not visit, such as Anxi (Parthia), Tiaozhi (Mesopotamia), Shendu (Pakistan) and the Wusun. Zhang Qian's report suggested the economic reason for Chinese expansion and wall-building westward, and trailblazed the silk road which is one of the most famous trade routes. After the defeat of the Xiongnu, however, Chinese armies established themselves in Central Asia, initiating the Silk Route as a major avenue of international trade. Some say that the Chinese Emperor Wu became interested in developing commercial relationships with the sophisticated urban civilizations of Ferghana, Bactria, and the Parthian Empire: "The Son of Heaven on hearing all this reasoned thus: Ferghana (Dayuan *"Great Ionians"*) and the possessions of Bactria (Ta-Hsia) and Parthian Empire (Anxi) are large countries, full of rare things, with a population living in fixed abodes and given to occupations somewhat identical with those of the Chinese people, but with weak armies, and placing great value on the rich produce of China" (*Hou Hanshu*, Later Han History). Others say that Emperor Wu was mainly interested infighting the Xiongnu and that major trade began only after the Chinese pacified the Hexi Corridor.

"China snatched control of the Silk Road from the Hsiung-nu", when the Chinese general Cheng Ki "installed himself as protector of the Tarim at Wu-lei, situated between Kara Shahr and Kucha." "China's control of the Silk Road at the time of the later Han, by ensuring the freedom of transcontinental trade along the double chain of oases north and south of theTarim, favoured the dissemination of Buddhism in the river basin, and with it Indian literature and Hellenistic art."

The Chinese were also strongly attracted by the tall and powerful horses (named "Heavenly horses") in the possession of the Dayuan (literally the "Great Ionians", theGreek kingdoms of Central Asia), which were of capital importance in fighting the nomadic Xiongnu. The Chinese subsequently sent numerous embassies, around ten every year, to these countries and as far as Seleucid Syria. "Thus more embassies were dispatched to Anxi [Parthia], Yancai [who later joined the Alans], Lijian [Syria under the Greek Seleucids], Tiaozhi (Mesopotamia), and Tianzhu [northwestern India]... As a rule, rather more than ten such missions went forward in the course of a year, and at the least five or six." (*Hou Hanshu*, Later Han History).These connections marked the beginning of the Silk Road trade network that extended to the Roman Empire. The Chinese campaigned in Central Asia on several occasions, and direct encounters between Han troops and Roman legionaries (probably captured or recruited as mercenaries by the Xiong Nu) are recorded, particularly in the 36 BCE battle of Sogdiana

(Joseph Needham, Sidney Shapiro). It has been suggested that the Chinese crossbow was transmitted to the Roman world on such occasions, although the Greekgastraphetes provides an alternative origin. R. Ernest Dupuy and Trevor N. Dupuy suggest that in 36 BCE, a "Han expedition into central Asia, west of Jaxartes River, apparently encountered and defeated a contingent of Roman legionaries. The Romans may have been part of Antony's army invading Parthia. Sogdiana (modern Bukhara), east of the Oxus River, on the Polytimetus River, was apparently the most easterly penetration ever made by Roman forces in Asia. The margin of Chinese victory appears to have been their crossbows, whose bolts and darts seem easily to have penetrated Roman shields and armour." The Roman historian Florus also describes the visit of numerous envoys, which included*Seres*(China), to the first Roman Emperor Augustus, who reigned between 27 BCE and 14 CE:

Even the rest of the nations of the world which were not subject to the imperial sway were sensible of its grandeur, and looked with reverence to the Roman people, the great conqueror of nations. Thus even Scythians and Sarmatians sent envoys to seek the friendship of Rome. Nay, the Seres came likewise, and the Indians who dwelt beneath the vertical sun, bringing presents of precious stones and pearls and elephants, but thinking all of less moment than the vastness of the journey which they had undertaken, and which they said had occupied four years. In truth it needed but to look at their complexion to see that they were people of another world than ours. — *Henry Yule, Cathay and the way thither*

The Han army regularly policed the trade route against nomadic bandit forces generally identified as Xiongnu. Han generalBan Chao led an army of 70,000 mounted infantry and light cavalry troops in the 1st century CE to secure the trade routes, reaching far west to the Tarim basin. Ban Chao expanded his conquests across the Pamirs to the shores of the Caspian Sea and the borders of Parthia. It was from here that the Han general dispatched envoy Gan Ying to Daqin (Rome).The Silk Road essentially came into being from the 1st century BCE, following these efforts by China to consolidate a road to the Western world and India, both through direct settlements in the area of the Tarim Basin and diplomatic relations with the countries of the Dayuan, Parthians and Bactrians further west. The Silk Roads were a "complex network of trade routes" that gave people the chance to exchange goods and culture.

A maritime Silk Route opened up between Chinese-controlled Giao ChÉ (centred in modern Vietnam, near Hanoi), probably by the 1st century. It extended, via ports on the coasts of India and Sri Lanka, all the way to Roman-controlled ports in Egyptand the Nabataean territories on the northeastern coast of the Red Sea.

Roman Empire

Soon after the Roman conquest of Egypt in 30 BCE, regular communications and trade between China, Southeast Asia, India, the Middle East, Africa, and Europe blossomed on an unprecedented scale. The eastern trade routes from the earlier Hellenistic powers and the Arabs that were part of the Silk Road were inherited by the Roman Empire. With control of these trade routes, citizens of the Roman Empire would receive new luxuries and greater prosperity for the Empire as a whole. The Greco-Roman trade with India started byEudoxus of Cyzicus in 130 BCE continued to increase, and according toStrabo (II.5.12), by the time of Augustus, up to 120 ships were setting sail every year from Myos Hormos in Roman Egypt to India. The Roman Empire connected with the Central Asian Silk Road through their ports in Barygaza (known today as Bharuch) and Barbaricum (known today as the cities of Karachi, Sindh, and Pakistan) and continued along the western coast of India. An ancient "travel guide" to this Indian Ocean trade route was the Greek Periplus of the Erythraean Sea written in 60 CE.

The travelling party of Maës Titianus penetrated farthest east along the Silk Road from the Mediterranean world, probably with the aim of regularising contacts and reducing the role of middlemen, during one of the lulls in Rome's intermittent wars with Parthia, which repeatedly obstructed movement along the

Silk Road. Intercontinental trade and communication became regular, organised, and protected by the 'Great Powers.' Intense trade with the Roman Empire soon followed, confirmed by the Roman craze for Chinese silk (supplied through the Parthians), even though the Romans thought silk was obtained from trees. This belief was affirmed by Seneca the Younger in his Phaedra and by Virgil in his Georgics. Notably, Pliny the Elderknew better. Speaking of the *bombyx* or silk moth, he wrote in his Natural Histories "They weave webs, like spiders, that become a luxurious clothing material for women, called silk." The Romans traded spices, perfumes, and silk.

Roman artisans began to replace yarn with valuable plain silk cloths from China.Chinese wealth grew as they delivered silk and other luxury goods to the Roman Empire, whose wealthy Roman women admired their beauty. The Roman Senate issued, in vain, several edicts to prohibit the wearing of silk, on economic and moral grounds: the import of Chinese silk caused a huge outflow of gold, and silk clothes were considered to be decadent and immoral.

If materials that do not hide the body, nor even one's decency, can be called clothes... Wretched flocks of maids labour so that the adulteress may be visible through her thin dress, so that her husband has no more acquaintance than any outsider or foreigner with his wife's body.

The Roman Empire, and its demand for sophisticated Asian products, crumbled in the West around the 5th century. The unification of Central Asia and Northern India within Kushan Empire in the 1st to 3rd centuries reinforced the role of the powerful merchants from Bactria and Taxila. They fostered multi-cultural interaction as indicated by their 2nd century treasure hoards filled with products from the Greco-Roman world, China, and India, such as in the archeological site of Begram.

Byzantine Empire

Byzantine Greek historian Procopius stated that two Nestorian Christian monks eventually uncovered the way of how silk was made. From this revelation monks were sent by the Byzantine Emperor Justinian (ruled 527 - 565) as spies on the Silk Road from Constantinople to China and back to steal the silkworm eggs, resulting in silk production in the Mediterranean, particularly in Thrace in northern Greece, and giving the Byzantine Empire a monopoly on silk production in medieval Europe.

Tang dynasty reopens the route

Although the Silk Road from China to the West was initially formulated during the reign ofEmperor Wu of Han (141 – 87 BCE), it was reopened by the Tang Empire in 639 when Hou Junji conquered the West, and remained open for almost four decades. It was closed after the Tibetans captured it in 678, but in 699, during Empress Wu's period, the Silk Road reopened when the Tang reconquered the Four Garrisons of Anxi originally installed in 640, once again connecting China directly to the West for land-based trade. The Tang captured the vital route through the Gilgit Valley from Tibet in 722, lost it to the Tibetans in 737, and regained it under the command of the Goguryeo-Korean General Gao Xianzhi.

While the Turks were settled in the Ordos region (former territory of the Xiongnu), the Tang government took on the military policy of dominating the central steppe. The Tang dynasty (along with Turkic allies) conquered and subdued Central Asia during the 640s and 650s.During Emperor Taizong's reign alone, large campaigns were launched against not only theGöktürks, but also separate campaigns against the Tuyuhun, the Xiyu states, and theXueyantuo. Under Emperor Gaozong, a campaign led by the general Su Dingfang waslaunched against the Western Turks ruled by Ashina Helu. The Silk Road was the most important pre-modern Eurasian trade route. The Tang dynasty established a second Pax Sinica, and the Silk Road reached its golden age, whereby Persian and Sogdian merchants benefited from the commerce between East and West. At the same time, the Chinese empire welcomed foreign cultures, making it very cosmopolitan in its urban centres. In addition to the land route, the Tang dynasty also developed the maritime Silk Route. Chinese envoys had been sailing through the Indian Ocean to India since perhaps the 2nd century BCE, yet it was during the Tang dynasty that a strong Chinese maritime presence could be found in the Persian Gulf and Red Sea, intoPersia, Mesopotamia (sailing up the Euphrates River in modern-day Iraq), Arabia, Egypt, Aksum (Ethiopia), and Somalia in the Horn of Africa.

Medieval

The Silk Road represents an early phenomenon of political and cultural integration due to inter-regional trade. In its heyday, it sustained an international culture that strung together groups as diverse as the Magyars, Armenians, and Chinese. The Silk Road reached its peak in the west during the time of the Byzantine Empire; in the Nile-Oxus section, from the Sassanid Empire period to the Il Khanate period; and in the sinitic zone from the Three Kingdoms period to the Yuan Dynasty period. Trade between East and West also developed across the Indian Ocean, between Alexandria in Egypt and Guangzhou in China. Persian Sassanid coins emerged as a means of currency, just as valuable as silk yarn and textiles.

Under its strong integrating dynamics on the one hand and the impacts of change it transmitted on the other, tribal societies previously living in isolation along the Silk Road, and pastoralists who were of barbarian cultural development, were drawn to the riches and opportunities of the civilisations connected by the routes, taking on the trades of marauders or mercenaries. Many barbarian tribes became skilled warriors able to conquer rich cities and fertile lands and to forge strong military empires.

The Sogdians dominated the East-West trade after the 4th century up to the 8th century, with Suyab and Talas ranking among their main centres in the north. They were the main caravan merchants of Central Asia. Their commercial interests were protected by the resurgent military power of theGöktürks, whose empire has been described as "the joint enterprise of theAshina clan and the Soghdians". A.V. Dybo noted that "according to historians, the main driving force of the Great Silk Road were not just Sogdians, but the carriers of a mixed Sogdian-Türkic culture that often came from mixed families." Their trade, with some interruptions, continued in the 9th century within the framework of the Uighur Empire, which until 840 extended across northern Central Asia and obtained from China enormous deliveries of silk in exchange for horses. At this time caravans of Sogdians travelling to Upper Mongolia are mentioned in Chinese sources. They played an equally important religious and cultural role. Part of the data about eastern Asia provided by Muslim geographers of the 10th century actually goes back to Sogdian data of the period 750–840 and thus shows the survival of links between east and west. However, after the end of the Uighur Empire, Sogdian trade went through a crisis. What mainly issued from Muslim Central Asia was the trade of theSamanids, which resumed the northwestern road leading to the Khazars and the Urals and the northeastern one toward the nearby Turkic tribes.

The Silk Road gave rise to the clusters of military states of nomadic origins in North China, ushered the Nestorian,Manichaean, Buddhist, and later Islamic religions into Central Asia and China.

Islamic era and the Silk Road

By the Umayyad era Damascus had overtaken Ctesiphon as a major trade center until the Abbasid dynasty built the city of Baghdad, which became the most important city along the silk road.

At the end of its glory, the routes brought about the largest continental empire ever, the Mongol Empire, with its political centres strung along the Silk Road (Beijing in North China, Karakorum in central Mongolia, Sarmakhand in Transoxiana, Tabriz in Northern Iran, Sarai and Astrakhan in lower Volga, Solkhat in Crimea, Kazan in Central Russia, Erzurum in eastern Anatolia), realising the political unification of zones previously loosely and intermittently connected by material and cultural goods. In Central Asia, Islam expanded from the 7th century onward, bringing a stop to Chinese westward expansion at the Battle of Talas in 751. Further expansion of the Islamic Turks in Central Asia from the 10th century finished disrupting trade in that part of the world, and Buddhism almost disappeared. For much of the Middle Ages, the IslamicCaliphate (centred in the Near East) often had a monopoly over much of the trade conducted across the Old World.

Mongol age

The Mongol expansion throughout the Asian continent from around 1207 to 1360 helped bring political stability and re-established the Silk Road (via Karakorum). It also brought an end to the dominance of the Islamic Caliphate over world trade. Because the Mongols came to control the trade routes, trade circulated throughout the region, though they never abandoned their nomadic lifestyle.

The Mongol diplomat Rabban Bar Sauma visited the courts of Europe in 1287–88 and provided a detailed written report to the Mongols. Around the same time, theVenetian explorer Marco Polo became one of the first Europeans to travel the Silk Road to China. His tales, documented in *The Travels of Marco Polo*, opened Western eyes to some of the customs of the Far East. He was not the first to bring back stories, but he was one of the most widely read. He had been preceded by numerous Christian missionaries to the East, such as William of Rubruck, Benedykt Polak, Giovanni da Pian del Carpine, and Andrew of Longjumeau. Later envoys included Odoric of Pordenone, Giovanni de' Marignolli, John of Montecorvino, Niccolò de' Conti, and Ibn Battuta, a MoroccanMuslim traveller who passed through the present-day Middle East and across the Silk Road from Tabriz between 1325–54.

In the 13th century efforts were made at forming a Franco-Mongol alliance, with an exchange of ambassadors and (failed) attempts at military collaboration in the Holy Land during the later Crusades. Eventually the Mongols in the Ilkhanate, after they had destroyed theAbbasid and Ayyubid dynasties, converted to Islam and signed the 1323 Treaty of Aleppo with the surviving Muslim power, the EgyptianMamluks.

Some studies indicate that the Black Death, which devastated Europe in the late 1340s, may have reached Europe from Central Asia (or China) along the trade routes of the Mongol Empire.

Decline and disintegration

The fragmentation of the Mongol Empire loosened the political, cultural, and economic unity of the Silk Road. Turkmenimarching lords seized land around the western part of the Silk Road from the decaying Byzantine Empire. After the fall of the Mongol Empire, the great political powers along the Silk Road became economically and culturally separated. Accompanying the crystallisation of regional states was the decline of nomad power, partly due to the devastation of the Black Death and partly due to the encroachment of sedentary civilisations equipped with gunpowder. Gunpowder and early modernity in Europe led to the integration of territorial states and increasing mercantilism. On the Silk Road, however, gunpowder and early modernity had the opposite impact: the level of integration of the Mongol Empire could not be maintained, and trade declined, partly because of an increase in European maritime exchanges.

The Silk Road stopped serving as a shipping route for silk about 1453 with the Ottoman supremacy at Constantinople. Ottoman rulers of the day were anti-western, countering the crusades and aware of the loss of Andalusia in the west. They expressed their displeasure by embargoing trade with the west. Tensions with the west had eased a bit a century later, and Venice was able to cut an uneasy deal with the Ottomans, regaining for a time some of their economic clout as middlemen.

New European routes

The disintegration of the Silk Road following the reign of the Mongols stimulated Europeans to reach the prosperous Chinese empire via a sea route. Tremendous profits were to be obtained by anyone who could achieve a direct trade connection with Asia. The ocean route from Europe to the East was initially discovered by the expeditions of Bartolomeu Dias (1488) and Vasco da Gama (1497-1499), via the Atlantic and Indian oceans. In 1500, an armada led by Pedro Álvares Cabral also linked for the first time on this new route the New World (South America) and Asia.

Trade was the primary motivation for Portuguese explorations of the Indian Ocean, including the sea of China, resulting in the arrival in 1513 of the first European trading ships to the coasts of China, under Jorge Álvares and Rafael Perestrello, sent by Afonso de Albuquerque. These were followed by the diplomatic and commercial mission of Fernão Pires de Andradeand Tomé Pires in 1517, under the orders of Manuel I of Portugal, which formally opened relations between the Portuguese Empire and the Ming dynasty during the reign of the Zhengde Emperor.

In 1557 the settlement of the Portuguese in Macau, who paid an annual lease of 500 taels (20 kilograms) of silver to the Emperor of China, established the first permanent European maritime trade post between Europe and China. Other European powers followed over the next centuries, which caused the eventual demise of the Silk Road, or its global diversification by trans-oceanic routes from the western Pacific to the Atlantic Ocean, via the Indian Ocean.

When Christopher Columbus sailed across the Atlantic Ocean in 1492, he was searching for an alternative trade route to China from Spain. When he discovered America, it was believed he had reached Asia and the search was interrupted.

However, the quest for a westward route was resumed a few years later after explorer Nuñez de Balboa crossed the Isthmus of Panama in 1513 and discovered, from there, the Pacific Ocean, proving that this was in fact a New World.

The western voyage from Europe to Asia was finally completed with the Spanish expedition of 1519-1522, led by the Portuguese Ferdinand Magellan, the first European voyage to cross the Pacific Ocean, and the first world circumnavigation in a single expedition, finished by 18 men led by Juan Sebastián Elcano.

In 1565 Spanish navigator Andrés de Urdaneta discovered a return route across the Pacific, from the Philippines to New Spain. This led to the first regular transpacific trade route, the Manila-Acapulco Galleon route, which lasted two and half centuries, until 1815.

This Pacific line was connected overland through Mexico with an Atlantic line, the Spanish West Indies Fleet, which in turn linked the Americas with Spain. The combined route was the longest trade route in history until the 19th century, and one of the first examples of globalisation.

The Netherlands and Britain followed beginning in the 17th century. The Netherlands made an unsuccessful attempt to find a northern sea route to Asia in 1594. Navigator Willem Barents left Amsterdam with two ships to search for theNortheast passage, north of Siberia and on to eastern Asia. He reached the west coast of Novaya Zemlya and followed it northwards but was finally forced to turn back when confronted with its northern extremity. By the end of the 17th century, the Russians re-established a land trade route between Europe and China under the name of the Great Siberian Road.

While Europeans were entering China from its southern coast, by the sea route, the question arose whether it was the same country as Cathay, which Marco Polo had reached by the overland route. By c. 1600, the Jesuits stationed in China, led byMatteo Ricci, were pretty sure that it was, but others were not convinced. To check the situation on the ground, Bento de Góis, a Portuguese former soldier and explorer who had joined the Jesuits as a Lay Brother in Goa, India, travelled in 1603–1605 from India via Afghanistan on one of the routes of the traditional Silk Road (via Badakhshan, the Pamirs, Yarkand,Kucha, and Turpan to the border of Ming China in Suzhou, Gansu).

Gottfried Leibniz, echoing the prevailing perception in Europe until the Industrial Revolution, wrote in the 17th century that, "Everything exquisite and admirable comes from the East Indies... Learned people have remarked that in the whole world there is no commerce comparable to that of China."

New Silk Road

The Eurasian Land Bridge (a railway through China, Kazakhstan, Mongolia and Russia) is sometimes referred to as the "New Silk Road". The last link in one of these two railway routes was completed in 1990, when the railway systems of China and Kazakhstan connected at Alataw Pass (Alashan Kou). In 2008 the line was used to connect the cities of Ürümqi in China's Xinjiang Province to Almaty and Astana in Kazakhstan. Starting in July 2011 the line has been used by a freight service that connects Chongqing, China with Duisburg, Germany, cutting travel time for cargo from about 36 days by container ship to just 13 days by freight train. In 2013 Hewlett-Packard began moving large freight trains of laptop computers and monitors along this rail route.

In September 2013, during a visit to Kazakhstan, Chinese President Xi Jinping introduced a plan for creating a New Silk Road from China to Europe. The latest iterations of this plan, dubbed "One Belt, One Road" (OBOR), includes a land-basedSilk Road Economic Belt and Maritime Silk Road, with primary points in Ürümqi, Dostyk, Astana, Gomel, Brest, and the Polishcities of Ma³aszewicze and £ódŸ, which would be hubs of logistics and transshipment to other countries of Europe.

On February 15, 2016, with a change in routing, the first train dispatched under the OBOR scheme arrived from easternZhejiang Province to Tehran. Though this chapter does not complete the Silk Road–style overland connection between China and Europe, plans are underway to extend the route past Tehran, through Istanbul, into Europe. The actual route went through Almaty, Bishkek, Samarkand, and Dushanbe.

Routes

The Silk Road consisted of several routes. As it extended westwards from the ancient commercial centres of China, the overland, intercontinental Silk Road divided into northern and southern routes bypassing the Taklimakan Desert and Lop Nur.

Northern route

The northern route started at Chang'an (now called Xi'an), an ancient capital of China that was moved further east during the Later Han toLuoyang. The route was defined around the 1st century BCE when Han Wudi put an end to harassment by nomadic tribes.

The northern route travelled northwest through the Chinese province ofGansu from Shaanxi Province and split into three further routes, two of them following the mountain ranges to the north and south of theTaklamakan Desert to rejoin at Kashgar, and the other going north of the Tian Shan mountains through Turpan, Talgar, and Almaty (in what is now southeast Kazakhstan). The routes split again west of Kashgar, with a southern branch heading down the Alai Valley towards Termez(in modern Uzbekistan) and Balkh (Afghanistan), while the other travelled through Kokand in the Fergana Valley (in present-day eastern Uzbekistan) and then west across the Karakum Desert.

Both routes joined the main southern route before reaching ancient Merv, Turkmenistan. Another branch of the northern route turned northwest past the Aral Sea and north of the Caspian Sea, then and on to theBlack Sea.

A route for caravans, the northern Silk Road brought to China many goods such as "dates, saffron powder and pistachio nuts from Persia;frankincense, aloes and myrrh from Somalia; sandalwood from India; glass bottles from Egypt, and other expensive and desirable goods from other parts of the world." In exchange, the caravans sent back bolts of silk brocade, lacquer-ware, and porcelain.

Southern route

The southern route or Karakoram route was mainly a single route running from China through the Karakoram mountains, where it persists in modern times as the international paved road connecting Pakistan and China as the Karakoram Highway. It then set off westwards, but with southward spurs enabling the journey to be completed by sea from various points.

Crossing the high mountains, it passed through northern Pakistan, over the Hindu Kush mountains, and into Afghanistan, rejoining the northern route near Merv, Turkmenistan. From Merv, it followed a nearly straight line west through mountainous northern Iran, Mesopotamia, and the northern tip of the Syrian Desert to the Levant, where Mediterraneantrading ships plied regular routes to Italy, while land routes went either north through Anatolia or south to North Africa. Another branch road travelled from Herat through Susa to Charax Spasinu at the head of the Persian Gulf and across toPetra and on to Alexandria and other eastern Mediterranean ports from where ships carried the cargoes to Rome.

Southwestern route

The southwestern route is believed to be the Ganges/ Brahmaputra Delta, which has been the subject of international interest for over two millennia. Strabo, the 1st-century Roman writer, mentions the deltaic lands: "Regarding merchants who now sail from Egypt...as far as the Ganges, they are only private citizens..." His comments are interesting as Roman beads and other materials are being found at Wari-Bateshwar ruins, the ancient city with roots from much earlier, before theBronze Age, presently being slowly excavated beside the Old Brahmaputra in Bangladesh. Ptolemy's map of the Ganges Delta, a remarkably accurate effort, showed that his informants knew all about the course of the Brahmaputra River, crossing through the Himalayas then bending westward to its source in Tibet.

It is doubtless that this delta was a major international trading center, almost certainly from much earlier than the Common Era. Gemstones and other merchandise from Thailand

and Java were traded in the delta and through it. Chinese archaeological writer Bin Yang and some earlier writers and archaeologists, such as Janice Stargardt, strongly suggest this route of international trade as Sichuan-Yunnan-Burma-Bangladesh route.

According to Bin Yang, especially from the 12th century the route was used to ship bullion from Yunnan (gold and silver are among the minerals in which Yunnan is rich), through northern Burma, into modern Bangladesh, making use of the ancient route, known as the 'Ledo' route. The emerging evidence of the ancient cities of Bangladesh, in particular Wari-Bateshwar ruins, Mahasthangarh, Bhitagarh, Bikrampur, Egarasindhur, and Sonargaon, are believed to be the international trade centers in this route.

21ST CENTURY MARITIME SILK ROAD FROM A GLOBAL PERSPECTIVE

In the twenty-first century, countries have become more inter-connected by the ocean in conducting market, technological and information exchanges. The world is now in an era that values maritime cooperation and development. China's proposal to build a Maritime Silk Road conforms with larger developments in economic globalization and taps into common interests that China shares with countries along the route. The goal is to forge a community of interest with political mutual trust, integrated economies, inclusive culture and inter-connectivity. The construction of a 21st Century Maritime Silk Road is a global ini-tiative that pursues win-win results through cross-border cooperation. It is thus of great importance to view it from the perspective of multi-polarization, economic globalization and the co-existence and ba-lancing of cooperation and competition.

Building a 21st Century Maritime Silk Road will help stimulate all-round maritime opening-up and benefit ASEAN and relevant countries. Oceans contain a treasure trove of resources for sustainable development. China is currently at a critical stage in its economic reform process and must pay more attention to the ocean. As mentioned in the resolution of the Third Plenum, "[China] needs to enhance opening-up in coastal regions and boost the connectivity construction with neighboring countries and regions to spur all-round opening-up."

The Maritime Silk Road of the 21st century will further unite and expand common interests between China and other countries situated along the route, activate potential growth and achieve mutual benefits in wider areas. The Maritime Silk Road will extend southward from China's ports, through the South China Sea, the Straits of Malacca, Lombok and Sunda and then along the north Indian Ocean to the Persian Gulf, Red Sea and Gulf of Aden. In other words, the Road will extend from Asia to the Middle East, East Africa and Europe, and it will mainly rely on ASEAN countries. Building the Maritime Silk Road will connect China's ports with other countries through maritime connectivity, intercity cooperation and economic cooperation. On the one hand, the Road will strengthen the economic basis for China to cooperate with countries along the route and better connect Europe and Asia. On the other hand, the Road will facilitate the development of the Regional Comprehensive Economic Partnership (RCEP), bringing benefits to China, ASEAN and other countries along the road.

The Maritime Silk Road will increase trust and regional peace and stability

As the world's economic and political center shifts towards the Asia Pacific, the region has stepped into a stage of geopolitics characterized by intersecting, overlapping and conflicting interests. By facilitating communication between countries along the road, the Maritime Silk Road will help build a community that represents the common concerns, interests and expectations of all countries. The community is expected to guide and support a peaceful and stable Asia Pacific landscape.

Moreover, the Maritime Silk Road will further bring together the "Silk Road Economic Belt," the "Bangladesh-China-India-

Myanmar Economic Corridor" and the "China-Pakistan Economic Corridor" that together connect Europe and Asia. Such connections will greatly enhance China and other countries' abilities to develop economically while limiting external risks. The Maritime Silk Road will also enhance cooperation in non-traditional security areas while maintaining maritime security.

MARITIME PARTNERSHIPS ARE THE KEY TO BUILDING THE MARITIME SILK ROAD

At a speech before the Indonesian parliament in 2013, President Xi Jinping stated that Southeast Asia has become an important hub for the maritime silk road and that China is willing to enhance maritime cooperation with ASEAN countries, boost maritime partnerships and build a 21st Century Maritime Silk Road. President Xi's speech set forth a clear path for developing road. Enhancing maritime cooperation will be a priority task in building the Maritime Silk Road. The first step will involve China and countries along the route promoting pragmatic maritime cooperation.

Connecting multiple regions and uniting wide areas of co-operation, the tasks put forth in the 21st Century Maritime Silk Road will not be achieved in the immediate future. Instead, these tasks call for China and relevant countries to work in a step-by-step and practical manner. Building the Maritime Silk road will require diverse forms of cooperation. With a focus on economic cooperation, the Road will give consideration to all parties involved. It will be based on the existing cooperation mechanisms and platforms and be promoted by China and other countries along the route.

The 21st Century Maritime Silk Road will cover more than 20 countries and regions that share a broad consensus on enhancing exchanges, friendship, promoting development, safety and stability within the region and beyond. The Silk Road has already received positive responses and support from many relevant countries. Greek Prime Minister Antonidis Samaras, for example, made it clear that Greece will "support and actively participate in building the 21st Century Maritime Silk Road proposed by China." The Road runs through a region that is sensitive to international strategy and has complex geopolitics. The countries in the region differ in size, development, history, religion, language and culture. Therefore, the 21st Century Maritime Silk Road will accommodate various countries' demands and apply suitable policies to each country. Meanwhile, the Road must change and consolidate new patterns of cooperation.

China has been building friendships and partnerships with nei-ghboring countries and developing maritime partnerships with its ocean neighbors, providing a solid foundation for cooperation with ASEAN and countries in the region. The 21st Century Maritime Silk Road requires the following efforts: First, consensus must be reached between major countries along the route to enhance maritime cooperation. During high-level dialogues in recent years, the Chinese leadership made maritime cooperation an important topic of bilateral discussions and established the China-ASEAN and China-Indonesia Maritime Cooperation Fund. At the same time, China has actively promoted maritime cooperation between Southeast Asia, South Asia and African countries and established high-level mechanisms between various national maritime departments.

Second, countries must engage in pragmatic cooperation along the route in the areas of trade, the economy, culture and infrastructure. In 2012, the trade volume of countries along the route accounted for 17.9 percent of China's total trade. The contracted turnover in countries along the route accounted for 37.9 percent of China's overseas contracted turnover. People-to-people exchanges between China and ASEAN recently topped 15 million, while two-way students reached more than 170,000.

Third, countries along the route must engage in effective cooperation on ocean and climate change, marine disaster prevention and mitigation, biodiversity preservation and other areas of maritime policy. In 2010, the Indonesia-China Center for Ocean & Climate (ICCOC) was established. In 2013, the China-Thailand Climate and Marine Ecosystem Joint Lab were both launched. In 2012, the Chinese government set up a Marine Scholarship, and from that year onward, the scholarship will sponsor young people from developing countries in Southeast Asia, Africa and Latin America to obtain a master's degree or doctorate in China to enhance the marine capabilities of their own countries.

SILK PRODUCTION AND THE SILK TRADE

Silk is a textile of ancient Chinese origin, woven from the protein fibre produced by the silkworm to make its cocoon, and was developed, according to Chinese tradition, sometime around the year 2,700 BC. Regarded as an extremely high value product, it was reserved for the exclusive usage of the Chinese imperial court for the making of cloths, drapes, banners, and other items of prestige. Its production was kept a fiercely guarded secret within China for some 3,000 years, with imperial decrees sentencing to death anyone who revealed to a foreigner the process of its production. Tombs in the Hubei province dating from the 4th and 3rdcenturies BC contain outstanding examples of silk work, including brocade, gauze and embroidered silk, and the first complete silk garments.

The Chinese monopoly on silk production however did not mean that the product was restricted to the Chinese Empire – on the contrary, silk was used as a diplomatic gift, and was also traded extensively, first of all with China's immediate neighbours, and subsequently further afield, becoming one of China's chief exports under the Han dynasty (206 BC –220 AD). Indeed, Chinese cloths from this period have been found in Egypt, in northern Mongolia, and elsewhere.

At some point during the 1st century BC, silk was introduced to the Roman Empire, where it was considered an exotic luxury and became extremely popular, with imperial edicts being issued to control prices. Its popularity continued throughout the Middle Ages, with detailed Byzantine regulations for the manufacture of silk clothes, illustrating its importance as a quintessentially royal fabric and an important source of revenue for the crown. Additionally, the needs of the Byzantine Church for silk garments and hangings were substantial. This luxury item was thus one of the early impetuses in the development of trading routes from Europe to the Far East.

Knowledge about silk production was very valuable and, despite the efforts of the Chinese emperor to keep it a closely guarded secret, it did eventually spread beyond China, first to India and Japan, then to the Persian Empire and finally to the west in the 6thcentury AD. This was described by the historian Procopius, writing in the 6th century:

Beyond Silk; a diversity of routes and cargos

However, whilst the silk trade was one of the earliest catalysts for the trade routes across Central Asia, it was only one of a wide range of products that was traded between east and west, and which included textiles, spices, grain, vegetables and fruit, animal hides, tools, wood work, metal work, religious objects, art work, precious stones and much more. Indeed, the Silk Roads became more popular and increasingly well-travelled over the course of the Middle Ages, and were still in use in the 19th century, a testimony not only to their usefulness but also to their flexibility and adaptability to the changing demands of society. Nor did these trading paths follow any one trail – merchants had a wide choice of different routes crossing a variety of regions of Eastern Europe, the Middle East, Central Asia and the Far East, as well as the maritime routes, which transported goods from China and South East Asia through the Indian Ocean to Africa, India and the Near East.

These routes developed over time and according to shifting geopolitical contexts throughout history. For example, merchants from the Roman Empire would try to avoid crossing the territory of the Parthians, Rome's enemies, and therefore took routes to the north, across the Caucasus region and over the Caspian Sea. Similarly, whilst extensive trade took place over the network of rivers that crossed the Central Asian steppes in the early Middle Ages, their water levels rose and fell, and sometimes dried up altogether, and trade routes shifted accordingly.

Maritime trade was another extremely important branch of this global trade network. Most famously used for the transportation of spices, the maritime trade routes have also been known as the Spice Roads, supplying markets across the world with cinnamon, pepper, ginger, cloves and nutmeg from the Moluccas islands in Indonesia (known as the Spice Islands), as well as a wide range of other goods. Textiles, woodwork, precious stones, metalwork, incense, timber, and saffron were all traded by the merchants travelling these routes, which stretched over 15,000 kilometres, from the west coast of Japan, past the Chinese coast, through South East Asia, and past India to reach the Middle East and so to the Mediterranean.

The history of these maritime routes can be traced back thousands of years, to links between the Arabian Peninsula, Mesopotamia and the Indus Valley Civilization. The early Middle Ages saw an expansion of this network, as sailors from the Arabian Peninsula forged new trading routes across the Arabian Sea and into the Indian Ocean. Indeed, maritime trading links were established between Arabia and China from as early as the 8th century AD. Technological advances in the science of navigation, in astronomy, and also in the techniques of ship building combined to make long-distance sea travel increasingly practical. Lively coastal cities grew up around the most frequently visited ports along these routes, such as Zanzibar, Alexandria, Muscat, and Goa, and these cities became wealthy centres for the exchange of goods, ideas, languages and beliefs, with large markets and continually changing populations of merchants and sailors.

In the late 15th century, the Portuguese explorer, Vasco da Gama, navigated round the Cape of Good Hope, thereby connecting European sailors with these South East Asian maritime routes for the first time and initiating direct European involvement in this trade. By the 16th and 17th centuries, these routes and their lucrative trade had become subject of fierce rivalries between the Portuguese, Dutch, and British. The conquest of ports along the maritime routes brought both wealth and security, as they effectively governed the passage of maritime trade and also allowed ruling powers to claim monopolies on these exotic and highly sought-after goods, as well as gathering the substantial taxes levied on merchant vessels.

The map above illustrates the great variety of routes that were available to merchants bearing a wide range of goods and travelling from different parts of the world, by both land and sea. Most often, individual merchant caravans would cover specific sections of the routes, pausing to rest and replenish supplies, or stopping altogether and selling on their cargos at points throughout the length of the roads, leading to the growth of lively trading cities and ports. The Silk Roads were dynamic and porous; goods were traded with local populations throughout, and local products were added into merchants' cargos. This process enriched not only the merchants' material wealth and the variety of their cargos, but also allowed for exchanges of culture, language and ideas to take place along the Silk Roads.

Routes of Dialogue

Perhaps the most lasting legacy of the Silk Roads has been their role in bringing cultures and peoples in contact with each other, and facilitating exchange between them. On a practical level, merchants had to learn the languages and customs of the countries they travelled through, in order to negotiate successfully. Cultural interaction was a vital aspect of material exchange. Moreover, many travellers ventured onto the Silk Roads in order to partake in this process of intellectual and cultural exchange that was taking place in cities along the routes. Knowledge about science, arts and literature, as well as crafts and technologies was shared across the Silk Roads, and in this way, languages, religions and cultures developed and influenced each other. One of the most famous technical advances to have been propagated worldwide by the Silk Roads was the technique of making paper, as well as the development of printing press technology. Similarly, irrigation systems across Central Asia share features that were spread by travellers who not only carried their own cultural knowledge, but also absorbed that of the societies in which they found themselves.

Indeed, the man who is often credited with founding the Silk Roads by opening up the first route from China to the West in the 2^{nd}century BC, General Zhang Qian, was on a diplomatic mission rather than a trading expedition. Sent to the West in 139 BC by the Han Emperor Wudi to ensure alliances against the Xiongnu, the hereditary enemies of the Chinese, Zhang Qian was captured and imprisoned by them. Thirteen years later he escaped and made his way back to China. Pleased with the wealth of detail and accuracy of his reports, the emperor sent Zhang Qian on another mission in 119 BC to visit several neighbouring peoples, establishing early routes from China to Central Asia.

Religion and a quest for knowledge were further inspirations to travel along these routes. Buddhist monks from China made pilgrimages to India to bring back sacred texts, and their travel diaries are an extraordinary source of information. The diary of Xuan Zang (whose 25-year journal lasted from 629 to 654 AD) not only has an enormous historical value, but also inspired a comic novel in the sixteenth century, the 'Pilgrimage to the West', which has become one of the great Chinese classics. During the Middle Ages, European monks undertook diplomatic and religious missions to the east, notably Giovanni da Pian del Carpini, sent by Pope Innocent IV on a mission to the Mongols from 1245 to 1247, and William of Rubruck, a Flemish Franciscan monk sent by King Louis IX of France again to the Mongol hordes from 1253 to 1255. Perhaps the most famous was the Venetian explorer, Marco Polo, whose travels lasted for more than 20 years between 1271 and 1292, and whose account of his experiences became extremely popular in Europe after his death. The routes were also fundamental in the dissemination of religions throughout Eurasia. Buddhism is one example of a religion that travelled the Silk Roads, with Buddhist art and shrines being found as far apart as Bamiyan in Afghanistan, Mount Wutai in China, and Borobudur in Indonesia. Christianity, Islam, Hinduism, Zoroastrianism and Manicheism spread in the same way, as travellers absorbed the cultures they encountered and then carried them back to their homelands with them. Thus, for example, Hinduism and subsequently Islam were introduced into Indonesia and Malaysia by Silk Road merchants travelling the maritime trade routes from India and Arabia.

THE NEW SILK ROAD CONCEPT AS A DOMESTIC POLICY INSTRUMENT

In the area of domestic policy, the New Silk Road concept is a personal project of China's new leader, Xi Jinping. This plan cannot fail mainly because its objectives are not clearly defined and it is based on an open concept. A whole range of moves made as part of foreign and economic policy can be included in the New Silk Road and presented as a success. Drawing on the glory days of Chinese civilisation is intended at legitimising the Communist Party and its achievements in the international arena.

In the area of economic policy, the New Silk Road will promote the development and economic growth of the central and western provinces of China. This concept is thus becoming an instrument in the policy of both Beijing (levelling out the differences on the scale of the whole country) and of individual provinces (competing with each other in the area of economic co-operation with foreign countries). The goals of Chinese provinces include promoting exports of goods and labour, and demonstrating their success in this area to the central government. However, subsidies for transport corridors offered by the central and western provinces and transport price competition adversely affect the rational use of the New Silk Road. The project can be used as an instrument in the policy of Chinese provinces allowing them to meet such criteria as export volume, export of workforce, and gaining experience in a given area. However, the Chinese government is likely to take action aimed at limiting this rivalry and the co-operation of individual provinces during the implementation of this concept.

Implementation of the New Silk Road's guidelines will also become a way to diversify investments and bring part of Chinese reserves into use. This will also contribute to boosting exports of capital and workforce and to diversifying investments. The construction of infrastructure will make it possible for Chinese firms to increase their engagement worldwide.

The prospects of the implementation of the New Silk Road

The implementation of the New Silk Road concept will to a huge extent depend on China. Building new connections makes sense at least because of the volume of Chinese trade with individual regions through which the land or the maritime variants of the New Silk Road will run: with Europe (US$559 billion), ASEAN (US$443 billion), the Middle East (US$257 billion), Africa (US$192 billion) and the CIS (US$150 billion). Given the open and imprecise nature of the concept, it may be expected that the concept will be implemented as part of bilateral relations, a formula now in use. The decision as to when the concept's success should be announced will be up to Beijing.

Previous experience also suggests that projects as part of the New Silk Road concept will be implemented in parallel rather than stage by stage. However, a number of limitations which may obstruct the process of the concept's implementation can be pointed to at the present stage.

The development of existing railway connections between China and Europe is the core of the land section's concept. At present, railway transport is used in only a small part of Chinese trade (3.5% of Chinese exports to the EU are transported by land). The main advantage of this is its much lower cost when compared to air transport and the fact that it is several times quicker than maritime transport. It takes 12-16 days to transport goods from central China to Germany by railway, and 50-60 days by ship. Railway transport will thus be appropriate for a specific group of goods, where it does not pay to transport them by air freight but maritime transport takes too long. The railway network will never be a predominant means of transport; it will remain an addition to maritime transport.

The most serious impediments to the implementation of the concept include customs procedures and differences in railway systems, which extend the time of transport. Interoperability of railway connections is difficult to achieve since the New Silk Road runs through three railway systems: the Chinese, the post-Soviet and the European. An additional challenge will be posed by Russia's integration projects as part of the Eurasian Economic Union, since this may impede the harmonisation and simplification of customs procedures. The decision to build new (standard gauge) railways in Eurasia may be of key importance in the context of the New Silk Road. Russia opposes such plans, especially with regard to Kazakhstan, and does not want a railway connection to be built from China to Kyrgyzstan and Uzbekistan. In addition to this, the various actors disagree about the shape of the route and its individual variants. The rivalry is especially evident between the EU and Russia. The New Silk Road also depends on the political developments in the numerous territories it runs through. Transport via Ukraine became less attractive when China withdrew from the plans to build a deep port in Crimea following its annexation. The lack of goods that could be exported to China is a great challenge, especially for Central Europe.

The trains go back empty, and the containers are often sent back to China by sea, which extends the time and increases the costs. The list of potential goods includes cars and medicines. Breaks need to be made in the winter season due to the low temperatures. As a consequence, some carriers started buying special thermo-insulated carriages that enable year-round transport.

6

Competing Visions for the Asia-Pacific

The US wants not only to be at the helm of the world's most economically dynamic region, but also to ensure that China's ascendancy does not go unchallenged. Beyond the reduction of tariffs, the TPP will thus intervene directly in the internal affairs of countries in the region.

From corporate governance and environmental standards to financial regulations, the agreement is seen by many as a means for the US to impose its vision on Asian trading partners. Some have even suggestedthat the TPP will leave certain emerging economies less competitive, while the US reaps the economic benefits.

The 'new Asian order'

The TPP is part of the US' vision for Asia. Specifically, it's an alternative to the economic future that the soon-to-be-operational China-led Asian Infrastructure Investment Bank (AIIB) proposes. Still smarting from its loss of face earlier this year – when US allies ignored pleas to refuse China's invitation to join the AIIB – the US may see the TPP as a way of tipping the balance back in its favour.

Announced as part of President Xi Jinping's ambitious "One Belt, One Road" (OBOR) initiative, the AIIB involves global co-operation to finance large-scale infrastructure projects in Asia. Its goal is the development of infrastructure and other productive sectors across the region. These include energy and power, transportation and telecommunications, rural infrastructure and agriculture development, water supply and sanitation, environmental protection and urban development and logistics.

More than 50 countries – including some of the US' closest allies, from Australia and Israel to South Korea and the UK – have signed the AIIB's Articles of Agreement. With US$50 billion of capital at its disposal (eventually $100 billion will be raised), the bank may soon rival the lending power of the World Bank's International Bank for Reconstruction and Development.

It's evidence that the "Chinese dream" has gone global. As one Wall Street Journal columnist put it, the AIIB and the OBOR represent a sinocentric "new Asian order".

Two visions for Asia - or just one?

But are these two instruments of free trade and development really incompatible? Is the US' pivot to Asia totally at odds with China's OBOR initiative? More importantly, will the US and China ultimately benefit as a result of their mutual exclusion from these agreements for Asian prosperity?

There's talk that the TPP will "advance democracy ... as an inevitable outcome" despite being largely silent on the matter. The free trade agreement may have democracy promotion as its implicit motivation.

Meanwhile, in line with China's regime-neutral approach to foreign policy – echoes of which can be found in Xi's recent UN General Assembly address – the AIIB may represent the newest arm of China's "no strings attached" model for international development aid. The investment bank could unintentionally promote, or at least sustain, autocracy.

Speculation aside, commentators are now making the case that the TPP and AIIB are not incompatible. Though they appear to represent conflicting visions for the Asia-Pacific, these two strategies are more complementary than we might think. Both the US and China – as well as much of Asia – would benefit from their mutual inclusion in these two trading and development initiatives. Despite being party to the TPP, it's clear many Asian nations aren't completely happy with its terms. Even the US' two closest allies in Asia – Australia and Japan – fear the TPP will be too intrusive in their domestic affairs.

Here, the US can perhaps learn something from China's more hands-off approach. Negotiating terms may be easier than believed, given top Chinese officials have already indicated that China would be "very open"to joining the TPP.

Similarly, the AIIB would only improve its credit rating and international legitimacy if it included countries such as the US and Japan. However tricky these negotiations may be, it is necessary for the AIIB to be seen as a true Asian alternative to the World Bank. Given that some Asian countries are already suspicious about what the flood of Chinese investment might do to local culture, the US' involvement might provide some reassurance.

More pragmatically, the TPP and the AIIB could together ensure greater trade and development than either would alone. With the TPP's focus on "software" (rules for commerce and trade) and the AIIB's emphasis on "hardware" (infrastructure and development initiatives), the two instruments could complement each other. In turn, they could ensure greater co-operation in Asia.

Countries like New Zealand, Singapore, South Korea, Malaysia and Australia have signed up to both the American and Chinese initiatives. Their vision for Asia sees both superpowers at the helm, sharing responsibility and counter-balancing power. Isn't it time the US and China accepted this too?

THE GROWING STRATEGIC IMPORTANCE OF BANGLADESH TO CHINA

The visit by Chinese President Xi Jinping to Bangladesh on October 14-15, 2016 had been dubbed as a 'historical state visit' poised to be a geopolitical game changer in South Asia and the Indian Ocean region. At the sidelines of Xi's visit, Bangladeshi and Chinese firms signed USD 13.6 billion worth of deals in trade and investment in addition to the USD 20 billion in loan agreements signed by the two governments. The inevitable question is why the world's second largest economy comprising of 1.37 billion people and an economy 67 times bigger than Bangladesh is cozying up to the world's 47th largest economy? What geopolitical importance does Bangladesh have to receive such enormous bilateral assistance from a nation aspiring to be the next world leader? Bangladesh's strategically important geographic location, physical and political proximity to India, availability of cheap labour, and proximity to the Bay of Bengal have considerable implications for Chinese regional geopolitics and geo-economics.

Consolidating sphere of influence in the Indian Ocean

The Chinese economy is heavily dependent on energy resources transported via the secure sea-lanes in the Indian Ocean. Around 80 percent of China's energy import from the Middle East pass through the Strait of Malacca, which is a narrow stretch of water connecting the Indian Ocean and Pacific Ocean. Malacca provides China the shortest maritime route to Europe, Africa and Middle East. China's ever increasing need for energy have increased the strategic importance of this maritime region and the importance of maintaining good relations with littoral states in and around the region. To consolidate influence in this critical trade route and at the same time shedding overdependence on it, China has been pledging investment to the littoral states around the Indian Ocean. It is due to this strategy, Bangladesh, owing to its geographic positioning in the Bay of Bengal, has been the recipient of investment pledges from China's deep pockets. Bangladesh is an important factor in the much touted 'string of pearls' theory, which explicates how China intends to exert more influence around the Malacca Strait and Indian Ocean through investment in development and infrastructural projects around Indian Ocean rim states.

To cut down over-reliance on the Strait of Malacca, China is already building oil pipelines from the Burmese port Kyakpiu to Kunming. In this context, China is also keen on developing the Chittagong port in the hopes of building a parallel pipeline connecting Chittagong-Kyakpiu-Kunming. If India ever, with US support, blocks the Malacca chokepoint through the Indian base in the Andaman Sea, it can have dire repercussions for the Chinese manufacturing base. Hence, it is important for China to gain more influence in the Indian Ocean region through bankrolling infrastructural investment in the coastal nations.

Conduit to South Asia

For long, China has invested much of its attention towards South East Asia but has now diverted towards South Asia, a region comprising of one-fourth of the world's population and housing the third largest economy by Purchasing Power Parity (PPP), which represents a lucrative market for Chinese products. Since connectivity at the moment is not feasible via the contentious Arunachal Pradesh or through Afghanistan or Pakistan, one way for China to reach mainland India is through Bangladesh, given the friendly relation the two countries maintain. Also, to activate the Bangladesh-China-India Myanmar (BCIM) sub-regional corridor, crucial for reaching South Asian markets, it is imperative to bring Bangladesh on board. China intends to draw in Bangladesh through massive infrastructural investment, an act touted by experts as China's 'checkbook diplomacy.'

Checking India's regional dominance and market for arms sale

China has been quietly checkmating India's regional dominance in South Asia through its arms sale in countries bordering India. While Beijing today is the third largest arms provider in the world, between 2011 and 2015, 71 percent of Chinese arms exports were to Pakistan, Myanmar, and Bangladesh – states proximate to both India and China. Although Bangladesh's USD 195 billion GDP is a meagre 0.017 percent of China's USD 11 trillion GDP, between 2011 and

2015 Bangladesh was the second largest recipient of Chinese arms in the world with Beijing supplying over 80 percent of the country's arms imports over the past decade.

When China sells heavy armaments like tanks and submarines to a country, the importing country becomes reliant on China for a long time for training, maintenance, and repair. This reliance inevitably results in certain degree of influence on the importing country. This makes it advantageous for China to be selling arms at low prices and on easy credit to countries bordering India as a way of checking India's geopolitical ambitions in the region. For China, growing ties with Bangladesh serves the dual purpose of revenue from sale of arms and checking Indian dominance in the region.

Key player in the One Belt One Road interconnection

During the 1960s, China was hesitant in forging regional cooperation with its Asian neighbours which changed during the 1990s after the Asian Financial Crisis. Since President Xi Jinping has come to power, China has taken a leadership role in forging community based regional integration in Asia. The geographical focus of integration for China has earlier been confined only to East Asia which has now been expanded to encompass South and Central Asia. China is currently expanding on two fronts; westward towards Eurasia and southward towards the Indian Ocean. Counterbalancing USA's influence in Asia Pacific is also one of many reasons why China is so persistently pushing for mega projects such as the One Belt One Road (OBOR).

Bangladesh is centrally situated along the BCIM Economic Corridor and retains a strategic position along the 21st Century Maritime Silk Road with Chittagong port as a major maritime pivot through the Indian Ocean, a very important factor for realisation of both the Economic Belt and Maritime Road initiatives.

Xi's 'One Belt, One Road' is his most ambitious foreign and economic policy till date. To solidify his second term, rejuvenate a slowing China, and to assume political leverage over its neighbors, Xi has already begun to vigorously market this flagship project. OBOR will support China in becoming the new leader of free trade in Asia Pacific with the US abandoning the TPP. It would also geo-economically assist China in dealing with its excess capacity, upgrade its industry, and develop its less prosperous regions. To materialise all interconnections under OBOR, Xi Jinping now needs to woo former Indian allies in South Asia to commit to his projects.

Relocating Sunset Industries

As labour costs rise in China, its declining sunset industries will be looking for places to relocate. China will continue to move away from labour intensive low-tech industries owing to its rising labour costs and cooling markets. It will gradually move towards high margin and high-end manufacturing like IT, aerospace, and telecommunication. Existing Chinese companies, producing low-end labour intensive products will be looking for places with cheap labour to relocate their plants. With almost a third of its population between the ages of 15-30, Bangladesh provides a huge young workforce at one of the cheapest rates in the world to the Chinese manufacturers of sunset industries wishing to carry forward with many of their labour intensive industries.

From the bigger scheme of regional power play to the unexplored potential in commerce and connectivity, Bangladesh is one of the most vital countries for China in expanding its sphere of influence in South and Southeast Asia. Hence, it is no surprise that the 2016 visit by President Xi Jinping, first in more than three decades, saw China-Bangladesh relations elevated to 'Strategic Partnership of Cooperation' from 'Comprehensive Partnership'. It is now for Bangladesh to gain leverage from China's checkbook diplomacy while maintaining the delicate balance of regional geopolitics.

ASIAN REGIONAL SHIFTS

In the early postwar period, prospects for Asia's security order were shaped by three dominant features: economic nationalism, security bilateralism, and political authoritarianism. Economic nationalism in Asia, spurred by a desire to enhance economic sovereignty to match political independence and aimed at reducing vulnerability to foreign economic forces, was clearly articulated at the historic Asian-African conference at Bandung in 1955. Subsequently, it produced a reliance on import-substitution strategies throughout Southeast Asia till the 1970s, when export-led growth models began to appear in that region. As James Kurth noted, "In regard to the international economy, the East Asian states are not international liberals but rather international mercantilists (1989). Security bilateralism emerged through America's bilateral military alliances in the region, termed as the "hub-and-spoke" system. This has been widely credited with providing not only the security of the alliance partners, but maintaining regional stability in Asia. Authoritarianism was Asia's dominant postwar political trend. Democratic leaders and political systems that emerged from the end of the colonial period found it difficult to get going. Communist takeovers in China, North Korea, and the Indochinese countries aside, democratic backsliding or the emergence of outright dictatorships occurred in practically every Asian country with the exception of Japan and India.

Half a century later, economic nationalism, security bilateralism, and political authoritarianism have given way to a complex mix of economic interdependence, security multipolarity (after a unipolar moment) multilateralism, and political pluralism, with profound consequences for regional order.

Economic Interdependence

Trade among the market-oriented economies of Asia and the Pacific nearly doubled as a proportion of their total trade between 1955 and 2005. Intra-East Asian trade today is higher than that in the NAFTA region (46%), and "very much comparable to intraregional trade in the European Union before the 1992 Maastricht treaty" (Kuroda 2005). China's trade with the United States in goods in 2009 was $366 billion, compared to $116 billion in 2000 (US Census Bureau). Foreign direct investment from the United States in China was over $45.7 billion in 2008 (Office of the US Trade Representative). In 2009, China's trade with Japan was $228.9 billion (The US-China Business Council), compared to $102 billion in 2002 (Ministry of Foreign Affairs of the People's Republic Of China's 2004), and with India $43.4 billion (The US-China Business Council), compared to $2.5 billion in 2000 (Brooks and Ferrarini 2010: 6). Mainland China–Taiwan trade in goods jumped from $25.83 billion in 1999 (Mastel 2001) to $106.2 billion in 2009 (The US-China Business Council). The level of two-way trade between China and ASEAN increased from US$8 billion in 1991 to over US$40 billion in 2001 and $231 billion in 2008 (People's Daily Online 2009). In 2008, China's trade with East Asia reached $757.5 billion (Asian Regional Integration Center).

Economic links in Asia have "moved beyond deepening intra-regional trade" and "become more *functionally integrative*" (Dent 2008: 46). Transnational production networks in East Asia cover both inter-industry and intra-industry or intra-firm trade (Bowles 1997: 223). Since the 1990s, China has joined Japan as another focal point of Asian regionalization, becoming a "regional integrator" (Lardy 2002). While Japanese FDI in the 1980s and 1990s encouraged a vertical or hierarchical structure in regionalized production (the so-called "flying geese"), with Japan producing the most advanced components, South Korea and Taiwan supplying intermediate components, and the ASEAN countries (except Singapore) producing lower-end parts and functioning as assembly sites, the production network emerging around China is more horizontal. Contrary to concerns that Southeast Asia may be reduced to a "semicolonial" status *vis-a-vis* China (which might support the scenario of a developing Chinese regional hegemony), China–ASEAN trade features export of manufactured products to each other. For example, the share of machinery and electrical appliances in China-ASEAN trade jumped from 12.41% in 1993 to 47.1% in ASEAN's total exports to China and from 20.78% in 1993 to 57.9% in

ASEAN's imports from China. This, demonstrating the importance of intra-industry trade, suggests the emergence of more horizontal, rather than hierarchical, production networks and supply chains between China and ASEAN (Men 2007: 266).

Financial interdependence and cooperation among Asian countries is growing as well. Chastened by the regional contagion effect of the financial crises of 1997 and 2008, Asian countries have set up currency swap arrangements under the Chiang Mai Initiative (now both bilateral and multilateral components, the former stood at US $90 billion in April 2009 [Ministry of Finance Japan] while the latter announced in 2010 amounts to $120 billion [People's Daily Online's 2010]). Moreover, the structure of economic interdependence is not intra-Asian, but also transpacific. Four Asian countries rank among the top ten nations holding US treasury securities (as of May 2009), with China topping the list at US $801.5 billion; Japan (2nd) at $677.2; Hong Kong (7th) at $93.2; Taiwan (9th) at $75.7 billion (US Department of the Treasury).

Further growth of economic interdependence in Asia is constrained by concerns about unequal benefits of regional trade agreements, fear of Chinese dominance, the rise of bilateral trade arrangements, and the launching of a separate trade liberalization track by the United States, the Trans-Pacific Partnership (TPP), that excludes China. Moreover, one of the more ambitious trade arrangements, the ASEAN Economic Community, is moving slower than envisaged. These trends might constrain the pacific effects of interdependence, which will be discussed in the following section.

Institutions

Regional institutions in Asia, stimulated by growing interdependence, today outnumber bilateral or multilateral alliances, reversing the situation that existed in the 1950s. The functions of multipurpose institutions have expanded to cover both interstate and transnational security issues. ASEAN, originally intended to reduce interstate tensions and promote economic cooperation, now tackles a wider variety of issues, admitted with a mixed record, environment, illegal migration, natural disasters, pandemics, terrorism. The ASEAN Regional Forum (ARF) has looked beyond confidence-building to a role in addressing transnational challenges such as disaster relief and terrorism. The Asia-Pacific Economic Cooperation's (APEC) summit serves an important political purpose. New and more specialized institutions have emerged to cover specific issue areas, the most notable being the Chiang Mai Initiative to address financial issues not handled by other regional bodies. The ASEAN Plus Three (APT) created in 1997, has also become the de facto regional framework for coordinating regional responses to pandemics and other nontraditional security threats. ASEAN is adopting greater institutionalization and legalization, especially with the adoption of ASEAN Free Trade Area (AFTA), Southeast Asia Nuclear Weapon-Free Zone, and the ASEAN Charter. The newest institution, the East Asian Summit, engages all the major powers in Asia, including the United States.

On the negative side, ASEAN and other multilateral bodies in Asia have a mixed record in carrying out their security functions, due to disagreements over regional definition, intra-mural territorial disputes and mistrust over historical memories, continued adherence of states to the principle of non-intervention, and an aversion to too much legalization. Moreover, there is a competitive aspect to regional institution-building, with China preferring an exclusively East Asian framework minus the United States, while Japan and others supporting an Asia-Pacific framework that includes the United States.

Multilateralism in Asia reshapes the purpose and function of the US bilateral alliance system, rendering US alliances in the region less exclusive, by encouraging them to develop a wider range of activities involving a greater number of actors, a well-known example being the expansion of the bilateral US-Thailand Cobra Gold exercise into a multilateral one, with China as an observer. Such trends also reflect what Admiral Dennis Blair (the former chief of the US Pacific Command and former Director of National Intelligence) termed as the "security community" approach, turning the "hub-and-spoke" of US bilateral alliances in Asia and the Pacific to a web of cross-cutting interactions and relationship that could form the basis for a Pacific community (Blair and Hanley Jr. 2000).

Democratization

Since 1986, democratic transitions have occurred in South Korea, Taiwan, Philippines, Thailand, Cambodia, and Indonesia. Data from Freedom House also show that between 1988 and 1989, the number of electoral democracies in Asia doubled from 5 to 10. From 1972 to 2010, the number of "free" countries increased from 5 to 6, while the number of "partly free" countries increased from 8 to 11 and the number of "not free" countries decreased from 11 to 7. The combined total of "free" and "partly free" countries in Asia now outnumber the total number of "not free" countries by 17 to 7, compared to 13–11 in 1972.

Democratization remains uneven in Asia, not just with China's remaining under authoritarian rule, but also recent reversals happening in Thailand (albeit briefly) and backsliding in Cambodia.

Moreover, it might be argued that Asia's new democracies are really semi-authoritarian, rather than liberal-democratic. On the positive side, East Asia refutes the view that democratization increases the danger of war. No two democratizing states in East Asia have fought a war against each other. While democratization has been accompanied by domestic violence, as in Indonesia following the downfall of Suharto, descent into authoritarian rule (the onset of the Suharto regime) produced even greater violence in Indonesia. Moreover, newly democratic nations in Asia have shown a tendency to pursue cooperative security strategies (marked by restraint and cooperation) toward their neighbors. Examples include Thailand's efforts in the late 1980s at turning Indo-China's "battlefields to market places," South Korea's policy under Kim Dae Jung in the later 1990s ("Sunshine policy") and Indonesia's efforts in the early 2000s to create an "ASEAN political-Security Community."

What are the implications of these trends? It is not that democracy is a prerequisite for a CSO. But democratization thwarts the alternative prospect of a regional hegemony under autocratic China by undercutting its normative and ideological legitimacy. An ideological Monroe Doctrine by China will be opposed as long as the trends toward greater political openness continue and Asia's largest economics and political players—India, Indonesia, Japan, and South Korea—remain democratic.

After outlining the trends favorable to a CSO and their limits, I now examine the implications of these trends for Asia's security order, especially how they might affect the conditions for a CSO in Asia. We will highlight trends that favor and those which inhibit those conditions.

CHINA AND INDIA TODAY: DIPLOMATS JOSTLE, MILITARIES PREPARE

Just as the Indian subcontinental plate has a tendency to constantly rub and push against the Eurasian tectonic plate, causing friction and volatility in the entire Himalayan mountain range, India's bilateral relationship with China is also a subtle, unseen, but ongoing and deeply felt collision, the affects of which have left a convoluted lineage. Tensions between the two powers have come to influence everything from their military and security decisionmaking to their economic and diplomatic maneuvering, with implications for wary neighbours and faraway allies alike. The relationship is complicated by layers of rivalry, mistrust, and occasional cooperation, not to mention actual geographical disputes.

Distant neighbours buffered by Tibet and the Himalayas for millennia, China and India became next-door neighbours with contested frontiers and disputed histories in 1950, following the occupation of Tibet by Mao's People's Liberation Army (PLA). While the rest of the world started taking note of China's rise during the last decade of the twentieth century, India has been warily watching China's rise ever since a territorial dispute erupted in a brief but full-scale war in 1962, followed by skirmishes in 1967 and 1987.

Several rounds of talks held since 1981 have failed to resolve the disputed claims. During his last visit to India, in 2010, Chinese Premier Wen Jiabao dashed any hopes of early border settlement, stating that it would take a very long time to settle the boundary issue—a situation that in many ways works to Beijing's advantage.

An unsettled border provides China the strategic leverage to keep India uncertain about its intentions, and nervous about its capabilities, while exposing India's vulnerabilities and weaknesses, and encouraging New Delhi's "good behavior" on issues of vital concern. Besides, as the ongoing unrest and growing incidents of self-immolations by Buddhist monks in Tibet show, Beijing has not yet succeeded in pacifying and Sinicizing Tibet, as it has Inner Mongolia. The net result is that the 2,520-mile Sino-Indian frontier, one of the longest inter-state boundaries in the world, remains China's only undefined land border. It is also becoming heavily militarized, as tensions rise over China's aggressive patrolling on the line of actual control (LAC) and its military drills, using live ammunition, for a potential air and land campaign to capture high-altitude mountain passes in Tibet.

Over the last decade, the Chinese have put in place a sophisticated military infrastructure in the Tibet Autonomous Region (TAR) adjoining India: five fully operational air bases, several helipads, an extensive rail network, and thirty thousand miles of roads—giving them the ability to rapidly deploy thirty divisions (fifteen thousand soldiers each) along the border, a three-to-one advantage over India. China has not only increased its military presence in Tibet but is also ramping up its nuclear arsenal. In addition, the PLA's strategic options against India are set to multiply as Chinese land and rail links with Pakistan, Nepal, Burma, and Bangladesh improve.

Developments on the disputed Himalayan borders are central to India's internal debate about the credibility of its strategic deterrent and whether to test nuclear weapons again. Being the weaker power, India is far more concerned about the overall military balance tilting to its disadvantage. India sees

China everywhere because of Beijing's "hexiao gongda" policy in South Asia: "uniting with the small"—Pakistan, Bangladesh, Nepal, Burma, and Sri Lanka—"to counter the big"—India. When combined with Chinese nuclear and missile transfers to Pakistan and building of port facilities around India's periphery, and a dramatic increase in the PLA's incursions and transgressions across the LAC, the official Indian perception of China has undergone a dramatic shift since 2006, with China now being widely seen as posing a major security threat in the short to medium term rather than over the long term. The Indian military, long preoccupied with war-fighting scenarios against Pakistan, has consequently turned its attention to the China border, and unveiled a massive force modernization program, to cost $100 billion over the next decade, that includes the construction of several strategic roads and the expansion of rail networks, helipads, and airfields all along the LAC. Other measures range from raising a new mountain strike corps and doubling force levels in the eastern sector by one hundred thousand troops to the deployment of Sukhoi Su-30MKI aircraft, spy drones, helicopters, and ballistic and cruise missile squadrons to defend its northeastern state of Arunachal Pradesh, territory three times the size of Taiwan that the Chinese invaded in 1962 and now claim sovereignty over as "Southern Tibet."

Propelled by incidents related to border disputes, Chinese opposition to the US-India nuclear energy deal, India's angst over the growing trade deficit due to perceived Chinese unfair trade practices, potential Chinese plans to dam the Brahmaputra River, and the "war talk" in the official Chinese media in the 2007 to 2009 period (reminding India not to forget "the lessons of 1962"), mutual distrust between the Indian and Chinese peoples is growing. Clearly, China's extraordinary economic performance over the last three decades has changed the dynamics of the relationship. China and India had similar average incomes in the late 1970s, but thirty years later they find themselves at completely different stages of development. China's economic reforms—launched in 1978, nearly thirteen years before India's in 1991—changed their subsequent growth trajectories by putting China far ahead of India in all socioeconomic indices. Both China's gross domestic product and military expenditure are now three times the size of India's; recent surveys conducted by Pew Global Research show a growth in popular distrust, with just twenty-five percent of Indians holding a favorable view of China in 2011, down from thirty-four percent in 2010 and fifty-seven percent in 2005. Likewise, just twenty-seven percent of Chinese hold a favorable view of India in 2011, down from thirty-two percent in 2010, with studies of Internet content showing a large degree of "hostility and contempt for India."

Nor is there much effort to keep these emotions submerged. Reacting to the test launch in mid-April of a long-range Agni-V ballistic missile, dubbed the "China killer" by India's news media, a Chinese daily wryly noted that "India stands no chance in an overall arms race with China," because "China's nuclear power is stronger and more reliable." The unequal strategic equation, in particular the Chinese perception of India as a land of irreconcilable socioreligious cleavages with an inherently unstable polity and weak leadership that is easily contained through proxies, aggravates tensions between the two. In 2008, an official reassessment of China's capabilities and intentions led the Indian military to adopt a "two-front war" doctrine against what is identified as a "collusive threat" posed by two closely aligned nuclear-armed neighbours, Pakistan and China. This doctrine validates the long-held belief of India's strategic community that China is following a protracted strategy of containing India's rise.

India is also responding by strengthening its strategic links with Afghanistan, Tajikistan, Mongolia, Vietnam, and Burma—countries on China's periphery. In testimony to the US Senate in February, James Clapper, the director of national intelligence, noted that "the Indian military is strengthening its forces in preparation to fight a limited conflict along the disputed border, and is working to balance Chinese power projection in the Indian Ocean." That "balance" includes a strategic tilt toward the United States that has also had a damaging effect on Sino-Indian relations. Although leaders from both countries often repeat the ritualized denials of conflict and emphasize burgeoning trade ties, such platitudes cannot obliterate the trust deficit. Few if any of China's strategic thinkers seem to hold positive views of India for China's future, and vice versa. Chinese strategists keep a wary eye on India's "great power dreams," its military spending and weapons acquisitions, and the developments in India's naval and nuclear doctrines. A dominant theme in Chinese commentary in the last decade is that India's growing strength—backed by the United States—could tip Asia's balance of power away from Beijing.

Not surprisingly, bilateral relations between Asia's giants remain, in the words of Zhang Yan, China's ambassador to India, "very fragile, very easy to be damaged, and very difficult to repair." Both have massive manpower resources, a scientific and industrial base, and million-plus militaries. For the first time in more than fifty years, both are moving upward simultaneously on their relative power trajectories. As the pivotal power in South Asia, India perceives itself much as China has traditionally perceived itself in relation to East Asia. Both desire a peaceful security environment to focus on economic development and avoid overt rivalry or conflict. Still, the volatile agents of nationalism, history, ambition, strength, and size produce a mysterious chemistry. Neither power is comfortable with the rise of the other. Both seek to envelop neighbours with their national economies. Both are nuclear and space powers with growing ambitions. Both yearn for a multipolar world that will provide them the space for growth and freedom of action. Both vie for leadership positions in global and regional organizations and have attempted to establish a sort of Monroe Doctrine in their respective neighbourhoods—without much success.

And both remain suspicious of each other's long-term agenda and intentions. Each perceives the other as pursuing hegemony and entertaining imperial ambitions. Both are non–status quo powers: China in terms of *territory*, power, and influence; India in terms of *status*, power, and influence. Both seek to expand their power and influence in and beyond their regions at each other's expense. China's "Malacca paranoia" is matched by India's "Hormuz dilemma." If China's navy is going south to the Indian Ocean, India's navy is going east to the Pacific Ocean. Both suffer from a siege mentality born out of their elites' acute consciousness of the divisive tendencies that make their countries' present political unity so fragile. After all, much of Chinese and Indian history is made up of long periods of internal disunity and turmoil, when centrifugal forces brought down even the most powerful empires. Each has its vulnerabilities—regional conflicts, poverty, and religious divisions for India; the contradiction between a market economy and Leninist politics for China. Both are plagued with domestic linguistic, ethno-religious, and politico-economic fault lines that could be their undoing if not managed properly.

In other words, China and India are locked in a classic security dilemma: one country sees its actions as defensive, but the same actions appear aggressive to the other. Beijing fears that an unrestrained Indian power—particularly one that is backed by the West and Japan—would not only threaten China's security along its restive southwestern frontiers (Tibet and Xinjiang) but also obstruct China's expansion southwards. Faced with exponential growth in China's power and influence, India feels the need to take counterbalancing measures and launch strategic initiatives to emerge as a great power, but these are perceived as challenging and threatening in China.

China's use of regional and international organizations to institutionalize its power while either denying India access to these organizations or marginalizing India within them has added a new competitive dynamic to the relationship. In the past decade, India has found itself ranged against China at the UN Security Council, East Asia Summit, the Asia-Pacific Economic Cooperation, the Nuclear Suppliers Group, and the Asian Development Bank. In 2009, China vetoed a development plan for India by the latter in the disputed Arunachal Pradesh, thereby internationalizing a bilateral territorial dispute. In a tit-for-tat response, New Delhi has kept Beijing out of India-led multilateral frameworks such as the Bay of Bengal Initiative for Multi-Sectoral Technical and Economic Cooperation, the India-Brazil-South Africa Dialogue, and the Mekong–Ganga Cooperation forums, and rejected China's request to be included as observer or associate member into the 33-member Indian Ocean Naval Symposium, started by India in 2008.

Resource scarcity has added a maritime dimension to this geopolitical rivalry. As China's and India's energy dependence on the Middle East and Africa increases, both are actively seeking to forge closer defence and security ties with resource supplier nations (e.g., Saudi Arabia and Iran), and to develop appropriate naval capabilities to dominate the sea lanes through which the bulk of their commerce flows. Since seventy-seven percent of China's oil comes from the Middle East and Africa, Beijing has increased its activities in the Indian Ocean region by investing in littoral states' economies, building ports and infrastructure, providing weaponry, and acquiring energy resources. Nearly ninety percent of Chinese arms sales go to countries located in the Indian Ocean region. Beijing is investing heavily in developing the Gwadar deep-sea port in Pakistan, and naval bases in Sri Lanka, Bangladesh, and Myanmar. Whether one calls it a "string of pearls" or a series of places at which China's navy can base or simply be resupplied, that navy is setting up support infrastructure in strategic locations along the same sea lanes of communication that could neutralize India's geographical advantage in the Indian Ocean region. A recent commentary from the official Xinhua news outlet called for setting up three lines of navy supply bases in the northern Indian Ocean, the western Indian Ocean, and the southern Indian Ocean. It stated: "China needs to establish overseas strategic support stations for adding ship fuel, re-supply of necessities, staff break time, repairs of equipment, and weapons in Pakistan, Sri Lanka, and Myanmar, which will be the core support bases in the North Indian Ocean supply line; Djibouti, Yemen, Oman, Kenya, Tanzania, and Mozambique, which will be the core support bases in the West Indian Ocean supply line;

and Seychelles and Madagascar, which will be the core support bases in the South Indian Ocean supply line."

For its part, New Delhi is pursuing the same strategy as Beijing and creating its own web of relationships with the littoral states, both bilaterally and multilaterally, through the Indian Ocean Naval Symposium, to ensure that if the military need arises, the necessary support infrastructure and network will be in place. India has also stepped up defence cooperation with Oman and Israel in the west, while upgrading military ties with the Maldives, Madagascar, and Myanmar in the Indian Ocean, and with Singapore, Indonesia, Thailand, Vietnam, Taiwan, the Philippines, Australia, Japan, and the United States in the east. In December 2006, Admiral Sureesh Mehta, then India's naval chief, expanded the conceptual construct of India's "greater strategic neighborhood" to include potential sources of oil and gas imports located across the globe—from Venezuela to the Sakhalin Islands in Russia. The Indian navy currently has a stronger naval presence on the Indian Ocean than does China. It is strengthening its port infrastructure with new southern ports, which allow greater projection into the ocean. Taking a leaf out of China's book, the new focus is to develop anti-access and area-denial capabilities that will thwart any Chinese attempt at encirclement or sea-access denial.

In short, maritime competition is intensifying as Indian and Chinese navies show the flag in the Pacific and Indian oceans with greater frequency. This rivalry could spill into the open after a couple of decades, when one Indian aircraft carrier will be deployed in the Pacific Ocean and one Chinese aircraft carrier in the Indian Ocean—ostensibly to safeguard their respective trade and energy routes.

In turn, India's "Look East" policy is a manifestation of its own strategic intent to compete for influence in the wider Asia-Pacific region. Just as China will not concede India's primacy in South Asia and the Indian Ocean region, India seems unwilling to accept Southeast and East Asia as China's sphere of influence. Just as China's rise is viewed positively in the

South Asian region among the small countries surrounding India with which New Delhi has had difficult relations, India's rise is viewed in positive-sum terms among China's neighbours throughout East and Southeast Asia. Over the last two decades, India has sought to enhance its economic and security ties with those Northeast and Southeast Asian nations (Mongolia, South Korea, Japan, Taiwan, Vietnam, Singapore, Thailand, Indonesia, and Australia) that worry about China more than any other major power. As China's growing strength creates uneasiness in the region, India's balancing role is welcome within the Association of Southeast Asian Nations (ASEAN) in order to influence China's behavior in cooperative directions. While the Southeast Asian leaders seek to deter China from utilizing its growing strength for coercive purposes and to maintain regional autonomy, Indian strategic analysts favour an Indian naval presence in the South China Sea and the Pacific Ocean to counter Chinese naval presence in the Indian Ocean. On maritime security, Southeast Asians seem more willing to cooperate with India than China, especially in the Strait of Malacca.

A key element of India's Pacific outreach has been regular naval exercises, port calls, security dialogues, and more than a dozen defence cooperation agreements. India has welcomed Vietnam's offer of berthing rights in Na Trang Port in the South China Sea, and news reports suggest that India might offer BrahMos cruise missiles and other military hardware at "friendship prices" to Vietnam. The conclusion of free-trade agreements with Singapore, South Korea, Malaysia, Japan, and the ASEAN, coupled with New Delhi's participation in multilateral forums such as the East Asia Summit and the ASEAN Plus Eight defence ministers' meetings, have also reinforced strategic ties. India's determination to strengthen its strategic partnership with Japan and Vietnam, commitment to pursue joint oil exploration with Hanoi in the South China Sea waters in the face of Chinese opposition, and an emphasis on the freedom of navigation are signs of India maneuvering to be seen as a counterweight to Chinese power in East Asia.

New Delhi is also scaling up defence ties with Tokyo, Seoul, and Canberra.

The US-India partnership is also emerging as an important component of India's strategy to balance China's power. India seeks US economic and technological assistance. It helps this relationship that India's longtime security concerns—China and Pakistan—also now happen to be the United States' long-term and immediate strategic concerns as well. Both the Bush and Obama administrations have encouraged India's involvement in a wider Asian security system to balance a rising China and declining Japan. Apparently, US weakness—real or perceived—invites Chinese assertiveness. Since the United States does not wish to see Asia dominated by a single hegemonic power or a coalition of states, India's economic rise is seen as serving Washington's long-term interests by ensuring that there be countervailing powers in Asia—China, Japan, and India, with the United States continuing to act as an "engaged offshore power balancer."

The "India factor" is increasingly entering the ongoing US policy debate over China. Asia-Pacific is now the Indo-Pacific, a term underlining the centrality of India in the new calculus of regional power. The 2010 US Quadrennial Defence Review talked of India's positive role as a "net security provider in the Indian Ocean and beyond."

India's "Look East" policy, which envisions high-level engagement with "China-wary" nations (South Korea, Japan, Taiwan, Vietnam, Thailand, Indonesia, and Australia), dovetails with the US policy of establishing closer ties with countries beyond Washington's traditional treaty partners to maintain US predominance. The US-Indian strategic engagement, coupled with India's expanding naval and nuclear capabilities and huge economic potential, have made India loom larger on China's radar screen. An editorial in a Shanghai daily last November lamented the fact that "India will not allow itself to stay quietly between the US and China. It wants to play triangle affairs with the duo, and will do anything it can to maximize its benefit out of it. Therefore, China will find it hard to buy India over." The Chinese fear that the Indian-American cooperation in defence, high-tech R&D, nuclear, space, and maritime spheres would prolong US hegemony and prevent the establishment of a post-American, Sino-centric hierarchical regional order in Asia. This tightening relationship, and the possibility that what is presently a tilt on India's part could turn into a full-fledged alignment, is a major reason for recent deterioration in Chinese-Indian relations.

Although these relations remain unstable and competitive, both have sought to reduce tensions. Despite border disputes, denial of market access, and harsh words against the Dalai Lama, leaders in both countries understand the dangers of allowing problems to overwhelm the relationship. Burgeoning economic ties between the world's two fastest-growing economies have become the most salient aspect of their bilateral relationship.

Trade flows have risen rapidly, from a paltry $350 million in 1993 to $70 billion in 2012, and could surpass $100 billion by 2015. Several joint ventures in power generation, consumer goods, steel, chemicals, minerals, mining, transport, infrastructure, info-tech, and telecommunication are in the works. Intensifying trade, commerce, and tourism could eventually raise the stakes for China in its relationship with India. On the positive side, both share common interests in maintaining regional stability (for example, combating Islamist fundamentalists), exploiting economic opportunities, and maintaining access to energy sources, capital, and markets.

Despite ever-increasing trade volumes, however, there is as yet no strategic congruence between China and India. As in the case of Sino-US and Sino-Japanese ties, Sino-Indian competitive tendencies, rooted in geopolitics and nationalism, are unlikely to be easily offset even by growing economic and trade links. In fact, the economic relationship is heavily skewed. The bulk of Indian exports to China consist of iron ore and other raw materials, while India imports mostly manufactured goods from China—a classic example of the dependency model. Most Indians see China as predatory in trade. New Delhi has lodged the largest number of anti-dumping cases against Beijing in the World Trade Organization. India is keener on pursuing mutual economic dependencies with Japan, South Korea, and Southeast Asian nations through increased trade, investment, infrastructure development, and aid to bolster economic and political ties across Asia that will counter Chinese power.

Even as a range of economic and transnational issues draw them closer together, the combination of internal issues of stability (Tibet and Kashmir), disputes over territory, competition over resources (oil, gas, and water), overseas markets and bases, external overlapping spheres of influence, rival alliance relationships, and ever-widening geopolitical horizons forestall the chances for a genuine Sino-Indian accommodation. Given the broad range of negative attitudes and perceptions each country has for the other, it is indeed remarkable that China and India have been able to keep diplomatic relations from fraying. How long this situation can last is more and more uncertain as each country is increasingly active in what would once have been seen as the other's "backyard" and both engage in strategic maneuvers to checkmate each other.

Just as China has become more assertive vis-à-vis the United States, Indian policy toward China is becoming tougher. India's evolving Asia strategy reflects the desire for an arc of partnerships with China's key neighbours—in Southeast Asia and further east along the Asia-Pacific rim—and the United States that would help neutralize the continuing Chinese military assistance and activity around its own territory and develop counter-leverages of its own vis-à-vis China to keep Beijing sober.

CHINA'S SHIFTING RELATIONSHIP WITH ASEAN

The history of China and its Southeast Asian neighbours during the Cold War years was one of both amity and animosity.

Indonesia (April 1950) and Burma (June 1950) were among the first few countries to recognize the People's Republic of China (PRC). From the early 1950s until the mid-1960s, Beijing enjoyed an especially warm relationship with Jakarta, most prominently displayed in the 1955 Bandung Conference of Asian-African Countries and continued during much of President Sukarno's reign. Beijing also maintained a close relationship with the fellow communist regime in North Vietnam and rendered significant support to its causes against France and the United States from the 1950s to the 1970s, including sizable material and human assistance. But China's relationships with many Southeast Asia's noncommunist states were decidedly estranged. Concerns over potential threats from communism led some of them to participate in and form alliance-like regional organizations (Southeast Asian Treaty Organization or SEATO, 1954-77; the Five-Power Defence Arrangements or FPDA, 1971-) with external powers—the United States in particular—to protect their interests. There were deep suspicions over China's motives and activities, especially as they related to the large number of overseas Chinese residing in these countries. Beijing's public support of the communist insurgents in the region only reinforced their perceptions and heightened their fears. Not surprisingly, many of them did not establish diplomatic relations with Beijing until the mid-1970s (Thailand, Malaysia, and the Philippines). Others only normalized ties with China in the 1990s (Singapore and Indonesia).

The Sino-U.S. rapprochement in the early 1970s led to the establishment of diplomatic ties between China and a number of ASEAN states. The emerging Chinese-ASEAN cooperation in the late 1970s ironically was prompted largely by their shared concerns over Vietnam's growing assertiveness and its attempt to establish hegemony in Indochina, in particular in the aftermath of its invasion of neighboring Cambodia. Thailand, being on the frontline of the Cambodian conflict, sought to develop security ties with China. China also coordinated with ASEAN in seeking a political settlement of the Cambodian issue and supported the latter's position that the Cambodian coalition government headed by Prince Sihanouk, not the Hanoi-backed Heng Samrin regime, should represent Phnom Penh in the United Nations (UN).

During the 1980s, Chinese policy toward Southeast Asia began to undergo important changes in two critical areas. Beijing started to place state-to-state relationships in precedence over ideological ties by halting its support to communist insurgence movements in the region. In 1989, it also passed laws on Chinese citizenship requiring overseas Chinese to adopt citizenship of their countries of residence. By taking these two important measures, major irritants effectively were removed from China's bilateral relationships with a number of Southeast Asian countries. Beijing now seemed more than ever eager to court better relationships with its Southern neighbours, and this has paved the way for improvement of political ties. Beijing's official contact with ASEAN as a group began in July 1991 when Chinese Foreign Minister Qian Qichen was invited to attend the opening ceremony of the 24th ASEAN Foreign Ministers' Meeting. Since then China has attended each ASEAN Foreign Ministers' Meeting consecutively. In 1994, China participated in the ASEAN Regional Forum (ARF) and became a consultative dialogue partner of ASEAN. This status was elevated in 1996, when China became a full dialogue partner with ASEAN. In December 1997, Chinese President Jiang Zemin and ASEAN leaders held their first ever summit in Malaysia and issued a joint statement announcing their decision to establish a partnership of good neighborliness and mutual trust between China and ASEAN oriented toward the 21st century. In October 2003, China and ASEAN signed the "Joint Declaration of the PRC and ASEAN State Leaders—A Strategic Partnership for Peace and Prosperity."

The emerging China-ASEAN ties were influenced by a number of developments at the time. One was Beijing's efforts, in the wake of the Tiananmen incident, in particular in response to the sanctions imposed by the West, to break the isolation. Southeast Asian countries, given their relative reticence regarding the June 4 Incident, became targets of the Chinese diplomatic good neighborly policy. Beijing and Jakarta restored, and China and Singapore established, diplomatic relations in 1990. Chinese Premier Li Peng visited Indonesia, the Philippines, Malaysia, and Laos as part of that diplomatic endeavor. A second reason was to sustain the cooperation between the two in the wake of the Cambodian settlement, in which China played a constructive role in the resolution of the dispute and had been in close consultation with ASEAN in the 1980s. But most important of all was Beijing's changing perception of its security environment and the relative place of Southeast Asia in its post-Cold War security policy. This resulted in the successful management of the territorial disputes in the South China Sea, Beijing's reassurance to ASEAN of its benign intentions and its acceptance of multilateralism and cooperative security, and China's growing economic ties with ASEAN.

CHINESE OVERTURES IN INDIA'S NEIGHBOURHOOD

China's interest in oil exploration in the Indian Ocean is a matter of strategic concern for India. Concerns have been expressed in India about what has come to be known as China's "string of pearls" strategy of bases and diplomatic ties stretching from the Middle East to southern China that includes Gwadar port in Pakistan, Chittagong in Bangladesh, and Hambantota in Sri Lanka. While Bangladesh has granted China exploration rights for developing natural gas fields of its own, friction in India-Bangladesh ties has precluded cooperation between India and Bangladesh on the issue of energy. China's activities near the Kenyan port of Mombasa will make India further wary of Chinese long-term plans vis-à-vis India.

After India realised that one of its closest neighbours and a major source of natural gas, Myanmar, is drifting towards China, it reversed its decades-old policy of isolating the Burmese junta and has now begun to deal with it directly.

New Delhi not only assured investment in developing the Sittwe Port and extended a $20 million credit for renovation of the Thanlyin Refinery, but it also supported Myanmar against the U.S. censure motion in an attempt to lure the junta to grant preferential treatment to India in the supply of natural gas.

But the Chinese firms were the ones that got preferential treatment in the award of blocks and gas, apparently in recognition of China's steady opposition to the United States moves against Myanmar's junta in the UN. This failure has further galvanised India into wooing Yangon even more aggressively.

Apart from India's existing infrastructure projects in Myanmar, which include the 160-kilometer India-Myanmar friendship road built by India's Border Roads Organisation in 2001, India is looking into the possibility of embarking on a second road project and investing in a deep-sea project (Sagar Samridhi) to explore oil and gas in the Bay of Bengal as well as the Shwe gas pipeline project in western Myanmar.

Even as the Burmese military junta was readying for a violent crackdown on monks and democracy activists, the Indian petroleum minister was in Yangon signing a production deal for three deep-water exploration blocks off the Rakhine coast. While India did support the United Nations Human Rights Council resolution against Myanmar, it tried to tone it down to little effect as it tried to balance its democratic credentials with its desire to retain its influence with the Burmese military government. India has found it difficult to counter Chinese influence in Myanmar, with China selling everything from weapons to food grains to Myanmar.

Emerging Competition in Central Asia

As the geopolitical importance of Central Asia has increased in recent years, all the major powers have been keen to expand their influence in the region, and India is no exception. It shares many of the interests of other major powers such as the United States, Russia, and China vis-à-vis Central Asia, including access to Central Asian energy resources, controlling the spread of radical Islam, ensuring political stability, and strengthening of regional economies. But unlike China and Russia, its interests converge with that of the United States in Central Asia and some have even suggested that it is in U.S. interests to have a greater Indian presence in Central Asia to counter growing Chinese or Russian involvement.

Central Asia is crucial for India not only because of its oil and gas reserves that India wishes to tap for its energy security but also because other major powers such as the United States, Russia, and China have already started competing for influence in the region. India's concern about rising Chinese influence in Central Asia was also reflected in India's desire to become a member of the Shanghai Cooperation Organisation (SCO). While ostensibly the SCO is aimed at tackling the security concerns in Central Asia, including extremism and separatism, it also serves as an important instrument in keeping control of the region and limiting U.S. influence there.

India has been granted an observer status, but China made sure that Pakistan was also invited, thereby diminishing India's influence. China has a major geopolitical advantage in Central Asian oil politics.

Oil resources in the region are of vital importance to China's future oil security and will become an important basis for China's future military strategy. In the event of an unexpected military crisis, China would have to rely heavily on oil resources in mid-Asia to sustain military operations. The extension of the pan-Asian global energy bridge from Central Asia to Iran would link China to the Middle East. This lifeline from the Caspian Sea to China, incorporating the Middle East, would most benefit China's long-term strategic energy security policy. It would leave China in a much less vulnerable position with respect to both oil reserve depletion and transportation risks.

By drastically shifting the most important and busiest global energy artery from the Strait of Malacca to a line across mainland China, the creation of new geopolitical tendencies inside Asia would be inevitable. China would undoubtedly benefit from such a pivotal geostrategic position, particularly as its coastal regions would serve as the refining link between

Middle Eastern and Central Asian crude oil—and the Asian-Pacific market.

Chinese aspirations as an "energy bridge" in Central Asia are long term and will require massive international investment in pipeline infrastructure and coastal refineries.

The Chinese National Petroleum Company (CNPC) has an oil-swap agreement with Iran. Oil purchased by China from the Uzen oil field in Kazakhstan is pumped to a refinery near Tehran, with China receiving an equivalent amount of Iranian crude exported from Iran's Gulf coast.

China's other deal with Kazakhstan includes a commitment to build a 3,000-kilometer pipeline from the oil fields to the Xinjiang province of China, and a 250-kilometer pipeline to the border of Iran (via Turkmenistan). Indian and Chinese state-owned oil companies were engaged in a bidding war to acquire a Canadian company with oil fields in Kazakhstan.

China's National Petroleum Corporation won the bid against India's ONGC after offering a higher sum for Petro Kazakhstan. The Caspian Sea region in Central Asia is another region that is going to see major powers, including China and India, jostling for influence, given its new-found importance as a still-growing source of oil and gas. The area is distant from world markets, generating uncertainty whether Caspian oil will increasingly be sent east or will continue to flow west through Russia or Turkey. In all probability, China is likely to emerge as a new energy hub for Caspian oil and more pipelines will be built to western China, even as India is yet to make any significant headway in exploiting the region's resources.

Courting of Russia

India's ONGC has a 20 per cent stake in exploration and development of the Sakhalin-I oil and gas fields in Russia and has been keen to import natural gas from Sakhalin. But China outmaneuvered India by offering a $6 billion loan offer to the Russian Oil company, Rosneft, which then asked India to outbid China if it wanted to be considered for the exports. India's OVL also lost out to China in the acquisition of BP's oil assets in Russia. In one of the first big-ticket oil asset acquisitions by China in Russia, TNK-BP, which controls the OAO Udmurtneft fields in Russia, decided to opt for China's Sinopec in the place of OVL. Though India has expressed its desire to buy nearly a quarter of its annual oil imports in the next decade from Russia, and Russia plans to increase the share of its energy exports to Asia from the current 5 per cent to around 25 per cent, India will have to compete with other Asian nations, most significantly China, which are as eager to court Russia.

While the Chinese have a natural advantage of having a common border with Russia, their diplomacy also seems to be more proactive. Energy issues are driving China and Russia into the arms of each other politically, leading to the mobilisation of the Shanghai Cooperation Council to focus on energy issues, with the possibility of it evolving into a military alliance to rival NATO.

Sino-Russian ties have improved considerably following a plethora of agreements and declarations on energy security cooperation. Russia could become an important supplier of oil to China in the coming years.

The two states have performed a feasibility study on a $1.6 billion, 2, 200-kilometer oil pipeline project to bring Serbian oil to northeast China which the Chinese government views as one way for alleviating its dependence on the Middle East oil supplies. Russia is a world-class gas producer, which fits well into the Chinese strategy to diversify its energy requirements and thus alleviate its dependence on oil. For such a venture to be economically viable, however, significant international confidence and cooperation is required at a multinational level; investment and demand by Japan and Korea is required to realise such a scheme. Russia is also investing in nuclear power reactors in China.

China, India, and the West

A key area of friction and a barrier to engagement between the democratic West and autocratic Beijing is China's relationship with energy-rich "rogue states." Chinese companies, backed by political intent and government finances, are willing to invest in countries with high political risk. With competition for scarce energy resources intense, China has pursued deals with international pariah states that are off limits to Western companies because of sanctions, security concerns, or ethical policy and the threat of international condemnation. China's relation with state sponsors of terrorism provides a great deal of money, allowing these countries to continue to harbour terrorists and to maintain a policy of oppression and exploitation of their people. This highlights the ideological affinity between China and other authoritarian regimes that are also anxious for market transition while maintaining singleparty rule—Myanmar, Vietnam, Cambodia, Laos, Iran, Sudan, and North Korea. China remains unconcerned as to the source of vital energy, whether Iranian, Kazakh, Sudanese, or Angolan. China considers anyone who helps with its oil security problem to be a friend of Beijing. China's unconditional assistance and opaque commercial transactions, which do little to encourage these rogue States to improve their governance systems, is viewed in Beijing as necessary in order to guarantee its own continued economic growth.

India, conversely, seems to be aligning itself with the West and is investing significantly in trying to evolve a strategic partnership with the United States. The desire of the George W. Bush administration to achieve full civil nuclear energy cooperation with India as part of its broader goals of promoting nuclear power and achieving nuclear security has marked a new phase in the rather unstable bilateral relationship between the world's oldest and the world's largest democracies. The nuclear agreement creates a major exception to the U.S. prohibition against nuclear assistance to any country that doesn't accept international monitoring of all its nuclear facilities. India, with sixteen nuclear plants, plans to build seven more and has been promised U.S. help to triple its collection by 2020. China remains the only major power that has taken an ambivalent stand of the nuclear deal. While it has indicated that it is willing to promote bilateral cooperation with India in civil nuclear energy, it has also hinted that it might step up its nuclear cooperation with Pakistan.

Given the strained relationship between Iran and the United States, India's traditionally close ties with Iran have emerged as a major factor that is influencing how certain sections of U.S. policymakers are evaluating the Indo-U.S. partnership. Though India has tried to carefully balance its relations with Iran and the United States, because of intense U.S. pressure, especially after the signing of the nuclear deal, India has moved closer to the United States on the issue of the Iranian nuclear programme.

The United States, preoccupied with the global war on terrorism, is becoming increasingly concerned with Chinese diplomatic activity, particularly in Asia and the Middle East, where its own presence in these regions could be marginalised. China's record of arms sales and support to energy-rich Middle Eastern countries and state sponsors of terrorism in the Gulf region continues to agitate Washington. Asia's oil imports from the Middle East are set to increase rapidly, primarily because of rising demand in China and India and Japan's continuing requirement to import all of its oil requirements.

Ensuring reliable and stable flows from the Gulf region will be Asia's biggest challenge. This may result in the political and economic dependence of many Middle East states shifting from the West towards Asia. As it is America's dependence on Middle East is much less than that of other major global economies as only 17 per cent of its oil imports flow from the region. In fact, it is China that will be importing almost 70 per cent of its oil from the Middle East by 2015. Unless new sources of oil production are exploited, Middle East reserves as a percentage of global stocks will be proportionally greater by 2025, as other key production areas see their resources dwindle. Middle East producers accounted for 31 per cent of the world's oil supply in 2000, and this figure could grow to 70 per cent by 2025. The Middle East will therefore continue to be the most significant region for oil-energy production.

China will continue to maintain a strong interest in oil production in both Iraq and Iran. These two energy partners are an insurance measure against reduced production from Central Asian oil fields. Iran has explicitly stated its desire for China to replace Japan as the country's largest energy trading partner. China is also considering to revive a $1.2 billion deal that it signed with Iraq during Saddam Hussein's regime in 1997 to develop the Iraqi oil field of al-Ahdab. Energy also remains the backbone of the Sino-Saudi relationship.

Until 1993 China was a net oil exporter, but it has since become the secondgreatest oil consumer after the United States. More than half of Chinese oil imports originate in the Persian Gulf, with 15 per cent in Saudi Arabia. Total Saudi-Chinese trade grew 59 per cent in 2005 to $14 billion and may reach $40 billion in the next four to five years. By 2010 the Middle East might account for 95 per cent of China's imported oil. Saudi Arabia has also emerged as a major investor in Chinese refineries. In 1999 Saudi Arabia's Aramco Overseas Company provided a $750 million investment—25 per cent of the total project—in a petrochemical complex in Fujian capable of processing eight million tons of Saudi crude oil per annum. Saudi Arabia, in cooperation with several members of OPEC, intends to build a new refinery in Guangzhou involving a total investment of $8 billion. China is assiduously attempting to enlarge its sphere of influence throughout the Persian Gulf, and its relationship with Saudi Arabia is a key component of this strategy.

The move in 2005 by the Chinese state-owned CNOOC to take control of the California-based oil exploration and production company Unocal Corporation in a $19 billion bid sent shock waves through the U.S. Congress. Although the Chinese maintain that their interest in Unocal was purely commercial in accessing substantial oil and gas reserves in Southeast Asia, the United States feared a broader Chinese strategy to secure global energy resources. China remains concerned over U.S. aspirations to dominate the Persian Gulf in order to secure its own energy requirements while simultaneously containing China's expansion in the region. Some in Beijing, therefore, consider the United States as a major threat to China's future energy security and remain reluctant to rely on the United States for the security of China's seaborne oil imports, thereby resulting in a focus on developing a blue-water navy to protect its sea lanes of communication. The Iraq war and its aftermath also seem to have reinforced China's fears that it is locked in a zero-sum contest for energy with the United States and added urgency to its mission to lessen dependence on Middle East oil supplies. However, if the American predominance of the Middle East weakens and China's global profile rises in region, India, along with several other regional states, will consider that a threat to its energy security with the distinct possibility of military conflict over the region's valuable resources.

ASEAN COUNTRIES' APPOINTMENT AND PREVARICATION STRATEGIES

Southeast Asia always has had to deal with the issue of living adjacent to a great power. Historically, there was the tributary system, and continental Southeast Asia (Vietnam in particular) lived under the constant shadow of the Chinese empires. While relations between China and ASEAN have become much more amicable, ASEAN countries continue to harbour a mixed reaction toward the rise of China, viewing this as both a challenge and opportunities. Hence ASEAN countries have adopted the dual-strategies of engagement and hedging to protect their interests in the face of a rising China. The former is intended to explore opportunities by integrating China into regional political, security, and economic arrangements, recognizing that a policy of isolating and alienating China is unsustainable. ASEAN's engagement strategy toward China since the mid-1990s has been driven largely by this consideration. The latter strategy emphasizes external balancing where ASEAN states seek to develop and strengthen relations with extra-regional powers such as the United States, Japan, India, and the EU, among others.

ASEAN Engages China

The ASEAN nations have always viewed China with both suspicion and some cautious optimism. Their threat perceptions are influenced by history, geography, and cultural factors. In the former sense, being small states vis-à-vis China, they have always harboured a suspicion of their giant northern neighbor for two reasons. One is historical precedent, in particular Beijing's past support of the insurgent movements in their countries; the other is uncertainty about how China will use its power in regional affairs. China's preponderance and its growing weight in the post-Cold War era create additional concerns. Territorial disputes in the South China Sea and China's military modernization programs, together with perceived U.S. drawdown of forces have further heightened the sense of insecurity. But ASEAN countries also recognize that, given their limited capabilities, they need to live with China, and one way of ensuring that China will act responsibly is to encourage greater integration between China and the region, thus increasing the stakes. Indeed, ASEAN has been pragmatic enough to recognize the importance of engagement rather than confrontation and hence adopted a strategy that aims at integrating China gradually into a regional web of economic interdependence, political dialogue, and security dialogue processes. They also reject the strategy of containment as the best way to deal with a rising China.

ASEAN's active engagement of China played a critical role in removing suspicions and encouraged Beijing to full participation in the regional multilateral security arrangement. Specifcally, three outstanding issues of particular concern to the Southeast Asian states were to be addressed: potential economic competition coming from China, territorial disputes, and lack of transparency in China's defence spending. Beijing began to address these concerns, winning ASEAN's confdence in the process.

There is no question that the ARF has performed a critical role in exposing and socializing China to the ideas of cooperative security, multilateralism, consultation and dialogue, consensus-building, and noncoercive ways of settling disputes. Beijing's early concerns fell in four areas: that the regional forum would be dominated by the United States or otherwise could provide the justification for Washington to intervene in the region's affairs; concern over the internationalization of territorial disputes; concern that the Taiwan issue might be brought on the table, hence interfering China's internal affairs; and concern that China would be pressured to display greater military transparency. ASEAN has been instrumental in engaging China and sensitizing Beijing to the values of the so-called ASEAN Way. This process has served to change China's perceptions of its interests and its policy choice preferences, leading to more moderate behavior as contrasted to its earlier assertive posture.

Over time, through participation in various ASEAN-led multilateral dialogues, China has moved from its early suspicion and resistance to gradual acceptance and embrace of the idea of cooperative security and multilateralism. However, China's interpretation of multilateralism is a rather limited one, in that it is considered to be a supplement, rather than a replacement of the traditional bilateral approach. It also has resisted the more formal institutionalization of the ARF, as desired by the western countries. Beijing's comfort level clearly has increased with the understanding that ASEAN will remain in the driver's seat, and the forum will not touch on issues of vital importance to China.

Indeed, while ASEAN could be credited with socializing China to the concept of multilateralism, one must acknowledge that the multilateralism Beijing embraces remains conditional, selective, and largely a way to counter U.S. power politics. State sovereignty is still the core of Chinese foreign policy and on fundamental issues such as territorial disputes and Taiwan, China's positions continue to be more realpolitik than receptive of multilateralism. What China pursues remains a notion of multipolarity, in which it will be recognized as an important actor. For ASEAN, this remains an issue to be reckoned with, but for the time being at least, Beijing is trying to reassure its southeastern neighbours. The 1997 financial crisis significantly weakened ASEAN's position. However, continued uncertainty in Sino-U.S. relations and their perceived competition for influence and primacy in Asia have given ASEAN some leverage, in so far as China's diplomacy is concerned. This has enabled the organization to remain in the driver's seat in regional security arrangements such as the ARF. At the same time, ASEAN also is reluctant to join U.S.-led military alliances due to ethnic sensitivity, as Southeast Asia is home to a large Islamic population. At a time when Beijing's relations with Tokyo also are experiencing difficulties, the value for Beijing of a better relationship with ASEAN has increased steadily. Beginning in the second half of the 1990s, the two sides moved to develop a number of institutionalized mechanisms to deepen bilateral relations, including the ASEAN+1, among others. In 2003, China and ASEAN signed the Joint Declaration on Strategic Partnership for Peace and Prosperity.

The Prevarication Strategy

International Relations theories long have debated the policy options of states facing an emerging power or hegemon. They invariably would either choose to balance (internally and/or externally) against the dominant power or bandwagon with that power. The latter is divided further into bandwagoning because of fear or bandwagoning for profits. In recent discussions, a new concept of hedging has emerged as yet another policy option for states facing uncertain international security environments. Denny Roy has further characterized the ASEAN strategy of hedging as "low-intensity balancing" that both seeks U.S. support and works with China. They encourage the United States to maintain a military presence in the region and provide support and base access but decline to form formal military alliances with Washington.

In Southeast Asia, hedging has been a particularly useful strategy for the region's small powers to manoeuvre among major powers to secure their interests. According to Robert Ross, the continental ASEAN and maritime ASEAN member states would have different attitudes toward China. The new ASEAN, which consists of Vietnam, Laos, Cambodia, and Myanmar, for instance, has special relationships with China due to history, geographical proximity, as well as unsettled issues. Wherever possible, ASEAN member states try not to be forced to choose sides, but opt for developing and maintaining good working relationships with as many major powers as possible. They all recognize the inevitability of China's rise and see in it both opportunities and challenges. In a certain way, ASEAN states realize that they cannot by themselves form an effective alliance to check China's rise; but neither do they want to ally themselves with external powers such as the United States for fear of provoking China. In addition to engagement with China, they therefore also seek to persuade the United States to stay engaged in the region to balance China's rise and to develop a network involving all major regional powers so they have stakes in regional order.

As pointed out above, since the end of the Cold War, ASEAN has pursued a dual-strategy of retaining U.S. security involvement in the region, including a military presence, and engaging China in diplomatic-political terms and expanding economic ties. While all member states recognize the importance of continued U.S. security involvement in the region, they also are concerned with Washington's penchant for unilateral use of force, in particular after the September 11, 2001 (9/11), terrorist attacks on the United States. Regarding China, ASEAN members have tried to refrain from identifying China as a threat; rather they talk about challenges and concerns, and their chosen strategy remains that of engagement rather than isolation, let alone containment. However, ASEAN also has reservations and appears uncertain about what a rising China will mean for them. If one could argue that ideology, overseas Chinese living in Southeast Asia, economic competition, and territorial disputes are the four key elements that could affect China-ASEAN relations, then it is clear that the first two, by and large, have been addressed, with the latter two constituting the remaining major challenges. But even here, the implications may be different for ASEAN member states; the more developed may see less of economic competition in a rising China but more opportunities; countries that have territorial disputes with China may view Beijing's policies and activities more suspiciously. This may explain why ASEAN member states have adopted different approaches, and applied the hedging strategies with varying degrees, in their handling of China. For instance, some look for closer U.S. ties, while others seek greater engagement with China; still others, living in China's shadow, are making the best of their situations.

Although China has developed extensive ties with ASEAN on political and economic fronts, Beijing also has maintained close relationships with specific member states, which remain essential in China's regional diplomacy, especially where territorial disputes are concerned. At the same time, it should also be understood that ASEAN itself has yet to develop its own identity apart from agreements on general principles and processes. Each member state has unique historical experiences dealing with China, with varying threat perceptions regarding China's rise, and has adopted different strategies in its respective China policy. ASEAN countries' threat perceptions of China vary depending on history, geography, and the extent and nature of unresolved disputes.

CHINA RISING POWER IN SOUTH ASIA

Beijing did not take too seriously ASEAN's growing role initially. Instead, it anticipated a greater role for the UN Security Council and a multipolar world when the Cold War ended. Within the Asian context, China saw the United States, Russia, Japan, and itself as the critical players, but not ASEAN, as it was deemed largely a subregional grouping with an inward-looking orientation. That began to change in the mid-1990s as Beijing both recognized and indeed appreciated the role that ASEAN could play. This became even more apparent with the expansion of the original ASEAN-6 to the Greater ASEAN of Ten by the decade's end.

Chinese analysts have characterized ASEAN's evolving regional role as evolving in four phases. In the first phase, which began in the late 1970s largely in response to Vietnam's invasion of Cambodia (and hence a direct threat to Thailand's security), the organization's major efforts were expended on seeking a peaceful solution of the Cambodian issue by engaging extra-regional powers. The Paris Agreement, to which ASEAN made a significant contribution, gave the organization a high profile in the international diplomatic arena and provided it with greater interest and the confidence to participate in and influence Southeast Asian affairs.

The second phase began in the early 1990s and focused mostly on ASEAN's effort to engage major powers in the development of a regional security dialogue that aimed at both socializing China to the benefit of multilateralism and cooperative security and keeping the other major powers engaged in the region's security to prevent the emergence of a power vacuum and hence invitation for competition. Through the Post-Ministerial Meetings, dialogues, and the establishment of the ARF, the group succeeded in bringing all major powers under the framework of a security dialogue that was subject to the ASEAN Way of gradualism, consensus-building, and nonuse of force in dispute settlement.

The third phase was characterized by ASEAN's continuing pursuit of multichannel, multilevel security dialogues that involved the Asia-Europe meeting (ASEM), ASEAN+1 and 3, and the organization's own plan toward greater integration, including the ASEAN FTA. The current phase involves ASEAN's efforts to move beyond Southeast Asia to launch a region-wide political forum that would include all major East Asian powers. Initially the brain-child of Malaysian Prime Minister Mahathir, the East Asia Summit was formally held in Kuala Lumpur in December 2005, but with the participation of Australia, India, and New Zealand, in addition to the originally conceived participating countries.

Over the years, ASEAN has debated, explored, and developed various strategies of dealing with major powers.

These strategies have been applied during different periods, depending on specific security circumstances of the time. Essentially, three approaches have been especially emphasized. One is the Non-Aligned Movement (NAM) approach promoted by Indonesia. This would be an effort to exclude major power interference in ASEAN's internal affairs. At the same time, it would sustain Jakarta's position within the organization. The second approach is favored by Malaysia, which advocates neutrality in two ways. One is noninterference and nonaggression in interstate relations to avoid being involved in great power conflicts; the other is to secure major powers' pledges not to intervene in Southeast Asian affairs, hence allowing the region to maintain autonomy and neutrality. The third is balancing, promoted by Singapore, between great powers. Singapore recognizes that major powers all have important interests in the region, therefore it is unrealistic to exclude their involvement. But efforts can be made to prevent one particular power from dominating the entire region.

The ASEAN Way of informality and noninterference in domestic affairs has served as the guiding principle in its approach to regional affairs. While this approach has served the organization well and provided a comfort level for member states to interact with each other without having to accept binding decisions, it is now facing increasing challenges. The tendency to hold meetings, talk, and sign documents but to be slow in implementation has begun to constrain ASEAN's ability to address real issues.

Beijing increasingly has viewed ASEAN as an important power centre in Asia. This is largely due to ASEAN's skillful diplomacy of balancing all the major powers, hence enhancing its own leverage. This is possible because major powers essentially have balanced out one another, with no one able to dominate. Finally, ASEAN itself since 1997 has sought to consolidate and achieve economic integration (ASEAN Economic Community) by 2015, with security and social community to follow. It hosted the first East Asia Summit in December 2005, and has over the years developed various ASEAN+1/3 meetings, with the ASEM playing a facilitating role in promoting regionalism.

At the same time, it should also be noted that ASEAN still harbours some suspicions toward China and likely will continue to resort to strategies of hedging or balancing through expanded ties with other external powers. In recent years, ASEAN member states have expanded their military cooperation greatly with the United States. Japan has been very active in regaining its influence in Southeast Asia and has offered a large economic aid package to the region. India also is actively engaging with ASEAN on greater economic, political, and military contacts. Finally, the East Asia Summit, originally billed as an exclusive regional event, had its inaugural meeting attended by Australia, India, and New Zealand, in addition to the ASEAN+3 countries. While a realpolitik assessment of these developments would alarm Beijing, as extra-regional forces would dilute China's own influence, Chinese officials and analysts seem not to be bothered by ASEAN's efforts to knit complex and overlapping arrangements and relationships with itself as the coordinating core.

Indeed, a major Chinese report on ASEAN recommended that Beijing respect ASEAN's position, including some member states' growing military ties with the United States; acknowledge and respect that the United States has legitimate interests in the region; and actually encourage better ASEAN-U.S. cooperation, especially in the context of fighting terrorism. In that context, U.S. deployment of military forces, dispatching of special force advisors, and specific arrangements for base access should not be viewed as targeted at China.

Nonetheless, Chinese analysts are monitoring these developments closely. The post-9/11 U.S. policy adjustment toward Southeast Asia could have a significant impact on issues of territorial disputes in the South China Sea, SLOCs, the cohesion of ASEAN as a group, and could cause domestic turmoil in some member states. Since 9/11, the United States has strengthened its military presence in the region and resumed and intensifed joint military exercises with a number of ASEAN member states, ostensibly aimed at fighting global terrorism. Meanwhile, the U.S. position on territorial disputes in the South China Sea has shifted from neutrality and nonintervention to "positive" mediation, with greater emphasis on freedom of navigation, including escorts.

What is most significant is a U.S. proposal for joint patrol of the Malacca Strait with the "Regional Maritime Security Initiative." While the proposal has been turned down by the three Strait countries—Malaysia, Singapore, and Indonesia—there has since been more cooperation between the United States and the regional militaries. For China, stable and uninterrupted supplies of oil through the Malacca Strait is critical to its economic security, and control by foreign powers could seriously undermine Chinese security interests.

Another issue of potential concern is Taiwan's activities in ASEAN countries. For various reasons, most of them economic, ASEAN has maintained rather close ties with Taipei. In fact, Taiwan has nine times the investment in the region than does China, and Taiwan was most active in the early to mid-1990s in pushing for more official contacts through "vacation diplomacy" and "golf diplomacy," among other tactics. Lee Hsien Loong's visit to Taiwan in the summer of 2004—billed as "private"—just before he became Singapore's prime minister triggered strong reactions from China, including cancellation of previously scheduled bilateral meetings and visits by Singaporean ministers. Managing such incidents requires delicate diplomacy as much as it demands a resolute stance on an issue for which China has no room for negotiation.

7

China's Rise and Asia's Emerging Security Order

The end of the Cold War and the rise of China have provoked widely divergent views about Asia's future security order. Some see the region heading toward major conflict and blame it on Asia's lack of European-style pacifying mechanisms of deep regional integration, multilateral institutions, and shared democratic politics. Asia's future may thus be likened to Europe's nineteenth-century and early twentieth-century past, a multipolar rivalry ending in two catastrophic wars. Another pessimistic view compares China's ascent to America's in the nineteenth century. Like the United States' pursuit of regional expansion and the Monroe Doctrine in the Western hemisphere, this view foresees China seeking a regional hegemony over its neighbors. On a cautiously optimistic note, some analysts foresee a balance of power order emerging in Asia, managed either by a concert of great powers or a Sino-US condominium (G-2). More optimistically, China's ascent is seen as reviving a benignly hierarchal regional order in East Asia under Chinese primacy that would bring in shared prosperity and peace. The most optimistic scenario raises the prospect of a regional community, in which economic integration, multilateral institutions, and shared norms and identity remove the danger of war.

We outline a different type of regional security order for Asia, one that differs not only from the images of a Hobbesian anarchy, but also from the benign visions of a Confucian hierarchy or a Kantian community. My perspective rests on two central arguments. The first is that while the rise of China is clearly reshaping the distribution of power in Asia, the region has also witnessed equally important and long-term changes to other determinants of security and stability. These changes, whose beginnings predate the rise of China, can be discerned by comparing Asia's security environment in the immediate aftermath of World War II and that of now. In the former period, Asian security was shaped by economic nationalism, security bilateralism, and political authoritarianism. These have gradually but unmistakably given way to market liberalism and economic interdependence, security multilateralism (coexisting with US-centric bilateralism), and growing domestic political pluralism. Together, they create those very mitigating factors for anarchy that the region was found to be wanting by the pessimists in the immediate aftermath of the Cold War's end and question the relevance of thinking about Asia's future security in terms of Europe's, America's, or Asia's own pasts.

Second, I do not believe that these changes, despite being consistent with the liberal theories of peace, would usher in a pluralistic security community in Asia, in which war becomes "unthinkable." The domestic (liberal-democratic) and international (integration) ingredients required for a Kantian peace in Asia would fall short. But they have the potential to constrain power maximizing behavior on the part of China on the one hand, and extreme balancing/containment postures on the part of the United States and its allies, on the other. Moreover, they would limit China's capacity to develop and legitimize a Sino-centric regional order (whether coercive Monroe Doctrine-like or a "benign" order similar to the old tributary system) and would prevent the development of a Sino-US duopoly or a multilateral Asian Concert system dominated by the great powers while marginalizing its weaker states. The purpose of this essay is to sketch out such a type of possible regional order in Asia, which I call a consociational security order (CSO).

In the following sections, I sketch out a theory of consociational security orders (CSOs), identify what makes them stable or unstable, and use this framework to analyze Asia's emerging security order. The next section outlines five main scenarios of conflict and order that have been suggested for Asia and discuss their limitations. Next, I elaborate the idea of CSO, differentiate it from other types of security orders, and discuss the conditions that need to be in place to make such an order possible. Then, I elaborate on the key changes occurring in Asia's long-term drivers of security. In reviewing the growing trend toward economic interdependence, multilateral institutions, and domestic politics (increasing democratization) in the region, I also assess how these changes impact Asia's security order, and whether and to what extent they may be shaping the prospects for the emergence of an Asian CSO.

Asian security order and their limitations. It is noteworthy that these perspectives focus either on power ("anarchy," "hegemony," and concert/condominium) or on culture/identity ("hierarchy" and "community"), as the basis of Asia's security order. Theories of domestic politics have been rarely employed. Yet, approaches derived from domestic politics can be very useful in analyzing Asian security order. And here, the theory that is especially relevant is not Democratic Peace, which concerns the relative absence of war among democracies, or why democracies avoid war among one another, but consociationalism, which concerns how ethnically diverse or "divided societies" can achieve stability (Cannon 1982). Asia, a region of tremendous cultural and political diversity, lends itself to the lens of consociational theory. Although widely debated among comparative politics scholars (Apter 1961; Lijphart 1962, 1977; Daalder 1974; Dekmejian 1978; Ganesan 1997; Lustick 1997), consociational theory has been generally ignored in the international relations literature. Yet, the theory identifies several conditions for achieving stability (Bogaards 1998) that are relevant for international relations scholars interested in understanding the requirements for regional and international security order. Moreover, these conditions resonate with IR theories, especially liberalism, defensive realism, and institutionalism, thereby creating an eclectic framework for the study of Asian security order.

Consociational Security Order: Definition and Enabling Conditions

To clarify the notion of a CSO, I offer a simple definition and differentiate it from other types of security orders. A consociational security order (CSO) is a relationship of mutual accommodation among unequal and culturally diverse groups that preserves each group's relative autonomy and prevents the hegemony of any particular group/s. CSOs differ from other types of security orders more familiar to international relations scholars: hegemony, concert/condominium, and community.

First, a CSO is different from a hegemonic security order. In the latter, only one power calls the shots, and balancing declines. Security management mechanisms, such as multilateral institutions, may exist, but they are created, maintained, and thoroughly dominated by the hegemon. Moreover, hegemonic orders seek to exclude other great powers by establishing and enforcing a sphere of influence, as was the case with the US Monroe Doctrine in the Western Hemisphere. By contrast, a key purpose of consociations is to avoid hegemony. "Rather than duality or hegemony of one group over others, multiplicity is preferred" (Dekmejian 1978).

Second, a CSO may be differentiated from a concert and its truncated version, a great power condominium. A concert is principally an arrangement in which great powers collectively assume the role of managing order to the exclusion of weaker states, which are thoroughly marginalized. While a consociation has its basis in an elite cartel, the dominant groups work with the weaker elements to manage political order. A CSO may be seen as a half-way house between a community and a concert. In a concert system, great powers cooperate to jointly manage international order and preserve stability. The relevant model here is the European concert system, which, involving the major powers of the day, assumed the primary responsibility for managing Europe's security problems and sought to "develop European solutions to European problems" (Elrod 1976). The system worked well between 1815 and 1823 but declined thereafter (prompting theoretical arguments regarding the durability of a concert approach in peacetime), suffering an eventual collapse with the Crimean War of 1854.

Third, a CSO is different from a community. The key attributes of a community are "trust, friendship, complementarity, and responsiveness" (Haas 1973: 116). The most relevant example of community in international relations, the "security community," is distinguished by deep levels of trust and collective identification ("we-feeling") that renders war unthinkable (Deutsch 1961: 98; Adler and Barnett 1998). A CSO has no natural sense of such identity or feeling. Cultural diversity, state sovereignty, and national autonomy remain important. A CSO does not make war unthinkable, nor does it abolish balancing behavior. A CSO is thus a "mixed" approach to political order, where competitive and cooperative behavior exists side by side, and the group holds together by a desire for avoiding system collapse. Competition is controlled for the sake of common survival.

How do CSOs engender stability? Drawing upon theories of both comparative politics and international relations, I identify four enabling conditions: interdependence, equilibrium, institutions under shared leadership, and elite restraint.

Interdependence among states helps to offset the centrifugal elements of cultural difference and animosity within CSOs and contributes to the imperative of common survival and well-being. Liberal theory points to the impact of economic interdependence in raising the cost of war and inducing restraint among actors (Keohane and Nye 1977). Consociational theory stresses political and security interdependence, not just economic. Such interdependence can be existential, based on the simple facts of geographic proximity, natural cross-border trade, migration, and communications. Or it is contrived by the group as a way of fostering a long-term rationale for coexistence and cooperation. In most cases, it tends to be both. Interdependence does not, however, imply integration, especially political integration. Just as domestic consociations respect the autonomy of constituents groups, international consociations must respect national independence and sovereignty.

Second, stability in a consociation comes from "equilibrium among the segments" (Bogaards 1998: 480). Unlike a security community, a consociational order does not transcend security competition (Bogaards 1998: 492). Instead, groups engage in coalitional politics to deny hegemony to any particular group. The key to consociational stability thus is the existence of "multiple balances of power." This assumption echoes defensive realism. Unlike offensive realists who argue that states go for "all they can get" with hegemony as their ultimate goal (Mearsheimer 2001), defensive realists maintain that states are generally satisfied with the status quo if their own security is not challenged and thus concentrate on maintaining a balance of power (Glaser 1996; Tang 2010). Structural conditions such as anarchy do not invariably lead to expansionism; but the fear of triggering a security dilemma, calculations of the balance of power, and domestic politics induce states to abstain from pre-emptive war and engage in reassurance policies.

A third condition relates to institutions. A consociation is "a management coalition of sovereign states" (Chryssochoou 1994: 18). Consociational international institutions are more likely to be intergovernmental, rather than supranational (as in a community). Theirs is a shared leadership system (also known as "joint consensual rule"), for example, no single power or a concert of great powers dominates them; instead, leadership is shared between weak and strong actors. For this reason, consociational institutions are normatively oriented to cooperative security, rather than collective security or collective defense. Collective security and collective defense institutions are usually geared to deterring and punishing aggression ("security against" an adversary) and require hard power or military action. Hence, essential to their success is the material capabilities that mainly the great powers can provide. By contrast, cooperative security stresses restraint, reassurance ("security with" a competitor or adversary, rather than security against), and relies on confidence-building measures and political-diplomatic means to mitigate conflict. Hence, cooperative security institutions are more amenable to pluralistic or shared leadership involving strong and weak actors, and their impact is usually more normative than regulatory. For this reason, weaker states lacking in material capabilities may prefer cooperative security institutions to collective defense systems that institutionalize their unequal relationship with the great powers.

A fourth conducive condition for stability identified by consociational theory is "individual and collective elite restraint" (Dekmejian 1978: 255). This restraint is not because of idealism or altruism, but as Lijphart noted, because the elites (leaders) "understand of the perils of political fragmentation." Hence, they "accommodate the divergent interests and demands of the subcultures" (Lijphart 1962: 216). The distribution of power in a consociation may be asymmetrical, and hierarchy exists as an objective fact, but the more powerful actors respect the rights and interests of the weaker segments. Decisions are not made unilaterally nor are imposed by the powerful actors on the weak, but are made and implemented through consultations and consensus. A system of mutual or minority veto, or "negative minority rule" (Lijphart 1979: 501), prevails, meaning the less powerful actors do retain a say over collective decisions. This allows different units of the consociation to "function without the anxiety of having its vital interests 'subsumed'" by any other member or combined strength of the other members (Chryssochoou 1995: 19). This aspect also differentiates consociations from concerts, where the most powerful actors collectively monopolize the management of order and marginalize weaker states.

The four stability conditions are mutually reinforcing, and they are also in a mutually offsetting relationship with factors conducive to instability. Growing interdependence encourages cooperative institution-building and "elite" (great power) restraint by raising the costs of conflict. Equilibrium through balancing (defensive realism) supports institutions by rendering unilateral or hegemonic strategies less fruitful and likely. Institutions promote "elite" restraint which in turn fosters cooperative security norms and shared leadership in institutions. Interdependence and institutions encourage strategies to achieve equilibrium through "defensive balancing" and discourage offensive strategies (like expansionism or containment) that might aggravate the security dilemma. Similarly, balancing ("equilibrium") prevents hegemonic orders, whether that of a single power, duopolies, or concerts. A key point here is that none of the elements of a CSO is likely to be sufficient by itself to ensure stability; prospects for stability are greater if all four are present to some degree.

After outlining the conditions that sustain a CSO, let me outline the strengths and limitations of a CSO approach vis-à-vis other theoretical approaches to Asian security. Four are important. First, unlike existing theoretical approaches to Asian security, it offers a framework to consider mixed scenarios of conflict and peace, between the extremes of realist pessimism and liberal and constructivist optimism. The dependent variable of a CSO is stability in the sense of avoiding system breakdown, not competition or small scale wars—if the relevant conditions are present. It is not a Hobbesian anarchy or a Kantian or a Deutschian community. This is one of the real benefits, or "value-addeds," of the CSO framework.

Second, it represents an attempt to employ a theory (consociationalism) specifically concerned with stability at the domestic level to the international level. This has been rarely attempted by IR scholars. One important exception is the Democratic Peace theory. This theory holds that liberal democracies enjoy peaceful relations because they reproduce their domestic norms and practices of peaceful competition and tolerance at the international level, especially when dealing with fellow democracies. But the democratic peace outcome requires a shared liberal normative and institutional setting among all the participating actors, which is hardly commonplace in world politics. Democratic Peace theory is not specifically relevant to the management of cultural diversity, where cultural and political norms may differ significantly among actors.

A third advantage of the CSO concept is that it departs from a parsimonious single theoretical lens and draws from multiple theoretical lenses: realism's balance of power, liberalism's economic interdependence, and constructivism's socialization and cooperative security institutions (which overlaps with liberal institutionalism, but focuses more on social influence as opposed to strategic bargaining in the former). As noted from the previous discussion, scenarios derived from single theoretical lenses have proven to be inadequate at capturing the complexity of Asian security. They identify single or convergent causal mechanisms of stability/instability, while the CSO framework, as noted, holds that no single factor is by itself sufficient to ensure stability; all four must be present to some degree. Hence, the CSO framework is consistent with "analytic eclecticism," a relatively new approach to international relations, which is especially relevant to the study of "mixed scenarios" of conflict and stability.

Finally, the CSO concept helps to place the discussion of the rise of China in a broader regional context. The recent discussions of Asian security "treat China as if it is the only country in the region and focus more on the US-China relationship than on East Asia itself...but the region comprises much more than China, and it is these interactions that are going to have the most impact on stability." The CSO framework is especially suitable for capturing the broader regional context, as CSOs imply a political canvass of multiple interests and identities and interactions among them.

Now I turn to the potential pitfalls and limitations of the CSO approach. Two are especially noteworthy. The first has to do with migrating a theoretical approach about ethnic competition and cooperation in the domestic politics to the international realm. In international relations, one does not have "multiple ethnic groups fighting for the control over a single state." This may be why the consociational theory has been rarely used by international relations scholars. But there are examples of security competition ("fighting") that feeds upon the multiple and competing ethnic and nationalist identities of states within a given region for the control of regional order. Asia as a multi-ethnic region provides one of the clearest examples, although one can find them in Africa. Moreover, as Martin and Simmons argue, concepts and approaches in domestic politics do yield valuable insights into international institutionalization and cooperation (Martin and Simmons 1998). Hence, the application of a domestic theory to Asian regional order is an important value-added to existing approaches to Asian security, especially when applied in conjunction with some international relations theories, which in this essay includes defensive realism, the liberal notion of interdependence, and the constructivist element of norms and socializing institutions.

A second potential liability of the CSO construct could be that it might introduce a "stability bias," predisposing one toward positive outcomes in security interactions. This risk is especially there because of the key theoretical foundations of the CSO approach: Defensive realism, interdependence, and social constructivism as applied to institutions all specify conditions for fostering stability. While acknowledging the risk that the CSO framework might predispose an analysis of security order toward optimistic predictions, I stress that my purpose here is not to predict the future, or assert that a CSO in Asia will emerge, but to use the CSO framework to identify the conditions which will determine the likelihood of its emergence. It is to look beyond available perspectives on Asian security with a framework that employs a more comprehensive range of drivers of regional order than the changing distribution of power, which is what most people mean by the "rise of China." To the extent that one finds these conditions to be present in Asian economic, political, and strategic trends, one might then expect greater stability. In the same vein, their relative absence or decline might lead one to expect conflict. With these, I now turn to a brief examination of these trends.

THE RISE OF CHINA

In 1999 the People's Republic of China celebrated the 50th anniversary of its founding, marking the end of a period corresponding almost exactly to the second half of the 20th century, in which China was restored to its role as a major player in international politics. Given that for the first 50 years of the 20th century China served simply as an arena in which the imperialist powers fought for spheres of influence, this transformation is of significance not only for China but also for international politics in East Asia. However, it was not until the 1960s that China stepped onto the international political stage as a more independent power. In the 1950s China had officially - though not always actually - adhered to a policy of "leaning towards the Soviet Union," and promoted a "China-Soviet Union monolith" during the Cold War as part of the Eastern bloc. The end of the 1950s saw this stance change to one of Sino-Soviet rivalry, and China's first successful nuclear test in 1964 introduced into the bipolar Cold War structure a new orientation towards "multi-polarity."

China's independence grew more prominent in the 1970s, as rapprochement with the US in 1971 brought considerable changes to the international political framework of East Asia. From that time until the early part of the 1980s, China adopted a policy of "a single line" to align with the US and Japan to oppose the Soviet Union's drive for domination. The increasing independence of China's foreign policy from the 1960s through the 1970s did not, however, reflect a similar expansion of China's own strength as a nation. China was during this time still suffering the aftereffects of the Great Leap Forward of the 1950s, the subsequent Great Famine, and the widespread chaos stemming from the self-destructive Cultural Revolution that began in the mid-1960s. China under Mao Zedong sought rapprochement with the US for no other reason than a very keen awareness of the threat posed by the Soviet Union in light of the domestic disorder in China. Thus, the Chinese threat perception of the Soviet Union and the US Asian Strategy seeking an "honorable withdrawal" from Vietnam, coincided well, leading to the Sino-US rapprochement in 1971. Deng Xiaoping, who after the death of Mao Zedong seized the reins of power, sought through a policy of "reform and opening to the outside world" to revolutionize the "self-reliance" economic approach that had been pursued theretofore. Beginning with the introduction of a "production by contract" system, he set out on a bold course to introduce into China elements of a market economy. This marked the country's first earnest attempts in the 20th century to establish the foundations for expanding its national strength. China began seeing the Soviet Union as somewhat less of a threat in the 1980s.

Although the Soviet invasion of Afghanistan did cause considerable alarm, reinforcing the view of the Soviets as a danger to Chinese security, it was apparent thereafter that the USSR had become bogged down in Afghanistan. Causing greater unease for the Chinese was the new Reagan administration, and above all its Taiwan policy, amid the building of a strong "new Cold War" structure to counter the Soviet Union. China began around 1982 unilaterally to revise its policy of rapprochement with the US, aspiring to what it termed "an independent and autonomous foreign policy," and sought to put a certain distance between itself and the US. Another factor behind these changes was that the China-Vietnam War, which had stemmed from an overwhelmingly powerful sense of the Soviet threat, had not gone as China had wished and, in fact, had for all practical purposes been a "defeat." China thus became more convinced that enhancing its own national power had to take precedence over pursuing an active foreign policy.

As China began making adjustments to its foreign policy, the new US-Soviet Cold War posed little direct threat, with China not particularly favoring either side. Over-dependence on the US might be seen as an attempt to intimidate the Soviet Union, and it might also leave China unable to speak out against US policy towards Taiwan. In any case, the success of the "reform and opening to the outside world" policy was Deng Xiaoping's highest priority, as he strove to increase the country's own strength. Apparently, China firmly believed that the "peaceful international environment" needed to achieve this aim could be established without drawing particularly close to the US. From that point on, China assumed a rather passive and reactive attitude towards foreign affairs.

The Tiananmen Square Incident of June 4, 1989, seriously impaired China in its pursuit of a peaceful international environment, as China found itself isolated internationally for about a year thereafter. Another factor setting China apart was its insistence that rule by the Communist Party would be maintained, by force if necessary, following the dramatic end to the Cold War in the latter half of 1989. There were those in the international community who hoped to sweep China into the subsequent wave of democratization, but the Japanese government and the Bush administration in the US feared that this would result in internal chaos, and both instead worked towards normalizing relations with China. As the country began normalizing its international relations, Deng Xiaoping at the beginning of 1992 again issued a dictate on reform and liberalization (during his inspection tour through the southern provinces of China), and the Chinese economy returned once more to rapid growth.

The growth of the Chinese economy in the 1990s allowed China for the first time in the 20th century to wield power as an important member of the international community on the sole basis of its own national power, free from alliances and partnerships with other countries. The Chinese economy began to grow at an annual rate of more than ten percent from 1992, and in that same year, the IMF and the World Bank released estimates of per capita GDP for individual countries calculated using purchasing power parity, the results of which astonished the world. On an exchange rate basis, China's per capita GDP at the time was less than US$500 but, using purchasing power parity, this figure climbs to about US$2000. Thus, the actual per capita GDP of China was more than four times the level calculated through exchange rates; multiplying this new per capita GDP by the population of China, the result is an economy on par with Japan and other major countries. If the present rapid growth continues, the Chinese economy someday might even surpass that of the US in scale.

Besides economic growth, there are other indicators showing China's growing national might, some of which could generate concern in other countries. Publicly released figures reveal a surprising 15% annual increase in defense expenditures. There have also been press reports of China eagerly buying up a vast supply of the weapons that Russia has been selling off since the end of the Cold War. 1992 saw the promulgation of the Law of the People's Republic of China on Its Territorial Seas and Adjacent Zones, and its activities in the Spratly Islands have sparked anxiety among the countries in Southeast Asia. Also noteworthy are the frequent proclamations of PLA naval personnel that their duty is the protection of the "maritime rights and interests" of China.

Given all of these trends, a perception of China as a threat has emerged in the post-Cold War era. Certainly there were those in the 1960s, even in Japan, who considered China a threat. The danger posed by China during this part of the Cold War, however, was an ideological one, which would at most constitute a threat through "indirect invasion." By contrast, the view of China as a threat in the 1990s arises entirely from the power and policies of China itself. Though not allied now with any other country, China's presence has become a concern to other countries, one important consequence of the reform and liberalization policy initiated by Deng Xiaoping.

What is one to make of the emergence of China in this fashion? Since the mid-1990s this question has become a key focus of attention among policymakers in countries such as the US and Japan with ties to East Asia. In the US the debate has centered on whether to opt for engagement with China or for containment of China, with much argument over whether to classify China as a "strategic partner" or a "competitor." The balance of military power between China and other countries, recent patterns of behavior exhibited by China, and other important elements.

CHANGE OF POWER STATUS AND THE SPEED OF CHINA'S RISE

Entering the 21st century, there are more and more predictions about when China will become a superpower. Some guess that China will be as strong as the United States in the coming decade, some bet that in 20 years and some predict its rise in year 2040. In spite of those disagreements among scholars, the forecasts were all based on the speed at which China's total power has been growing in recent years, without any consideration of the influences of the other powers' growth. As we are aware that China's power status is related to that of the other states, when forecasting China's future power status, we should not only take account of the speed of China's power growth but also the growth of the other states' power. To foresee the future change of China's power status, we should clarify the conditions for ascent and descent of international power status.

Conditions for Ascent and Descent of Power Status

As a state's power status is determined by quantitative comparisons of powers among states, the change in power status of a state depends on the difference in power growth rates between two states in a given period of time. Based on the afore-mentioned formula of a state's power status, the expression for the change of a state's power status should be $Sc = A(1 + Ra)/B(1 + Rb) - A/B$, (here Sc refers to the result of a change in power status of two states A and B; where A and B indicate the original power for State A and State B respectively; while Ra and Rb indicate the actual growth rates of the two states, respectively). The expression shows that the change of a state's power status depends entirely upon the power growth rates (Ra and Rb) of the two states over a certain period of time. That is, the state with a faster power growth rate will rise, and the other will fall, and the statuses remain unchanged if the growth rates of the two state powers are the same. Over a fixed time period, the difference in power growth rates for the two states may result in three possibilities for change of a side's power status: rising, falling or unchanged. The three scenarios may result from 13 different situations, in which there are five for ascent, five for descent and three for no change.

It will be a political issue if a state is able to rise to a superpower in a few decades, but only an historical issue if a state rises to a hegemon over hundreds of years. As the atrophy of a state's power is a significant factor for the rapid rise of other states' power statuses, it creates an important scenario for a shift of power between two states. Therefore, power atrophy is an important political issue deserving more attention than power growth. A state's power increases in most years, decreases occasionally and very rarely has zero growth. Thus, the probability of the 10 scenarios of power-status change varies. Often both states enjoy positive power growth simultaneously; it is less common for one state to have a positive power growth while the other has a negative one; it is rare for both states to have negative power growth and is even less common that one state incurs zero power growth. When two states simultaneously have positive or negative power growth, it takes a longer time for their power gap to change and their power statuses to shift, and the probability of power-status shift is small. If one of the two states incurs zero power growth, their power gap will change relatively rapidly and there will be a higher probability for their power status to shift. However, the fastest change in the two states' power gap or their power statuses will occur when the two states have opposite power growths, i.e. one state's power increases and the other's decreases ($Ra > 0 > Rb$ or $Ra < 0 < Rb$). Because national power grows in most years and opposite power growths of two states tend to shift power statuses easily, the factors leading to power atrophy are more significant than the factors enhancing national power in terms of changing the power gap and power status between states.

Political turbulence can cause a state's comprehensive power to diminish severely and rapidly, and it alters a state's power status at a faster rate than does economic development. Being defeated in a war, state disintegration, civil war, social turmoil and political movements all work effectively in shifting power status. The shift of power status between China and the Soviet Union after the Cold War serves as a typical example. In 1991, prior to collapse, the Soviet Union was the only competing superpower in the world rivalling the United States, and its power status drastically differed from that of China. However, as the succeeding state of the former Soviet Union after its collapse, Russia's comprehensive power endured a drastic fall and as a result its geographical area was reduced by about 24%, its population reduced by 48%, its economy decreased by 11%, and the size of its military was cut by 33.7%. At that time Russian comprehensive power was still greater than China's, however, its power status fell into the same class that China belonged to. The power gap between them was only in degree and no longer in character. Thereafter, Russia's economy declined for years, its military capability was severely weakened, and its political power was diminished internationally. Even though it is hard for us to figure out in which specific year the power-status shift occurred, we are quite certain that China's comprehensive power surpassed that of Russia during the 1990s. Up to 1999, sustaining only military superiority over China, Russia fell far behind China in aspects of political power and economic power. In 1999, Russia's GDP accounted for only one-fourth or one-third of China's GDP of $1 trillion.

Economic crisis can cause a nation's power to decrease rapidly and it works as a faster agent than economic development in changing the power gap or power status between two states. The East Asian Financial Crisis during 1997–98 widened the power gap between China and the Southeast Asian countries and meanwhile reduced the disparity of economic power between China and Japan. The East Asian Financial Crisis decreased China's annual economic growth rate to 7% from 9% prior to the crisis while it caused negative and zero economic growth, respectively, for Indonesia and Japan. Indonesian GDP fell to $50 billion in 1998 from $190.3 billion in 1995 (in 1998 its currency exchange rate fell to US$1:IDR7500 from $1:IDR2321 in 1996) and it recovered to $208.3 billion in 2003, with only a 9.5% increase from its GDP in 1995. In that period, Japan's GDP reduced from $5083.1 billion in 1995 to $4326.4 billion in 2003, a total reduction of 15%. During the same period, China's GDP (by currency exchange rate) doubled from $704.1 billion in 1995 to $1409.9 billion in 2003. Therefore, in the eight years from 1995 to 2003, the economic gap between Indonesia and China had been widened from 3.7 times to 6.8 times, while the economic gap between China and Japan narrowed from 7.2 to 3.0 times. In terms of PPP, China's economy even surpassed Japan's, causing a shift in their economic power rankings.

Political Factors Determining the Fluctuation of China's Power Status

According to the principle that opposite power growths among states tend to change power status between states easily, we come to realize that in 10 years (by 2015) whether China can sustain the existing power status will be determined mainly by the likelihood of political crisis that may cause China's power status to descend. Since its foundation in 1949, China's power status has undergone a spell of four rising and three falling periods. During 1950–58 China's power status had been rising. During that period, the Korean War tremendously raised both China's military power status and her domestic and international capabilities of political mobilization. Between 1952 and 1958, China's GDP increased by as much as 1.9 times. During 1959–63 China's comprehensive power atrophied severely.

The Anti-Rightwing Movement led the Chinese government to adopt the policies of 'Great Leap' and 'People's Commune', which resulted in an overall economic crisis. It was not until 1964 that China's economy recovered to the same level of 1960. In 1959, Sino–Soviet relations began to deteriorate and China was facing joint pressures from both the United States and the Soviet Union. During 1964 and 1965, China's national power enjoyed a brief rising period but fell again during 1966–76. In May 1966, the Cultural Revolution occurred and the country was immersed in turbulence and chaos when the government's ability to maintain order was severely hampered, economic activities stagnated, and the military weakened. However, in the same period of time, many Asian states such as Japan, South Korea and Singapore had industrialized their countries and their power status was rising rapidly in relation to China's. From 1978 to 1988 was a period when China restored its social order, increased its domestic mobilization capability and normalized relations with the United States and the Soviet Union. Consequently, China had again enhanced its international political capability, and its economy sustained an average annual growth as high as 10.2%. The political events of 1989–93 slowed China's economic growth, and dramatically reduced its domestic and international political mobilization capabilities.

Thus, China's power status fell as her political power diminished in such a drastic manner. From 1993 to 2004 was the third period when China's power status ascended. During this interval, China gradually emerged from the international isolation which had started in 1989 and its capabilities of domestic and international mobilization once again increased. During 1993–2004, China's economy sustained an annual growth of 9.2% and the 1997 East Asian Financial Crisis accelerated the ascendance of China's economic power status. Ever since the founding of the People's Republic of China, each of the three major descents of China's power status was traced back to a political crisis rather than wars or economic difficulties. Therefore, we can believe that as long as there is no future political crisis, China will be able to avoid a fall in its power status.

Based on the principle that national power usually sustains growth in the majority of years, the author argues that the major external elements affecting the speed of rise of China's power status will be: (1) US military commitments and an increase or decrease of its international mobilization capabilities, and (2) the pace of political integration of the European Union (EU). According to the current growth of the comprehensive strengths of major powers, the author assumes that no other single nation, except the United States, could have larger comprehensive power than China in the next 10 years. Although each individual European state has smaller comprehensive power than China, the EU as a unified power will have a superior status to China's. If the political integration of the EU results in an international player with national character in the next 10 years, our references for judging China's future power status should include both the United States and the EU. Some people suppose that China's future power status would fundamentally depend upon China's economic growth. They obviously have neglected the political and military powers of the United States and the EU. China possesses a huge supply of low-paid labour, therefore in the next 10 years China's economic growth will be faster than that of the United States and the EU. It is also quite possible for China to narrow its economic gap with the United States and the EU. Nevertheless, there is uncertainty with regard to the development of the military and political powers of China, the United States and the EU in next 10 years.

In 10 years from now, China may narrow its military gap with the EU but the change of its military gap with the United States will depend on its military containment against Taiwanese secessionists. A favourable security environment will constrain the EU from large military expenditure.

Therefore, in the next 10 years, China's military strength will grow faster than that of the EU and will reduce the military gap between the two. Nevertheless, the change of military disparity between China and the Unites States will be determined by the rates of military investment of the two sides. As a result of the pro-independence group introducing a timetable for Taiwan to achieve legitimate independence by 2008, the Chinese government will inevitably enhance its military capability to contain Taiwanese secessionists. If the Chinese government was to launch a military attack against

Taiwan's independence, it would be possible for China to narrow its military gap with the United States. If the United States continues to wage wars against smaller states while China has no need to attack Taiwanese secessionists militarily, the US military budget will increase faster than that of China's, thus the military power gap between China and the United States would be enlarged.

In the coming decade, China will probably reduce the disparity of its political power with that of the United States, but in the meantime her advantageous political power with relevance to the EU may diminish. In the 1990s, global democratization and marketization increased the US international mobilization capability to a historical peak. With little resistance from the UN Security Council, the United States obtained UN authorizations on waging the Gulf War in 1991, the Somali War in 1996, the war in Kosovo in 1999 as well as the war in Afghanistan in 2001.

Many countries provided military and economic support to the United States during these wars. However, the United States current unilateral policy caused its international political mobilizing capability to fall sharply from 2003. Without any UN authorization, the United States waged war in Iraq under the excuse of alleged Iraqi possession of weapons of mass destruction. The US action encountered strenuous objections from many traditional European allies, headed by France and Germany.

As no weapons of mass destruction have been discovered in Iraq, US international influence has been seriously weakened. In the next 10 years, hegemonic position will drive the United States to continue its unilateralist foreign policy. Meanwhile, China will maintain its multilateral diplomacy to harmonize relationships with her neighbours, the EU and the developing countries of other regions.

Their opposite foreign policies will reduce the political power disparity between China and the United States. Presently, China has greater political power than the EU because China is a single state while the EU is a regional organization with inconsistent foreign policies adopted by its member states. In 1999, the EU introduced the Euro which entered circulation in 2002 and finally established a single currency system on the EU market. In the year 2004, the political leaders of EU member states signed the European Constitution laying a legislative foundation for the EU to become a single state entity. If the EU constitution is approved by its member states, it will establish its own three-in-one entity of administrative institutions including a council, a committee and a foreign ministry. Future political integration of the EU will enhance its character as a large national state, which may help it to narrow its political power disparity with China.

Based on the above analysis, if we assume that both the United States and the EU act as single states, the comprehensive national power gap between either China and the United States or the EU and China will probably be narrowed by the year 2015. China's comprehensive power status may rank third in the world. In 10 years and beyond, it may be possible for China to reduce its economic power disparity with the United States and the EU even though its economic power may still be smaller than theirs. China will narrow its military power gap with the EU but its overall military strength will still be weaker than that of the United States or the EU. In terms of political power, China will narrow the gap but still cannot catch up with the United States. China may maintain her political power superiority over the EU but the disparity between the two may be reduced by further political integration of the EU if all its member states ratify the EU Constitution before 2015.

We have discussed why China enjoys the leading power status among the major powers with the exception of the United States. Based on the principle that a nation's power status ascends in accordance with a faster growth rate, we may presume that China will strengthen its power superiority over Japan, Russia and India within the next 10 years. If the EU becomes a single state entity by 2015, Britain, France and Germany will no longer be regarded as individual international players. Thus, we only assess here the power status between China and three other states: Japan, Russia and India.

With regards to economic power, low-cost labour and a rapidly expanding domestic market will ensure China a faster economic growth than Japan and Russia in the next 10 years. According to World Bank data based on PPP calculations, Japan, Russia and China have GDP per capita in 2001 of $26,940, $8230 and $4580, respectively. This indicates that China's labour wage level was less than 18% of Japan's and 56% of Russia's. Low-cost labour guarantees foreign investors long-term high profits in China. At the end of 2005, China adopted a floating exchange rate according to World Trade Organization regulations and the Renmenbi (RMB) will appreciate continuously over the next 10 years. The increase in RMB exchange rate will make China's economic growth appear even faster. Although it enjoys the same advantage of low-cost labour as China, India is far behind China in aspects of opening-up to foreign investment as well as other economic reforms. Therefore, the Indian economy will continue to grow at a slower pace than that of China.

In terms of military power, it is anticipated over the next decade none of the three states, namely Japan, Russia and India, will be involved in military conflict with the United States. Therefore, the military spending of these states will increase slower than China's. Even though India and Russia are both faced with the threat of separatism in Kashmir and Chechnya, respectively, they do not face direct military protection of these separatists by the United States. As a result, the threat to Russia and India, from the separatists in these two regions, will not be comparable to that caused by the Taiwanese secessionists. Japan is under US military protection, hence its military investment will not increase as fast as that of China. The Japanese government has decided to reduce its 2005–09 military expenditures to $233 billion, i.e. 3.7% less than its average annual military spending in the previous five years. As a result of the danger of Taiwanese independence, China is faced with potential military clashes with the United

States in the Taiwan Straight. China's military spending in the next 10 years will increase much faster than that of Japan, Russia and India. This will in turn reduce the military disparity between China and Russia and at the same time make its military superior to Japan and India.

In terms of political power, China's endeavours in East Asian regionalization will effectively enhance its ability for political mobilization over the next 10 years. China will have the opportunity to further improve its relations with the EU and that will strengthen China's influence on global affairs. India, Russia and Japan, however, will have few chances to further enhance political influence in their own regions. Although India has already been a leading nation in South Asia, the South Asian regionalization has much less momentum than the East Asian. The Eastern expansion of the EU is constraining Russian political influence in East Europe and the former Soviet Republics. To sustain its special relationship with the United States, Japan has adopted a policy undermining the establishment of the East Asian Community. This policy is similar to that adopted by Great Britain with regard to the EU. Japan's policy against East Asian regionalization may ultimately weaken its political influence in East Asia. In terms of global affairs, both India and Japan may have the opportunity to become permanent members of the UN Security Council but they will have little chance of obtaining the power of veto. What they actually obtain may only be a position of permanent/non-permanent membership without substantially increased power. Russian political impact on global affairs will further diminish as it is still trapped in a regressive inertia following the collapse of the Soviet Union.

CHINA'S POWER STATUS AND ITS IMPLICATIONS

The author believes that in order to study China's power status objectively, we should first understand the true nature of international power and clarify our goal for measuring the differences of national powers. If we fail to do this, then as complexity in these measurements increases, their pragmatic value actually decreases. Therefore, the results of assessment will not benefit us at all in understanding national power status.

Relativity in Assessing China's Power Status

Power status connotes relativity. It refers to ranking the power status of one state with relevance to that of other states in an international sphere. The power status of a state can be understood only through a simultaneous comparative assessment of the power status of other nations. If there is only one nation in the world, then there is no frame of reference with which we can decide if a country's power status is high or low. This means that only when there are two or more countries in the world, that the study of a state's power status and its comprehensive national power has significance.

The term 'power status' contains a connotation of both 'the rank of power status' and 'the differences in power status'. Whereas the difference in power status decides the rank of power status, the rank of power status cannot always truly reflect the real nature and degrees of difference in power status. During the Cold War period, the United States and the Soviet Union ranked first and second, respectively, in their power status. However, the difference in power between them remained at a hierarchical level of superpowers. But in the 1990s, while the United States still kept its top ranking (regardless of which major power stayed in second: Russia, Japan or China), the nature of the ranking gap between the first and the second power states changed substantially, because it became a difference in power status between a superpower and a major power.

The power status of a state is based on, but not decided by, its national power. In other words, the increase of a state's power does not necessarily elevate that state's power status. For example, in the late 19th century during the Qing Dynasty, China had enough industrial capacity to arm its military. Its overall national power was far larger than that of the early

Qing Dynasty when there was no modern industry. However, internationally, China's power status during the late Qing Dynasty was far behind that of the early Qing Dynasty. Take the current cases of The Netherlands and South Korea. In 1999, GDP in The Netherlands grew from $393.5 billion to $398.1 billion, with an absolute increase of $4.6 billion. However, according to World Bank statistics, the ranking of The Netherlands fell below that of South Korea, whose GDP in the same period increased from $317.1 billion to $406.1 billion.

The rank of a state's power status is decided by the difference between its own power status and that of other states. However, this absolute difference does not indicate the nature and extent of power differences between states. The absolute value of the disparity in power status between two states indicates which state possesses a mightier power status. Therefore, it reflects the rank of the power status of the two states. However, this absolute difference hardly displays the true nature and class difference of a state's power status. For instance, according to the 2003 World Bank GDP statistics, by currency exchange rates, the GDP difference between Japan and Germany was $1.93 trillion while the GDP difference between Germany and Brazil was $1.97 trillion. The absolute values of the two differences vary little, but this by no means indicates that the difference in economic power between Germany and Japan shares any similarity with the difference between Brazil and Germany. Common sense leads us to conclude that Germany and Japan share the same class status, but that Brazil and Germany do not.

The power status of a state depends on how its national power compares with that of other nations. We can clarify this further by looking at GDP comparisons for Japan, Germany and Brazil. In 2003, Japan's GDP amounted to $4.3 trillion, Germany's to $2.4 trillion and Brazil's to $0.5 trillion. Despite the fact that the difference in GDP between Germany and Japan almost equals that between Brazil and Germany, Japan's GDP was only 1.8 times Germany's GDP while Germany's GDP amounted to 4.8 times that of Brazil.

This helps us understand that using common knowledge leads us to conclude that Germany and Japan share the same economic class, whereas Brazil and Germany are quite different.

In short, it is the proportional relationship between the power statuses of two states, not the absolute quantity of difference that decides a state's power status. It can be expressed as: $S = A/B$, (where S indicates power status of State A in proportion to that of State B; A refers to the power of State A, and B to the power of State B.) In the reality of international politics, when two states confront each other on a specific issue, the advantages and disadvantages of their powers depend largely on one state's power in proportion to the other.

As an example, assume a small military skirmish along a common border between two nations, Side A has three soldiers and Side B only one. Although Side A has only two more soldiers than Side B in absolute number, its power is 200% greater than that of Side B (i.e. the possibility of winning for Side A is three times as much as that for Side B). To cite another example, Side A has 102 soldiers and Side B 100; even if Side A has two more soldiers than Side B, its power strength gains only a 2% advantage. Therefore, the possibility of winning for either side is almost equal. In this analogy, to assess China's power status and its progression, one should focus on China's power status in proportion to the power status of other states, instead of solely on the absolute differences in the power of two states.

Importance of Assessing China's Power Status

Because power status is relative, recognizing China's power status in relation to that of other states is of immediate significance in our study. In order to further understand China's power status we consider the following three aspects. First, by understanding the relativity of power status, we can better understand the major difference in defining the 'Rejuvenation' or 'Rise' of China. In 2003, the Chinese leaders first introduced the term 'Peaceful Rise'. However, in April 2004 at the Boao Asia Forum, it was replaced by 'Peaceful Development'. This was mainly because 'Rise' has a relative meaning in terms of power status. Despite the often heated debates on 'Peaceful Rise', scholars on all sides acknowledge that the word 'Rise' implies attaining superpower status. For the Chinese, 'rejuvenation' bears a similar connotation to 'rise'. Both mean to restore China's power status to the prosperity enjoyed during the prime of the Han, Tang and early Qing Dynasties. It does not simply refer to a regression of China's comprehensive national power down to the ancient level. By early 21st century standards, China's comprehensive national power in the aforementioned ancient periods was only equivalent to a state of low power status in the current international system. As power status changes with time and the international environment, China's national rejuvenation will be realized only if its pace of national power growth is faster than that of other countries. Growth at any slower pace will weaken China's power status gradually and thus diminish the hopes of national rejuvenation and rise.

Second, the zero-sum nature of power status helps us understand that there will be no win–win situation in conflicts among international political entities accompanying the rise of China. Power status and international politics share the same zero-sum characteristic.

The rise of a state's power status indicates an expansion of its political power. This in turn causes the fall of other states' power status and political power. Powerful states remain a minority in the world while weaker states remain a majority. Until September 2002, no more than 10 global or regional major powers had been listed among 191 member countries of the UN.

The middle and small powers are represented in greater numbers in this ranking. As the power status of one small state increases, the relative power it gains is drawn from many other middle or small states of similar power status. Thus, an evenly spread decrease in power in every small power is not obvious, and so is unlikely to cause conflict among these states. For instance, the sum of international political power for 100 small states is fixed and stable, and each small state holds 1% of this power sum. When one small state increases its power status to 1.9% of the total power, the share for each of the remaining 99 countries is decreased to 0.99%, i.e. each country loses only 1% of its original power.

On the other hand, an increase in power status for a major state usually conveys serious outcomes in this aspect. Great powers are few in number. Therefore, as a major power gains an advantage in its power status, the remainder of the few major powers feel a tremendous loss of their original power.

If the dominant world power belongs to a single state, then this hegemony holds 100% of the power. When the power status of another state increases to the same level, there are two states sharing this world dominant power.

That means, among those with dominant power, the former hegemony will be diminished to half, or only 50%. Since a change in a major power's power status may result in the restructuring of international relations and a rearrangement of world resources, studies on comprehensive national strength and power status are of the utmost importance only for those few major powers.

The zero-sum nature in power status gives us the insight that a majority of political conflicts along China's path to her rise will bear this zero-sum nature as well. In other words, there will be few win–win situations in China's ascent to a superpower.

Third, by recognizing China's current power status, we can better perceive the strategic relationship between China and the other major powers in the post-Cold War era.

In a world configured with one superpower against several major powers, the United States is destined to defend its status against any possible challenging states in the future. As one of the major powers after the Cold War, China automatically becomes an opponent of the United States.

None the less, the United States will decide whether to interpret China as its number one rival on the basis of how China's power status changes. Although China and the Western European major powers have been categorized as regional powers, the geographical distances between them cause fewer conflicts of interest. Thus they may even forge a strategic alliance against the United States' hegemonic pressures. However, in East Asia, China and Japan have fundamental conflicts that will cause inevitable confrontations between the two. In the early post-Cold War period, Japan was the world's second economic power after the United States, and the number one economic power in East Asia.

If its economic power status decreases due to an increase in power status of other states, both globally and regionally, Japan may take several measures to protect its existing international status by strengthening its political and military power. Thus, if China's economic power status replaces that of Japan, Japan may confront China politically. A better understanding of China's power status enables us to know why structural conflicts exist in China's strategic relationships with the United States and Japan but not with the major European powers.

CHINA'S CURRENT SECURITY POLICY

In response to the attacks in Africa during the last five years, China has confronted the problem of nontraditional security threats in several ways. The PRC's initial reaction is to work with local governments. "China will cooperate closely with immigration departments of African countries in tackling the problem of illegal migration, improve exchange of immigration control information, and set up an unimpeded and efficient channel for intelligence and information exchange," China's 2006 *Africa Policy* stated.

"In order to enhance the ability of both sides to address nontraditional security threats, it is necessary to increase intelligence exchange, explore more effective ways and means for closer cooperation in combating terrorism, small-arms smuggling, drug trafficking, transnational economic crimes, etc." Beijing has instructed its embassies in Africa to keep a close watch on local security. The swift and successful evacuation of Chinese citizens from Chad also demonstrated that China has developed operational scenarios to deal with these emergencies. The Chinese government has also started issuing travel advisories.

In Sudan and Kenya, state-owned companies receive protection from local armed forces against attacks by rebels. Beijing has signed an agreement with South Africa to prevent the Chinese diaspora from turning into a target for armed gangs. Such measures are designed to help Chinese citizens and companies avoid some of the risks related to operating in Africa, but they do not provide any guarantee for safeguarding China's economic activities if the situation keeps deteriorating. In the case of Sudan, China learned the hard way that prodding instable governments can have drastic consequences. If problems start to occur at the regional level, supporting these emerging states might prove even riskier.

Nor does this narrow security response address China's uncertainty about the military capability of African nations. The dilemma reverts back to the realistic supposition of self-help. Is the PRC trying to safeguard its interests by building up its own military presence in Africa?

Bilateral military exchanges are a first indicator to test whether this assumption holds true. According to the Chinese government, interaction with other armed forces expanded significantly, with 174 high-level visits in 2001 and more than 210 in 2006. This upward trend was not maintained in Africa, however, where such bilateral exchanges have remained stable at an annual average of 26. Beijing has established a permanent military dialogue only with South Africa. Interviews with European diplomats in ten randomly chosen African countries also reveal that the number of accredited military officers in Chinese embassies, i.e., military attachés and their support staff, has barely or not expanded at all in the last few years. In fact, only in 15 countries are Chinese military attachés assigned on a permanent basis. China's military diplomacy in Africa remains modest, and it has not kept up with the impressive number of Chinese trade officials posted in African nations to strengthen economic ties in the last few years. Military aid is another indicator. Providing military hardware to partner nations can serve various objectives. In a context of competition, it helps to thwart defence cooperation with other states or to prevent other powers' attempts to alter the regional military balance. Defence aid might help a privileged political partner to safeguard economic interests. Whereas these three objectives are motivated by security issues and long-term economic interests, defence aid may well be the result of more short-sighted aspirations. There is no evidence that China's military aid successfully counterbalances other powers, such as the United States.

Apart from Sudan and Zimbabwe, most countries that have received Chinese military aid in the last few years are also supplied by Washington. In 2007, Beijing temporarily froze the supply of heavy arms to Khartoum after pressure from the West. When Nigeria's Vice President, Atiku Abubakar, announced that his nation would turn to China instead of the United States for arms, Beijing's response was reluctant, and no major supply operations materialized. China's military aid programs should not be considered as support for its forays into the mining industry. For instance, between 2004 and 2008, resource-rich Nigeria received only half as much military aid as Ghana or Uganda. During this period, China provided more military assistance to Angola than to Sudan, even though the security challenges in the latter were much greater.

Although violence in Somalia has threatened China's oil exploration activities in both Ethiopia and Kenya, China only made a commitment to Kenya to help in protecting its border. China has, at times, provided military aid, but such assistance does not seem to be part of any coherent strategy related to protecting its security interests.

Finally, self-help would imply the deployment of military forces whenever China's interests are threatened, possibly in an attempt to train friendly armed forces and dissuade any challengers. Yet, such a Chinese military presence is negligible. China has no bases in Africa, as does the United States and France, nor has it trained African soldiers to counter threats to its national interests.

In Sudan, Zimbabwe, Cameroon, and Gabon, China has employed teams of three to ten instructors, but they are assisting in the maintenance of equipment, rather than providing training for combat missions. In Zambia and Algeria, similar examples of cooperation exist but are limited to medical activities. Other major powers deployed naval vessels in an effort to combat piracy and to maintain the maritime supply lines surrounding Africa. During such operations, the Chinese Navy has rarely shown its flag.

In 2000, China sent its newest *Luhai*-class guided missile destroyer and a supply ship to Tanzania and South Africa. A 2002 fleet composed of a guided missile destroyer, the *Qingdao*, and a supply ship, the *Taicang*, visited Egypt. These voyages were gestures of courtesy rather than a reaction to security challenges. They were limited in duration, and no actions were attempted against pirates or poachers. In December 2008, however, the Chinese government did deploy two destroyers and a replenishment ship in the Gulf of Aden to participate in the United Nations-backed mission against piracy. A mission that was only undertaken after receiving a positive signal from US Pacific Command chief Admiral Timothy Keating.

Instead of dealing with security threats unilaterally, China has resorted to bandwagoning. Although in the 1980s and early 1990s, Beijing opposed attempts by the international community to intervene in African security issues, nowadays it tends to join them. Beijing is increasingly recognizing the United Nations' role in resolving the numerous conflicts and safeguarding the sovereignty of developing nations. In the 1990s, China began supporting United Nations (UN) missions designed to implement peace agreements between rivalling parties, on the condition that a well-defined and restricted mandate was included. Traditional peacekeeping operations such as those in Somalia (UNSOM I), Mozambique, Rwanda, and Sierra Leone all were supported. When the UN Security Council decided to dispatch forces to Liberia in 2003, China offered to support the mission and gradually increased the number of its peacekeepers to 1,300 in 2007.

At the same time, however, failed states and national governments that had actively participated in atrocities challenged the efficacy of many of the traditional UN operations. China's focus on the primacy of sovereignty, requiring at a minimum the state's consent, collided with the willingness of other nations to intervene aggressively under the UN Charter's Chapter VII mandate.

Beijing loudly opposed the move by European countries to push for Operation Turquoise in Rwanda, Washington's call to broaden the UNSOM mandate, or France's demand for a troop increase in the 2004 UN operation in Ivory Coast. Despite its strong concerns, China did not veto these interventions at the UN Security Council, but rather abstained and remained aloof from implementation. Sudan was the first instance where China actively lobbied an African government to permit a UN mission on its soil. Via active brokering and indirect pressure, China succeeded in neutralizing the incompatibility between its economic interests and the principle of noninterference on the one hand, and western appeals for intervening in Darfur and the need for long-term stability on the other.

That Beijing recognizes the importance of collective security became apparent in 2006, when China was the first nation to ask the UN Security Council for a peacekeeping mission in Somalia. In June that year, at a Security Council meeting in Addis Ababa, China's Permanent Representative to the UN, Wang Guangya, scolded other diplomats for neglecting Somalia and urged them to support the deployment of peacekeepers. "I was reluctant to take on this role," said Wang, explaining that

African governments had been pushing China to raise the issue in the Council, "but there was a lack of interest by the other major powers." Initially, the proposal was tentatively received by Great Britain and the United States, but after various talks in New York, Beijing and Washington jointly sponsored a resolution for the deployment of a UN mission. In 2007, in early consultations with France, China supported a French draft resolution on Chad calling for the dispatch of mainly European peacekeepers under the auspices of Chapter VII. It was significant that China approved the "close liaising" with the Hybrid Operation in Darfur (UNAMID), where earlier it had objected to the development of links between UNAMID and UN missions. "Our support for the resolution on Chad shows that we are prepared to cooperate to tackle security issues at a regional level and that our awareness on the increasing complexity of violent conflicts in Africa grows," a Chinese diplomat explained.

China is also turning to African regional organizations to collaborate on security issues. In the China-Africa Action Plan, approved in November 2006, Beijing vowed "to support Africa in the areas of logistics" as well as "to continue its active participation in the peacekeeping operations and demining process in Africa and provide, within the limits of its capabilities, financial and material assistance as well as relevant training to the Peace and Security Council of the African Union." In June 2006, the Chinese government granted the African Union's Mission in Sudan \$3.5 million in budgetary support and humanitarian aid. Earlier, it provided financial and technical support to the Association for West African States.

Slowly but surely, China is showing itself ready to participate in international efforts to prevent conflicts, fueled by the easy availability of small arms and illegally exported natural resources. In 2002, for instance, Beijing revised its regulation on the control of military products for export and published the "Military Products Export Control List" supplying guidelines for the export of military-related products. In the same year, it signed the "Protocol Against the Illicit Manufacturing of and

Trafficking in Firearms," which committed the People's Republic to control the manufacturing, marking, import, and export of firearms, and to confiscate and destroy all illicit firearms. In 2005, the government launched a national information management system for the production, possession, and trade of light arms, and it introduced a system to monitor end-users of Chinese-made weapons to prevent the arms from finding their way to "sensitive regions" around the world via third parties. In 2006, China supported a draft UN resolution on the illicit trade of small arms and light weapons, in contrast to the United States. In 2002, China joined the Kimberley Process, a joint government, international diamond industry, and civil initiative designed to stem the flow of conflict diamonds originating from Africa. In 2005, China allowed a voluntary peer review of its support for the Kimberly Process. Although these actions still have many flaws, they seem to prove that China wishes to do more than just put "boots on the ground" in response to Africa's internal conflicts.

Despite the strategic importance of Africa, China does not try to safeguard its foothold in the region by unilaterally projecting military power. In Africa, its military diplomacy remains limited when compared with defence initiatives in other regions. If the PRC does pursue bilateral cooperation programs, these are more likely to be a part of its diplomatic charm offensive, rather than addressing threats to China's economic and security interests. Instead of relying on a military presence to counterbalance other powers, the PRC tends to join collective security efforts within the framework of the United Nations and African regional organizations. Over the past few years, this strategy of joint ventures has evolved from passive support to active cooperation. Beijing has softened its devotion to noninterference. While maintaining the primacy of sovereignty, it has become willing to support interventions whenever regional stability is at stake.

Although China has become a revisionist power in terms of its economic aspirations on the continent, it is acting as a status-quo power in terms of security objectives. There are several explanations for this stance. First, China only recently began its economic focus on the African continent. For the past two decades, China concentrated on curbing the military and diplomatic influence of Taiwan; the focus on "economization" of its Africa policy only began in the late 1990s.

Hence, the security challenges it is facing now are a recent phenomena, and solutions to these challenges are just starting to be explored. The PRC is going through the early stage of resecuritization of its Africa strategy, and joining with other nations in an allied strategy can be considered the easiest immediate response. Second, and related to this point, China has not developed sufficient means to back up its security policy with military power. This is a matter of budgetary constraints. Building an independent and sustained military presence is a costly affair and would, at present, overstretch the PLA's capabilities, while Asia remains its primary focus. The PLA does not possess the logistical capacity to support sustained region wide deployment in Africa. Its long-range airlift and sealift, as well as its intelligence and command capabilities, are not up to the task. Third, the Chinese government wants to avoid the People's Republic being perceived as a hegemonic power.

In the initial stage of its economic charm offensive, the PRC tried to pursue a business-as-usual approach, maintaining a low profile and steering clear of political entanglements. That approach is no longer possible now that China stands at the forefront of Africa's political scene, actively altering the economic balance of power. Beijing is well aware of the dichotomy between its weak and strong identities and is reluctant to demonstrate any independent military capacity. Such a show of strength might reduce its diplomatic maneuverability, increase resistance from African nations-just as Washington is now experiencing-and raise suspicions elsewhere regarding Chinese intentions. Yet, as interests, perceptions, and capacities are susceptible to change, the question remains whether China will stay on this track of cooperative security.

China's interests in Africa have changed over the past decades and will undoubtedly continue to evolve. The concept for its security policy in the region will depend on the role that Africa plays as a supplier of natural resources. Africa currently supplies approximately 30 percent of China's oil imports. Beijing and its African partners announced that they are preparing to increase bilateral trade to $100 billion by the year 2010. Most of this increase will come from the import of raw commodities. In recent years, Chinese companies have laid the foundation for a substantial increase in the production of resource industries. Exploration in the Gulf of Guinea, Angola, and the Horn of Africa have the potential for an increase in oil exports to China of more than 80 percent in the next ten years. Chinese companies are just starting to tap the large mines that were recently acquired in Gabon, the Democratic Republic of Congo, Namibia, and elsewhere on the continent. Given the fact that other emerging markets such as India and Brazil are shifting the use of their raw materials from export to domestic consumption, the economic relevance of Africa to China cannot be overstated.

How necessary it is to back up these Chinese economic ventures with more overt security measures is yet to be seen. The incidents described in the first section of this article, the persistent instability in nations, as well as the weak position of amicable political leaders will undoubtedly position Africa higher on Beijing's foreign security agenda and require a more complete approach. The question again arises whether it is in China's best interest to apply its African policy independently or in synergy with other nations. The short-term costs of any unilateral action would certainly exceed those of collective action, but long-term uncertainty about the intentions of other major players might influence any concerns related to cost-effectiveness. If Washington or Delhi decides to change course and contain China's expanding influence in Africa by pursing a strategy of counterbalancing and sea denial, the repercussions for the People's Republic will be dramatic. The concerns of the national security establishments in India and the United States and their expanding military presence in Africa are not unnoticed in China, and they highlight the necessity for the PRC to build a legitimate capacity to deal with crises unilaterally. China's diplomatic identity will help shape policy decisions in support of a more active and autonomous security strategy. Beijing is realizing that the comfortable cloak of frailty it previously presented to the world no longer fits. African partners do not attach much value to China's diplomatic schizophrenia and the complex image of an economic giant, political dwarf, and minor military player it projects. When mayhem erupts, China automatically ends up on the frontline, finding itself hounded by African governments asking it to exercise its leverage. The cases of Chad and Somalia are not the only examples of this. South Africa has accosted China regarding illegal immigrants from Zimbabwe. Central Africa has carefully examined the violent incursions from Sudan. The African Union has called upon China several times to play a more active role in promoting security. The possibility exists that individual countries may be compelled to form a closer alliance with China in order to reduce their current reliance on the European Union and United States for security. Nigeria's announcement that it would rely on China instead of the United States for military support hints at this direction. The ability of the PRC to keep a low military profile is diminishing.

On the other hand, China's self-perception is also in transition. The "Century of Humiliation" is far behind and is being replaced by a national attitude of confidence and assertiveness. Chinese leaders have built on the success of their policy of good neighbour diplomacy that resulted in fewer frictions and more influence in Asia. The People's Republic has drawn confidence from the successful launch of a number of new defence systems. As China sees its diplomatic leverage expanding geographically from the Strait of Formosa, via Asia to the rest of the developing world, its ability to deal with emerging security issues is likely to follow suit.

Finally, there is the factor of capacity. China is gearing its military for a greater deployment capability. Its large immobile army is gradually being converted into a highly specialized and flexible organization. Simultaneously, the PLA is launching new military systems that will enhance its capacity to transport these forces. In 2007, the Chinese government approved the development of large passenger jets, including military transport variants similar to the American C-17 Globemaster III. Beijing has also ordered several new ships in an effort to enhance its naval transport capacity. In 2006, the hull of the first T-071 vessel was laid. This landing-platform dock has a range that goes far beyond Taiwan, with the aim of providing sea-based support to operations on land, humanitarian aid, and assisting in evacuations and disaster management. These vessels will be supported by a new generation of large replenishment ships and could be escorted by advanced frigates and destroyers. The Chinese flotilla that was sent to Somalia demonstrates China's new blue-water capacity. The type 052C *Lanzhou*, for instance, is a showcase of the advanced detection capacity for China's Navy. Its multifunction, active phased-array radar has a detection range of 450 kilometers and is complemented with a long-range, two-dimensional air search radar that has a 350-kilometer range and three additional systems to detect incoming missiles and aircraft. China is advancing its ability to pursue a more confident and independent security policy in Africa.

Will all this newfound military activity be sufficient to offset the antagonistic response it is likely to provoke? Probably not. If China decides to go solo and to pursue a more aggressive security policy in Africa, it is improbable that it will be able to overcome countermoves by India and the United States. It will be difficult for China to safeguard maritime trade with Africa if India exercises its naval dominance in the Indian Ocean. The sheer geographical divide between the PRC and the African continent makes it extremely difficult to support military activities if the United States or India opposes them. Contrary to China's revolutionary phase of the 1950s and 1960s when trade and economic interests only played a small part, China's increasing reliance on Africa renders it highly vulnerable to sea denial operations or a *guerre de course*. The fragile Cold War balance between the United States and the Soviet Union that allowed Mao to meddle with America's interests in Africa without having to fear political or economic reprisals can no longer be counted on. These days China has much to lose if it provokes Washington or Delhi.

CHINA'S SECURITY ENVIRONMENT

China and India, the two largest developing countries in the world, have a commonality of history, culture, economy and social characteristics, and profiles of development. Each applies itself to internal economic development, carries out an independent foreign policy and strives for a peaceful international environment. China and India are among what Brzezinski described as "five geo-strategic players", what Henry Kissinger listed as the "six big powers", and what Samuel Huntington pointed out are "core states of seven civilizations." China is a big power in East Asia while India is a big power in South Asia. Each has advantages and influence in their respective regions.

However, they are not world powers that have global influence. In terms of institution and comprehensive strength, they cannot even be ranked as strong powers. For America, China and India, at one end, are two emerging markets offering economic benefits and developing opportunities. At the other end, China and India are also two transitional countries demonstrating uncertainty, from the United States' strategic point of view. What Washington fears most is the possibility of China and India, with Russia, forming an alliance based on a common understanding and interests of a new international political and economical order and a multi-polar world. The United States and India, the largest democracies in the world, share common political values and strategic interests. Their common geo-political, economic and socio-political interests are advancing a co-operative agenda (which their differences over nuclear proliferation may not be able to halt). With the US–India relationship moving forward over the past two years, the two countries have developed a comprehensive co-operative framework covering democracy, economy and security.

The United States now pays more attention to India's role as the largest democracy than it did before. India's continuous and fast-growing economy, especially its information technology industry, attracts great investment from transnational corporations based in America.

In the security arena, the U.S. leadership has gradually begun to 'forget' India's nuclear tests and has come to recognize India as a *de facto* nuclear power, as also its preponderant position in South Asia. With India's support for America's unilateral action in missile defence, the US and India moved from divergence to co-operation in the field of non-proliferation. After 9/11, counter-terrorism has been a new field of strategic co-operation for U.S. and India. In a related development, Pakistan turns out to be less of an 'obstacle' for the US–India framework of relationships.

China and the United States, the largest developing and developed countries respectively, also have comprehensive common strategic interests. Besides large potential economic cooperation, they also share broad interests in other fields such as regional stability and the role and reform of the United Nations.

What is more likely is the emergence of a "soft balance of power" system among the three countries. Alternately, at one end, a vicious competitive relationship among the three countries may emerge, and the "soft balance of power" may be changed into a "hard balance of power" similar to that in the Cold War era, if one of them regards the development of relations between the two other countries as a challenge to its national interests, or if any two in this triad forge a relationship as a means to contain the third country. At the other end, it is possible for China, the US and India to establish a relatively harmonious relationship if they can seek out common views and interests, and push their differences aside to deal with bilateral and trilateral relations within a strategic perspective.

BUILDING SECURITY AND CONFIDENCE WITH CHINA

Except for the brief period of confrontation between 19591992 and the diplomatic freeze that followed for next few years the relations between China and India had never been conflictual in nature. But because of the complicated colonial legacies - which were further compounded by the Cold War dynamics and by the border war of 1962 - mutual distrust and threat perceptions have continued to undermine all efforts towards building confidence. One may ask why confidence and security building measures (CSBMs) between India and China are so critical to the evolution of their multifaceted and multilayered *rapprochement*? The one line answer would be that these CSBMs present a perfect barometer for any crystal gazing into the future of these two Asian giants. However, this answer remains far too simplistic to explain the complexity of Go-Indian ties. And it is in this context of complications that this essay tries to examine and highlight Sino-Indian CSBMs in terms of their being the first significant step forward untying the knots in the bilateral relations and mutual perceptions.

Firstly, to deal with the theoretical elements of Sine-Indian CSBMs, it has been unjustifiably fashionable to view Sino-Indian CSBMs essentially in the framework of western ready-made models. If anything, the CSBMs in the Asian context have far preceded all western models and, therefore, are neither borrowed from nor identical to those leading to the Final Act of the Helsinki process of the Conference on Security and Cooperation in Europe (CSCE) that was concluded in 1975. Beginning from the Joint Defence Council of 1948 that effected the division of assets and armed forces between India and Pakistan to the Sino-Indian *Panchsheel* Agreement of 1954, and later the Indo-Pak Simla agreement of 1971, various formal and informal agreements had already effected these CSBMs like "non-use", or the "selective use" of armed force and created various other mechanisms. Therefore these CSBMs had been institutionalised in Asia far earlier. Besides, these were also far more broad based than the Western CSBMs, including those that were later incorporated the Document of the Conference on Disarmament in Europe held in 1986 at Stockholm (Sweden).

Coming to the salient features of what can be described as the Asian CSBMs that distinguish the Sino-Indian CSBMs from most of their comparable Western models, one sees the near absence of a subjective feeling in the Asian context of an imminent threat which is so central to all those Western conceptions of CSBMs. In Asia's rather lose polycentric situation, nations had never been so clearly divided as are the communist and liberal democratic traditions that characterise the bipolar division of the West. Similarly, the second basic condition of equality of the military strength between the potential parties to the conflict, again seems very much a Eurocentric feature of CSBMs and is generally missing in the Asian situation. China, India and Pakistan can themselves be cited as ideal examples of this asymmetry of power. Nevertheless, CSBMs have continued to evolve amongst these three countries. Thirdly, the inter-state boundaries which form the basic element of European CSBMs are itself a major problem and therefore the very objective towards which most Asian CSBMs seek to provide solutions, Also, Asian CSBMs are generally backed by ever widening network of measures like state sponsored people-to-people contacts which are aimed at expanding mutual trust and understanding between the entire social elite on both sides.

Nor should we regard the Asian CSBMs in general and the Sino-Indian CSBMs in particular as the byproduct of the post-Cold War peace dividend although the global factors, have surely been much more influential in moulding the European CSBMs than those between Asian countries. This is because unlike Europe, (a) the conflicts in Asia were never seen to be vital to the national interests of both the super powers: and, (b) the middle ranking powers like China and India have become increasingly independent from the regimented bipolar world order of the Cold War years. To give two most apt examples, contrary to Cold War trends, India had initiated its CSBMs during the mid-1970s and India's Foreign Minister, Atal Behari Vajpai, paid his first visit to Beijing at the lime when China was launching its war against Vietnam and the Soviet forces were about to enter Afghanistan yet, despite India's closeness to Moscow, the new Cold War of the early 1980s did not disturb the smooth evolution of Sine-Indian *rapprochement* Similarly, following the June 1989 Tiananmen Square incident, while most of world powers had imposed sanctions thus completely isolating China, the relations between China and India not only continued to be smooth but experienced a greater momentum: the period from the second half through 1989 and 1990 saw 10 high-level visits between the two countries that included visits to New Delhi by Vice Premier Wu Xueqian in October 1989 and by Foreign Minister Qian Qichen in March 1990.

The credit for this goes to (a) this unique Asian way of trial and error which, therefore, lends some sort of originality of these Sino-Indian CSBMs, and (b) to the political leadership of both the countries who were able to take and stand by such bold initiatives.

If anything, it is their expanding interactions at various levels that has been the greatest single factor behind the evolution of Sino-Indian CSBMs. Starting from their exchange of Ambassadors in 1976, these expanding official and business interactions can be divided into three major phases. The first phase (1976-1988), was characterised by both *China and lndia looking at* each *other* simply gauging the potential for expanding mutual goodwill and trust. Second phase (1988-1996), which witnessed five formal summits interspersed by hectic initiatives and agreements towards evolving and consolidating CSBMs. Then having established this strong network of CSBMs the recent four agreements signed during President Jiang Zemin's visit to New Delhi in November 1996, Sino-Indian *rapprochement* has now entered into its third and final phase where the two are expected to take concrete decisions on more difficult issues like the boundary question.

A quick glance through this evolution from freeze to fervour shows how, though no breakthrough has yet been achieved on the crucial boundary question quite a substantial progress has been made considering the complicated and knotty ground realities. The historic f 988 visit to Beijing by Prime Minister Rajiv Gandhi had worked as a catalyst in facilitating a U-turn in Sino- Indian relations. Especially, considering Indian sensitivities vis-a-vis China, this visit itself was an extremely bold initiative. But more than this, in the Joint Communiqué at the end of this visit India agreed, for the first time, to dropping its earlier policy stance of asking for settlement of the border as a precondition for any improvement in relations in other fields. Secondly, India not only agreed to describe Tibet as an integral part of (not just an autonomous region) of China but also expressed "concern over anti-Chinese activities by some Tibetan elements in India" -a proviso which was criticised by some as a clear sell-out of the Tibetan interests. India's over-reaction towards Tibetan protesters during the visit by Premier Li Peng in 1991 was another demonstration of India's resolve in not letting Tibet become a problem in the way of Sino-Indian *rapprochement*. All this meant that, Rajiv Gandhi's visit had finally abandoned India's discredited forwards policy and, at least during the interim, accepted China's long-standing demand for the maintenance of tranquillity on the line of actual control (LoAC).

There were also some legal hurdles to this visit. The historic November 1962 resolution of Indian Parliament had bound successive Indian leaders from making any move towards improving Sino-Indian ties until they had obtained every inch of India's sacred land claimed or taken by the Chinese. But this December 1988 visit by Rajiv Gandhi to Beijing became possible because of another major resolution that was passed by the All India Congress Working Committee on November 5, 1988 urging the government to seek a settlement through "peaceful negotiations" based on "mutual interest" and "acceptable to the peoples of both countries" even if it took time. Apart from minor objections, no main national political parties raised any hue and cry against these "concession" by Rajiv Gandhi. This was because (a) the Congress Party, at this time, had an overwhelming majority in Indian Parliament and (b) the earlier major, initiative towards building peace with China had been taken during the Janata Party government in February 1979. Moreover, eight rounds of border talks (initiated during Foreign Minister, Huang Hua's visit to New Delhi in 1981) had already created some sort of favourable backdrop.

Apart from these interactions at the political level, Rajiv Gandhi's visit also opened avenues for direct military interactions. Because of the 1962 war, any interaction between the military personnel or on defence related matters remained a taboo until the early 1990s. The first exchange in this direction was made by the senior serving officials of the National Defence College (New Delhi) and the National Defence University (Beijing) respectively visiting each other in 1990 and 1992.The two have also since been considering undertaking an arrangement for an institutional exchange wherein at least one officer could attend the others training courses. The military-to-military dialogue was taken to a higher level by India's Defence Minister, Sharad Pawar's visit to China in July 1992. This opened the way and was followed by Vice Chief of China's People's Liberation Army, Lt. General Xu Huizi, visiting India in December 1993 followed by a visit by their Defence Minister, Chi Haotian's visit to India during September 7-13, 1994. From the Indian side, Chief of Army Staff, General B.C. Joshi and Chief of Naval Staff, Admiral V.S. Shekhawat paid reciprocal visits to various defence facilities in China during July 1994 and March 1996 respectively. This increasing interaction and transparency between the two military establishments has surely contributed to the building up of mutual confidence.

Once again, just like the lack of interactions and other historical legacies had coloured their visions during the earlier years, increasing information and confidence has led to revision and rectification of various policies on both sides. One good example of this spectrum of biases in perceptions can be seen in the way various China watchers interpreted the incident when in May 1992 China detonated a 150 megaton nuclear device just hours after President R. Venkatraman arrived in Beijing. While some called it an act of intimidation, others described it as an expression of China's solidarity with India in their strategic defiance of Washington. However, with persistent efforts from both sides, a relatively more objective understanding of each other has started to emerge during the 1990s. Observing the tenor of policy pronouncements from both sides there appears to be an obvious shift of emphasis away from the assertion of huge territorial claims or high moral principles increasingly towards "mutual concessions" and "accommodation "from the Chinese side and on historical, legal, geographical realities from the Indian side with both now calling for a "fair, reasonable, and mutually acceptable" compromise solution to their boundary question.

Also both sides today have far greater mutual understanding on various issues ranging from global problematic like the US nuclear non-proliferation to regional and bilateral contentions like Kashmir, Tibet, and border. As a result, while owing to their ideological systems and methods of operation the two had appeared to be dramatical opposites during the 1950s over the years the two sides have begun to appreciate and emphasise on their similarities and evolved common approach on certain issues like nuclear disarmament, trade and human rights. On the nuclear question, for example, while China has sought to keep its own nuclear build-up completely insulated from the ongoing disarmament debates between Moscow and Washington: yet, Beijing has also generally kept a low profile on India's nuclear and missile programme and, in fact, assisted India by supplying heavy water at a crucial stage in January 1995. Nevertheless, there still exist differences of approach on various issues and inspite of substaintial improvement, India has continued to be deeply concerned about China's supplies of nuclear components, materials and knowhow to other countries in India's neighbourhood. This is especially true of China's indulgence with Pakistan. Yet, in the end, all this has never discouraged India from making efforts at improving ties with both Beijing and Islamabad.

From the Indian side, these efforts for *rapprochement* had all started as early as late 1960s. Later, starting from Sardar Swaran Singh's (then Foreign Minister) offer in August 1970 "to settle all matters...peacefully through bilateral negotiations," India not only became the first one to take many major initiatives but also became the first one to declare and actually resume its Ambassadorial level diplomatic relations with Beijing. Besides, India also made many other goodwill gestures towards China like installing telex links in each others embassies, supporting China's candidacy for the Manila-based Asian Development Bank, inviting China to a regional UNESCO conference in New Delhi, and Prime Minister Mrs. Indira Gandhi herself making a personal gesture by visiting and signing the book of condolences in the Chinese embassy in New Delhi as mark of respect for the late Premier Zhou Enlai. The first feelers from the Chinese side came in May 1960 and April 1961 from then Vice Premier Deng

Xiaoping who revived Zhou Enlai's 1960 proposal for a package deal on the boundary question. Here, Deng proposed Chinese recognition of the McMahon Line in the eastern sector in return for Indian acceptance of the status quo along the LoAC in the western sector. In fact, according to Mrs. Gandhi's foreign policy Advisor, G. Parthasarthy, Mrs. Gandhi had even agreed to accept the Chinese package deal only that, with the Chinese assent, the formal announcement had been postponed until after December 1985 general elections. Soon the assassination of Mrs. Gandhi in October 1984 and later the Sumdorong Chu valley incident in July 1966 completely rocked this spirit of accommodation and delayed major initiatives by f9w more years.

A clear shift in China's South Asia policy, however, began to occur from late 1960s when Beijing gradually gave up its earlier post-1962 tactics of providing moral and material support to India's smaller neighbours which was aimed at: (a) tying New Delhi down to the South Asian region and, (b) trying to offset India's preeminence even in this smaller region. In 1969, for example, China not only refused to supply weapons to

Nepal and gave only muted response to India's peacekeeping in Sri Lanka, it even told General Ershad of Bangladesh to expect no more Chinese support on their river water dispute with New Delhi. This has since resulted in improving India's relations with both Bangladesh and Nepal. Putting an end to its dilly-dallying of late 1980s, the Rao-Li joint statement of December 1991 clearly told China's closest ally Pakistan that Beijing now regards Kashmir as a bilateral issue between India and Pakistan. Since then China's position on Kashmir has also undergone a marked change on at least two basic counts: (a) by describing it as a bilateral issue between India and Pakistan that should be dealt not under UN resolutions of 1954 but the 1972 Simla Agreement, and (b) by broadly agreeing to underline the fear from "Islamic fundamentalism". In the second case, the Joint Statement did not directly mention either India's Kashmir or China's Xinjiang yet, as both these provinces share common borders with Pakistan, the statement has clear implications for Islamabad. But nothing perhaps stands comparison to the first Magna Carta on Sine-Indian CSBMs that came two years later and was a part of the next Rat-Li Joint Statement from Beijing.

By any standards, this nine-point "Agreement on Maintenance of Peace and Tranquillity along the Line of Actual Control (henceforth MPTA), signed between two Prime Ministers Narasimha Rao and Li Peng at Beijing's Great Hall of the People on September 7, 1993 has been the corner-stone of Sine-Indian CSBMs. Though already in vogue since the Rajiv Gandhi visit to Beijing in 1988, it was this agreement that formally institutionalised the process of Sine-Indian CSBMs.19 Picking up strings from India's first CSBM agreement of April 1954, the MPTA reiterates its faith in *Panchsheel* and asserts that these Five Principles of Peaceful Coexistence should form the basis of all inter-state relations. But unlike in the earlier Sino-Indian *Panchsheel* agreement where India unilaterally made major concessions, the MPTA clearly represents equality of two nations and lays out various CSBMs that should further buttress Sino-Indian rapprcchement. This business-like spirit is crystal clear throughout its concise text that details on number of specific points. The second CSBMs agreement was signed during President Jiang Zemin's visit to New Delhi in November 1998. This is a 12 Article document that partly fulfils the agenda of their first CSBM agreement of 1993 and it further seeks to extend the CBMs to more specific and sensitive areas in the military field. Going by its first Article that reads "Neither side shall use its military capability against the other side", it virtually stands out as a No War Pact and both sides have also projected it in that light. The agreement begins with (Article II) recognising that both have "different perceptions" on certain segments of border for which the two have agreed "to speed up the process of clarification" and under Article X both sides agree 40 exchange maps indicating their respective perceptions... as soon as possible." It is this businesslike approach to these sensitive questions that gives hope for the future as it depicts !heir growing mutual confidence on the current pace of their *rapprochement*.

As regards evolving CBMs in the military field, the agreement makes a serious attempt at effecting reductions in their military manpower and equipment deployed in the border areas. There had been major confusion as China does not consider their deployments in Tibet as being open for mutual reductions where India believes that Chinese forces on the Tibetan plateau have clear one-to-ten advantage against Indian forces. Accordingly, Article III provides that keeping with "the principle of mutual and equal security" all future ceilings are expected to be based on "perimeters such as the nature of terrain, road communications and other infrastructure and time taken to induct/deinduct troops and armaments." Article IV clearly categonses certain type of offensive weapons withdrawal of which will be given priority These include combat tanks, infantry combat vehicles, guns (including howitzers) with 75 mm or bigger calibre, mortars with 120 mm or bigger calibre, surface-to-surface missiles, surface-to- air missiles and to start with the two sides will "exchange data on the military forces and armament" that are to be reduced. It also exhorts the two sides to 'avoid holding large scale military exercises involving more than one Division (15,000 troops) in close proximity to the LoAc" and to inform the other side on "type, level, planned duration and areas of exercise" in case it involves more than a Brigade (5,000 troops) and about deinduction "within five days of completion." The other side is free to seek any number of clarifications as it deems necessary. Taking a major step forward, the two agree that no combat aircraft which "include fighter, bomber, reconnaissance, military trainer, armed helicopter and other armed aircraft" shall be allowed to fly "within ten kilometers" of the LoAC "except by prior permission" from the other side (Article V).

Similarly, Article VI prohibits any use of "hazardous chemicals, conduct blast operations or hunt with guns or explosives within two kilometers" of the LoAC unless it is "part of developmental activities" in which case the other side shall be informed "through diplomatic channels or by convening a border personnel meeting, preferably five days in advance." Then to "strengthen exchanges and cooperation between their military personnel and establishments" Article VII provides that the two sides shall (a) increase "meetings between their border representatives at designated places, (b) expand "telecommunication links" between these border points, and (c) establish "step-by-step medium and high-level contacts between the border authorities" of the two sides. Should any land or air intrusions take place "because of unavoidable circumstances like natural disasters" the other side is expected under Article VIII to "extend all possible assistance to them" and the two shall exchange information and have consultations to work out "modalities of return of the concerned personnel." And finally, as won as the Sino-Indian Joint Working Group on Boundary Question starts "mutual consultations" (Article Xl) for "detailed implementation measures", each side shall have (Article IX) "the right to seek clarification" regarding the "manner in which the other side is observing the agreement" or on any "doubtful situation" in the border region. Finally, under Article XII though all Hindi, Chinese and English versions are "equally authentic", but "in case of divergence, the English text shall prevail." This agreement has since been ratified by both sides and instrument of ratification were exchanged at the JWG's tenth meeting in New Delhi in August 1997.

These two agreements apart from being a major take-off point for many fresh initiatives, have also provided a major boost to existing "mechanisms" for their border related CSBMs. The Joint Working Group on Boundary Question has been one most effective and generic forum for implementing Sino-Indian CSBMs. To begin with, the JWG has institutionalised regular meetings of military commanders from both sides at the following four points: Bumla and Dichu in the eastern sector, Lipulekh near Pithoragarh (U.P.) in the middle sector and Spanggur near Chushul in the western sector.

These meetings are organised and conducted by these area commanders from the two sides to establish facts on the ground and can also be held more than once in case of any exigencies. Besides, commanders on both sides are now provided with "hotline" links to ensure consultations in case of any intrusions or other emergencies. Advance notices of proposed military manoeuvres on one side is provided to the other and mechanisms for handling possible intrusions on either side are put in place. The high point of these JWG meetings occurred during its eighth meeting during August 1995 at New Delhi where the two sides agreed to actually dismantle four border posts in the Wangdong tract where troops had been deployed at an alarming proximity to each other. Apart from their land-based troops, the two air forces have also been building ties and officers of the People's Liberation Army-Air Force (PLAAF) have already visited India's Air Force bases in 1995. Similarly, the two navies have also been working together allaying each others doubts about Chinese naval presence in Myanmar or India's maritime capabilities at its Fortress Andaman. India has offered to China's envoy to visit Indian naval base at Port Blair in Andaman and Nicobar. At a certain stage there were even reports of China and India preparing for joint military and naval exercises which, however, was denied by the Chinese side.

Then there are various other bold initiatives that come about from outside the framework of JWG. Within less than two months of the MPTA, for example, a Chinese ship "Zheng He" made a port visit to Bombay, which was the first of its kind in last 35 years. Before this only INS Mysore had visited Shanghai in 1958. Also, working on the basis of Chiunese *guanxi* (personal contacts) principle, exchanges between other opinion makers and members of strategic research institutions (like Institute for Defence Studies & Analyses, United Services Institution of India, Centre for Policy Research, and Rajiv Gandhi Foundation from India and China institute for Contemporary International Relations, China Association for Friendly International Contact, Fudan University etc. from China) have also been increasingly formalised. Similarly, *Xinhua, People's Dai and Beijing Review* have their accredited correspondents in India and India's *Press Trust of India* has a resident reporter in Beijing. The agreements on exchange of scholars (between the Indian Council for Social Science Research and Chinese Academy of Social Sciences signed at New Delhi in January 1992) and their Agreement on Radio and Television Cooperation (signed in Beijing on September 7, 1993) have broadly contributed to expanding mutual awareness. The Festival of China was staged in India in 1992 and Festival of India was held in China in April 1994. In fact, the Communist Party of China now has direct links with the Indian National Congress, the Bharatiya Janata Party and the Communist Party of India (Marxists). The two had also tried opening up direct flights between New Delhi and Beijing and now have telecom lines between various cities of the two countries. Contact have also evolved between various NGOs like trade unions and woman organisations, stimulating a great deal of interest and confidence.

In the de-ideologised post-Cold War world, trade has come to be perhaps the most durable CSBM which raises stakes in mutual security and peace amongst states, Though compared to their size and total foreign trade, the volume of Sino-Indian bilateral trade remains still very small yet, more than what is visible in terms of statistics, their border trade has substantially increased the traffic of goods and people in their border regions thus consolidating their border related CSBMs.

Garbyang (in Uttar Pradesh) was the first border port to be opened in February 1991 followed by Gunji (in Uttar Pradesh) in 1992 and later Shipki La (in Himachal Pradesh) in 1994. A fourth border point agreed upon in principle is yet to be opened. India has suggested an eastern route originating in Sikkim on which China has been evasive as it means recognising Sikkim's accession to India.

As an alternative, a route from Kalimpong in Dajeeling District in West Bengal, passing through Sikkim to Yatung in Chumbi Valley, is likely to be agreed upon. Amongst its other intangibles, in 1994, India became China's largest trading partner in South Asia overtaking China's long-standing close friend and ally Pakistan, This obtains for India a greater leverage and psychological advantage vis-a-vis Sine-Pakistan ties. And finally, talking of statistics, according to a recent study by US based Centre for Global Trade Development that monitors trade patterns of 220 countries, has predicted that trade between China and India may cross $ 25 billion by the year 2000. According to the study, this is possible because at their current rate of growth India's total annual exports are expected to reach $ 90 billion and that of China (plus Hong Kong $225 billion after 1997) to $425 billion per annum. The Sino-Indian Joint Business Council has, however, put the figure at a much moderate level of $ 5 billion by 2000.

IMPLICATIONS FOR CONSOCIATIONAL SECURITY IN ASIA

Interdependence

Opinion is divided on the pacific impact of economic interdependence. Skeptics argue that growing economic ties has a poor record in preventing conflict in the past (the two world wars) and that it can create new forms of competition and conflict now, such as competition over resources and markets. Believers in economic interdependence see it otherwise. To quote President Obama, "economic ties and commercial ties that are taking place in this region are helping to lower a lot of the tensions that date back before you were born or even before I was born… there's something about when people think that they can do business and make money that makes them think very clearly and not worry as much about ideology. And I think that that's starting to happen in this region" (The White House 2009). The historical analogy may not be entirely accurate, given the broader and deeper structure of economic interdependence that obtains in Asia today compared to nineteenth-century Europe. Capital flows today are more in the form of *foreign direct investment* (FDI), which create an international division of labor whose "impact on security relations will indeed be transformative" (Pollins 2008: 3, 9). As regards new forms of conflict, while competition for resources does exist in Asia, for example, the Sino-Indian competition for energy resources, it is a far cry from the "orgy of imperialism" that swept Europe in the late nineteenth and early twentieth century, creating an "international tension which made everyone conscious of war" (Stone 1983: 96–107).

Equilibrium

China poses the most powerful challenge to Asia's balance of power. But despite its growing economy (likely to be the number 1 in the world in the next decade) and military spending, the United States remains and is likely to remain for a long time, the preeminent military player in Asia. While China's naval build-up gives it an increasing capacity for denying areas close to its shore to the United States and its allies, any effort by it to dominate the sea lanes of Asia and the Indian Ocean can be countered by the naval forces of the United States, in cooperation with Japan and India. The balancing between China and the United States is consistent with defensive realism, rather than offensive realism (which would imply aggressive expansionism and power maximization by China and preemptive containment by the United States). The United States' strategic concepts of "hedging" and "pivot" (renamed as "rebalancing") support this. In 2006, the United States outlined a policy of "encouraging China to play a constructive, peaceful role in the Asia-Pacific region" while creating "prudent hedges against the possibility that cooperative approaches by themselves may fail to preclude future conflict" (Stewart 2009). This strategy involved deploying six carrier battle groups in the Pacific and 60% of its attack submarine fleet (the *Washington Times*2006). Under "rebalancing," the US navy would shift by 2020 from a 50/50% split between the Pacific and the Atlantic to a 60/40% split, including six aircraft carriers. The aim of rebalancing is to "maintain a nuanced balance" against China while averting "the potential for a...slippery slope toward growing confrontation with China" (The Brookings Institution 2012: 9). While the new US strategy faces budgetary challenges, it also has significant bipartisan support.

Shared leadership

Asia's regional institutions provide the main avenue for shared, rather than hegemonic, leadership. They lack collective security/defense functions, which would require hegemonic leadership—single or collective (concert). Instead, they promote cooperative security. This has allowed ASEAN to stay in the driver's seat of Asian institutions and helped the engagement of China, Vietnam, and India into the region. In the 1990s, they helped to overcome Beijing's initial suspicion of multilateralism as well as America's initial leaning toward a containment strategy (Shambaugh 2004–2005). Arguably, Asia's regional institutions did a better job of dealing with China than Europe's in dealing with Russia. NATO's expansion excluding Russia undermined Europe's cooperative security doctrine promoted by the OSCE. Asia's institutions followed the norm of "security with" in spirit, if not in its legalistic form, by offering full membership to China. ASEAN's strategy continues to engage all the great powers so that no single power can dominate them. This was what led it to invite Australia, India, Russia, and the United States into the EAS, despite the latter being East Asian in geographic scope.

Some wonder if ASEAN might lose its unity and ability to lead, not the least due to a Chinese assertiveness and "divide and rule" strategy. If this happens, and if ASEAN and related institutions are marginalized or replaced by an Asian concert of powers or a Sino-US G-2, or an Asian NATO, the prospects for an Asian CSO would be seriously damaged. So far, these ideas have found little support in the region. ASEAN has value to China's effort to legitimize its "peaceful rise" concept. And ASEAN's continued leadership survives by default because no great power—the United States, China, Japan, or India—is in a position to develop a multilateral security institution under its own imprint either due to historical baggage or the level of mistrust among them.

Elite Restraint

As discussed, all the great powers recognize the "centrality" of ASEAN in the regional security architecture, a sign of restraint or even respect toward a coalition of weaker actors. But there is uncertainty over Chinese restraint. After a period of "charm offensive" in the 1990s and early 2000s and growing engagement with ASEAN-led regional bodies to demonstrate its "peaceful rise," China has become more assertive especially in the South China Sea dispute. China's role in the East China Sea island dispute (over Senkaku/Diaoyu) with Japan has also raised concern regarding Chinese intentions.

Yet, in the South China Sea issue, which presents a critical test of Chinese restraint because of China's huge military superiority over the ASEAN claimants, China has not invaded any island by force since 1974, only occupied islands that were previously unoccupied. China also relented in its initial refusal to discuss this dispute multilaterally with ASEAN (which includes non-claimant states) or at the ASEAN Regional Forum, which includes non-regional states including the United States. It has not closed the door to negotiations. After renewed tensions with Philippines and ASEAN in 2012, Beijing "backed off" from its hardline stance and diplomatically reassured Vietnam, Philippines, and ASEAN. In Northeast Asia, China has worked to restrain North Korea's nuclear ambitions and moved some distance away from the use of force in dealing with Taiwan.

Moreover, Chinese restraint stems not from altruism, but from strategic calculations and normative pressure that the conditions of a CSO—balance of power, interdependence, institutions—provide.Strategically, Chinese leaders realize that assertiveness would push the ASEAN countries closer to the United States (a balancing factor). China's engagement with ASEAN since the mid-1990s has been a source of normative and diplomatic pressure; China has engaged regional institutions to sell its peaceful rise policy and deny other powers, such as Japan and the United States, the opportunity to take over the show. Another source of Chinese restraint lies more in its dependence on Middle Eastern and African oil imports via the Indian Ocean, whose sea lanes are controlled by the US and Indian navies. Hence, while uncertainty over Chinese restraint is a significant challenge to an Asian CSO, Chinese calculations in the context of the US "rebalancing" strategy and the political and normative costs of a war with ASEAN members make it more, rather than less likely.

8

Sino-Indian Convergence: Bilateral and Global Vision

Bilateral relations between India and the People's Republic of China (PRC) have indeed come a long way after they touched their nadir in the immediate aftermath of India's nuclear tests in May 1998. China had been singled out as the "number one" security threat for India by India's Defence Minister just before the nuclear tests.

After the tests, the Indian Prime Minister wrote to the US President justifying Indian nuclear tests as a response to the threat posed by China. Unsurprisingly, China reacted strongly and diplomatic relations between the two countries plummeted to an all time low.

However, some six years later, the relations between the two countries seem to be on an upswing. The visit of the Indian External Affairs Minister to China in 1999 marked the resumption of high-level dialogue and the two sides declared that they were not threats to each other. A bilateral security dialogue was also initiated that has helped the two countries in openly expressing and sharing their security concerns with each other. India and China also decided to expedite the process of demarcation of the Line of Actual Control (LAC) and the Joint Working Group (JWG) on the boundary question, set up in 1988, has been meeting regularly. As a first step in this direction, the two countries exchanged border maps on the least controversial middle sector of the LAC. The Indian Prime Minister visited China in June 2003, the first such visit in a decade. The joint declaration signed during the visit stated that China was not a threat to India. The two states appointed special representatives in order to impart momentum to border negotiations that have lasted twenty two years, with the Prime Minister's principal secretary becoming India's political-level negotiator, replacing the India-China JWG.

India and China also decided to hold their first joint naval exercise later in the year and discussions on joint air exercise continue.

India also acknowledged China's sovereignty over Tibet and pledged not to allow "anti-China" political activities in India. On its part, China has acknowledged India's 1975 annexation of the former monarchy of Sikkim by agreeing to open a trading post along the border with the former kingdom and later rectified official maps to include Sikkim as part of India.

India and China have found substantial convergence of interests at the international level. Both share similar concerns about the growing international dominance of the US, the threat of terrorism disguised as religious and ethnic movements and the need to accord primacy to economic development.

India and China have both expressed concern about the US ' use of military power around the world and publicly opposed the war in Iraq. This was merely a continuation of the desire of both states to oppose the US *hyperpuissance* ever since the end of the Cold War.

Like other major powers in the international system, India and China favour a multi-polar world order where US unipolarity remains constrained by the other "poles" in the system.

China and India zealously guard their national sovereignty and have been wary of US attempts to interfere in what they see as domestic affairs of other stares, be it Serbia, Kosovo or Iraq. Both took strong exception to the US air strikes on Iraq in 1998, the US-led air campaign against Yugoslavia in 1999, and more recently the US campaign against Saddam Hussein arguing that these violated the national sovereignty and undermined the authority of the United Nations system.

Both nations also favour more democratic international economic regimes. They have strongly resisted efforts by the US and other developed nations to link global trade to labour and environmental standards, realizing clearly that this would put them at a huge disadvantage vis-a-vis the developed world, thereby hampering their drive towards economic development, a top priority.

Both have committed themselves to crafting joint Sino-Indian positions in the World Trade Organization (WTO) and global trade negotiations in the hope that this might provide them greater negotiating leverage over the developed states. They would like to see further liberalization of agricultural trade in the developed countries, tightening of the rules on anti-dumping measures and ensuring that non-trade related issues such as labour and environment are not allowed to come to the WTO.

In recent years, India and China have attempted to build their bilateral relationship on the basis of their larger worldview of international politics.

As they have found a distinct convergence of their interests on world stage, they have used it to strengthen their bilateral relations. They have established and maintained regular reciprocal high-level visits between political leaders. There has been a sincere attempt to improve trade relations and to compartmentalize intractable issues that make it difficult for their bilateral relationship to move forward.

India and China have strengthened their bilateral relationship in areas as distinct as cultural and educational exchanges, military exchanges, and science and technology cooperation. Bilateral trade has recorded rapid growth from a trade volume of US $265 million in 1991 to US $3596 million in 2001.

In 2001, bilateral trade saw an increase of 23.4 percent over 2000. It is expected to rise to $10 billion this year. The two nations are even evaluating the possibility of signing a comprehensive economic cooperation agreement and a free trade agreement by the end of this year, thereby building on strong complementarities between the two. Both states are also taking steps to upgrade their military-related cooperation, leading to greater understanding on the bilateral military front, something that would have been unthinkable just a few years ago.

As a first step in this direction, the Chinese and Indian navies carried out joint search and rescue operations off the Shanghai coast in November 2003. Both states are also seeking to cooperate on the nuclear front with China planning to import heavy water from India to be utilized in the pressurized heavy water reactors near Shanghai.

Many observers have also pointed out a subtle shift in Beijing's stance on Pakistan vis-a-vis India. China's "neutral" position during the Kargil conflict and the intense Indo-Pak crisis following the terrorist attack on the India's Parliament is seen by many as a reflection of China's sincerity in its attempts to improve ties.

In keeping with China's attempts to project itself as a responsible regional player, China is seen by some as supporting peace and anti-terrorist efforts in South Asia by cooperating with the US and India. China is also seen as playing a central role in encouraging Pakistan to negotiate with India by using its leverage over Pakistan. After assuming office Prime Minister Manmohan Singh's government made it clear that it favoured closer ties with China and would continue to work towards improving bilateral relations with China. In his first address to the nation, the Prime Minister, Manmohan Singh, also emphasized the carrying forward of the process of further development and diversification of Sino-Indian relations. The late J.N. Dixit, National Security Advisor in the current government, wrote that "the Congress will continue the process of normalizing, strengthening and expanding India's relations with China, which is the most important factor affecting Asian security and stability". One of the first foreign visits of the new

Indian foreign minister, Natwar Singh, was to China to attend the Asia Cooperation Dialogue in Qingdao, in East China's Shandong province and apparently had "substantive discussions" with his Chinese counterpart.

All this reflects on India continuing to build its relations with China on the convergence of interests that the two nations have achieved in recent years.

Aside from the positive developments, one should not ignore the enormous obstacles that confront this bilateral relationship. There has been a dominant tendency in the Indian foreign policy establishment to focus on the strengths of its bilateral relations with China while pretending that problems confronting the relationship would somehow take care of themselves. The challenges in the Sino-Indian relationship are by no means insignificant nor will China take care of Indian interests. It is for India to recognize them for what they are and evolve a coherent strategy to tackle them.

GREAT ASIAN POWER : CHINA AND INDIA

A shifting global power balance from West to East has become a much remarked upon phenomenon of recent years, but it has antecedents in earlier decades. The first country to present a modern "Asian challenge" was Japan, one of the defeated powers of World War II. In 1960, Japan was still considered to be a struggling developing country, poorer than Argentina. By the 1970s it had emerged as the leading Asian economy, welcomed as a founding member of the elite club of the Group of Seven industrialized nations (G7) and en route to global great-power status. On a lesser scale, South Korea was also being recognized as a low-income nation that was lifting itself up mightily and moving to the head of the class of the newly industrializing countries.

What is different about the current attention to rising Asia is the sheer magnitude of the transformational processes occurring simultaneously in the world's two most populous countries. Much of the globalization with which we are familiar has been led by the G7 and OECD countries. In the future, globalization could have more of an Asian face. In the words of the U.S. National Intelligence Council study, "Asia will alter the rules of the globalizing process. By having the fastest-growing consumer markets, more firms becoming world-class multinationals, and greater S&T [science and technology] stature, Asia looks set to displace Western countries as the focus for international economic dynamism – provided Asia's rapid economic growth continues." Asian powers are also expected to dominate global politics later in this century. The ability of Western countries, notably the United States, to accommodate that fact could therefore be crucial to the future of world order.

Within Asia, the most attention is clearly focused on its pre-eminent emerging global players China and India, both of which are adding enormous numbers of new workers and consumers to the global economy while developing huge middle classes larger than the entire populations of most G7 countries. As a recent business article surveyed the prospect:

The postwar era witnessed economic miracles in Japan and South Korea. But neither was populous enough to power worldwide growth or change the game in a complete spectrum of industries. China and India, by contrast, possess the weight and dynamism to transform the 21st-century global economy. ... even America's rise falls short in comparison to what's happening now. Never has the world seen the simultaneous, sustained takeoffs of two nations that together account for one-third of the planet's population. For the past two decades, China has been growing at an astounding 9.5% a year, and India by 6%. Given their young populations, high savings, and the sheer amount of catching up they still have to do, most economists figure China and India possess the fundamentals to keep growing in the 7%-to-8% range for decades. (...) In the coming decades, China and India will disrupt workforces, industries, companies, and markets in ways that we can barely begin to imagine.

Other projections have come to similarly dramatic conclusions about the impacts of these two emerging powers on both the geo-economic and geo-political global landscape. The NIC study suggests that a combination of sustained high economic growth, active promotion of high technologies, population size, expanding military capabilities and international policy ambitions will fuel their rising power on the world stage. Among the expected manifestations are the following:

- The demographic weight of China and India will be such that they will not need to approach Western standards of living to achieve great-power standing.
- China will become the leading centre of world manufacturing and exports. ("Competition from 'the China price' already powerfully restrains manufactures prices worldwide.")
- "China's and India's perceived need to secure access to energy supplies will propel these countries to become more global rather than just regional powers ...."
- "China's desire to gain 'great power' status on the world stage will be reflected in its greater economic leverage over countries in the region and elsewhere as well as its steps to strengthen its military. East Asian states are adapting to the advent of a more powerful China by forging closer economic and political ties with Beijing, potentially accommodating themselves to its preferences, particularly on sensitive issues like Taiwan."
- "China will overtake Russia and others as the second largest defence spender after the United States over the next two decades and will be, by any measure, a first-rate military power."
- "The rise of India also will present strategic complications for the region. Like China, India will be an economic magnet for the region, and its rise will have an impact not only in Asia but also to the north – Central Asia, Iran, and other countries of the Middle East."

- The China-India relationship will be one to watch. Some may see India as a potential "counterweight" to China's influence. But their trade with each other will rise rapidly and they could form a potent strategic alliance.
- "The United States and China have strong incentives to avoid confrontation, but rising nationalism in China and fears in the US of China as an emerging strategic competitor could fuel an increasingly antagonistic relationship."
- Since "China's ability to sustain its current pace is probably more at risk than is India's ... India could emerge as the world's fastest-growing economy as we head towards 2020."

So far there is little sign that China's torrid economic pace is slowing, with the latest figures showing an expansion of 9.9% in 2005, recently overtaking the United Kingdom and France in economic size, and likely Germany in 2008. However, there are a number of downside risks and disruptions that accompany this extraordinary rise: massive internal migration from the countryside to the cities, fragile financial systems and state-owned enterprises, pervasive corruption, rising socio-economic inequalities, inadequate social safety nets and health-care systems in the face of an ageing population and epidemic diseases, growing levels of unemployment and civil unrest, demands for political as well as economic liberalization, for democracy and rights as well as market freedoms, and the spectre of conflicts involving Taiwan or North Korea.

Indeed, some argue that China's combination of a neo-Leninist state and rampant crony capitalism is not sustainable and is more likely to lead to decay than democratic transition. As one sceptic puts it: "For the moment, China's strong economic fundamentals and the boundless energy of its people have concealed and offset its poor governance, but they will carry China only so far.

Someday soon, we will know whether such a flawed system can pass a stress test: a severe economic shock, political upheaval, a public health crisis, or an ecological catastrophe. China may be rising, but no one really knows whether it can fly." About 800 million people, 70% of the population, still live in the countryside, and the gap between the rural poor and urban elites is larger than at any time since the 1949 revolution. As a recent *Economist* article put it: "A spectre is haunting China – the spectre of rural unrest." How well, or badly, China is able to manage multiple transitions and surmount potential internal challenges will be critical to its role in shaping world politics in the coming years. At the same time, it is undeniable that China's growing weight in political and military as well as economic terms is already reshaping the strategic balance in Asia and globally. Much of the attention has focused on China's aggressive diplomacy, an uneasy United States-China relationship and closer United States-India relations. A report prepared for members of the U.S. Congress prior to the first East Asia Summit in mid-December 2005 – a new formation that excludes the United States, unlike broader forums such as APEC (Asia Pacific Economic Cooperation) – suggests that: "Fundamental shifts underway in Asia could constrain the U.S. role in the multilateral affairs of Asia. The centrality of the United States is now being challenged by renewed regionalism in Asia and by China's rising influence."

According to James Hoge: "Suspicious Americans have interpreted larger Chinese military budgets as signs of Beijing's intention to roll back America's presence in East Asia. Washington is thus eager to use India, which appears set to grow in economic and military strength, as a counterbalance to China as well as a strong proponent of democracy in its own right."

That in turn feeds Chinese suspicions of current United States-India military cooperation (which also raises sensitive nuclear nonproliferation issues) as part of a policy of "soft containment of China." An article on the eve of President Bush's March 2006 visit to India refers to "China's fear that America's grand strategic design is to encircle it and block its rise as a great power."

Military historian and journalist Gwynne Dyer goes so far as to suggest that "Washington and New Delhi are laying the foundations for a new Cold War in Asia." But other analysts point out that "India is far too canny, and cares too much about its own China relationship, to be drawn into such a game." (Interestingly, India has also been improving relations with Taiwan, with the launching of a Taiwan-India Cooperation Council in February 2006.)

Implications for Canada

Canada is not a major player in any of the above strategic manoeuvres and calculations, but it will be affected by their result. And like all countries, including the United States, Canada will have to adjust its policies to accommodate the "Asian face" of globalization and the growing global power and influence of China. That includes coming to terms with China's inroads into Canada's principal market, the United States. In July 2005, for the first time, China overtook Canada to become the largest exporter of goods to the United States. While China does not yet tend to compete in the same products as Canada, its continued rapid rise does raise concerns about whether Canada will remain up to the competition in future. Even Canada's established markets cannot be taken for granted. Moreover, China has now replaced Japan as Canada's second-largest trading partner. According to a March 2006 Statistics Canada study, China's growing role in global trade is a main factor in the U.S. share of Canada's imports dropping to its lowest level since the 1930s.

An awareness of the rising role of Asia goes back some decades. For example, a 1975 study sponsored by the Ottawa Defence Research Board and the Canadian Institute of International Affairs described both Japan and China as having "entered officially a new age of global influence and responsibility."

As well, it was foreseen that "the Chinese seem certain to widen their lead over the Japanese in terms of regional power and global political-diplomatic influence." Recognition of the importance of Asia was advanced by the creation of the Vancouver-based Asia Pacific Foundation of Canada (APFC) by Act of Parliament in 1984 and by Canada's multilateral participation in APEC.

However, as several recent APFC publications warn, Canada could be sidelined politically by the advent of new Asia-only forums; and given that Canada's share of the Chinese market is actually declining, a broader, more strategic approach is needed to the region than just occasional "Team Canada" trade missions. Canadian experts on the region have argued that, notwithstanding official recognition of the importance of emerging powers in the 2005 *International Policy Statement*, Canada still lacks a significant presence. As a recent roundtable report put it: A point that came out more than once during the discussion of our relations with China and India is that people in those countries, and elsewhere in Asia, have no very clear impressions of Canada. In economic terms we are still seen as a vast repository of natural resources. We have to do a much better job of 'branding' ourselves, or portraying ourselves as more than that, as a country with many strengths and much to offer.

Promotion of new technologies, including for environmentally sustainable development, of globally competitive education and skills development, and of a western Canadian "Gateway" to the Asia Pacific are some of the initiatives being advanced to respond to this challenge.

China is clearly the most important Asian country in terms of building a beneficial long-term relationship, and it represents a challenge that engages every facet of international policy: not only diplomacy, development, and trade and commerce (including controversial investments in Canada by Chinese state-owned firms), but also security, human rights, democratization and governance issues, the environment and climate change, public health concerns, and so on.

In terms of the bilateral economic relationship, as previously noted, China is by far Canada's dominant partner among the

BRIĊSAM countries. But even so, China still accounts for only about 4% (2004 figures) of Canada's total two-way global trade flows (in a substantial deficit position, given a trade imbalance of just 1.6% of Canadian exports compared to 6.8% of imports). And looked at from China's perspective, Canada has only a 1.5% share of Chinese trade with the world. The investment relationship is even less, with Canada receiving under 0.1 % of China's overseas foreign direct investment (FDI) and Canadian FDI in China still small at US$500 million in 2004.

During 2005, which marked 35 years of official diplomatic relations with the People's Republic under the "One China" policy, the Canadian government made a commitment to double economic ties by 2010 and to upgrade relations to the level of a "strategic partnership." Strategic working groups were launched in January 2005 in the areas of trade and investment, energy and resources, science and technology, and multilateral cooperation. According to Paul Evans of the Asia Pacific Foundation, China's rise as a world economic power and global diplomatic player carries a number of implications for Canada:

- Increasing prices for commodities, natural resources and energy based in large part on growing Chinese demand.
- Increasing trade and investment volumes with China accompanied by a growing trade and, at least in the short term, investment deficit. In addition to formulating rules to protect Canadian investment in China, a major new development is the prospect of increasing substantially larger Chinese investment and acquisitions in Canada. The increased volume of trade poses major issues for air and port infrastructure and has the potential to affect the course of deeper North American integration.
- Increased pressure for Chinese professional and business people to emigrate to Canada and to press for more flexible visa, taxation and citizenship rules.
- Increased opportunities in areas of non-tradable service including education, health care and tourism. The level

of human interactions is destined to grow, perhaps dramatically, with significant implications for new opportunities in connecting immigration, education and tourism. There will be new pressures for alterations in visa, citizenship and taxation rules.

- Increased opportunity, and need, for working with Chinese officials on virtually the full spectrum of Canadian diplomatic and developmental priorities.

Canada's engagement with India is at a considerably lower level despite the fact that India is the world's largest democratic emerging power. The relationship has never been very deep and was vexed for decades following 1974 when India exploded a nuclear device using Canadian technology. Canada has had to come to terms with India as a nuclear power. While bilateral sanctions were lifted several years ago, diplomatic strains remain in a number of areas notwithstanding recent prime ministerial and ministerial visits and trade missions. Moreover, India, unlike China, is no longer a direct recipient of Canadian official development assistance. Canada's trade and investment relationship with India is growing but remains very small. India is only Canada's 18th-largest export market, and India accounted for just 0.3% of Canada's two-way trade flows in 2004 (0.2% of exports and 0.4% of imports). Canada in turn represents about 1.0% of India's global trade.

The investment relationship is even smaller, with about $250 million of Canadian FDI in India in 2004, versus only $62 million of Indian investment in Canada, mostly in the information technology sector. At the same time, a significant trade developing in commercial services is probably under-reported in the official statistics. In contrast to China's reliance on low-cost manufacturing, much of India's dynamism is due to the burgeoning services and high technology sectors.

SINO-INDIAN RELATIONS: A GROWING UNEASE

The dramatic rise of two Asian giants set against the backdrop of a troubled diplomatic history has propelled India and China into a trajectory that will likely prove difficult to navigate in the coming years. With the world riveted by Chinese aggression against Japan and Southeast Asian states in recent months, one country was not surprised: India. After all, New Delhi has been grappling with the challenge of China's rapid rise for some time. Bilateral ties between China and India nosedived so dramatically last year that Indian strategists were even predicting 'the year of the Chinese attack on India'; it was suggested that China would attack India by 2012 primarily to divert attention from its growing domestic troubles. This suggestion received widespread coverage in the Indian media, which was more interested in sensationalizing the issue than interrogating the claims.

Meanwhile, the official Chinese media picked up the story and gave it another spin. It argued that while a Chinese attack on India is highly unlikely, a conflict between the two neighbours could occur in one scenario: an aggressive Indian policy toward China about their border dispute, forcing China to take military action. The Chinese media went on to speculate that the 'China will attack India' line might just be a pretext for India to deploy more troops to the border areas.

A Growing Unease

This curious exchange reflects an uneasiness that exists between the two Asian giants as they continue their ascent in the global inter-state hierarchy. Even as they sign loftily worded documents year after year, the distrust between the two is actually growing at an alarming rate. True, economic cooperation and bilateral political, as well as socio-cultural exchanges are at an all time high; China is India's largest trading partner. Yet this cooperation has done little to assuage each country's concerns about the other's intentions. The two sides are locked in a classic security dilemma, where any action taken by one is immediately interpreted by the other as a threat to its interests. At the global level, the rhetoric is all about cooperation, and indeed the two sides have worked together on climate change, global trade negotiations and demanding a restructuring of global financial institutions in view of the global economy's shifting centre of gravity. At the bilateral level, however, mounting tensions reached an impasse last year, when China took its territorial dispute with India all the way to the Asian Development Bank. There China blocked India's application for a loan that included money for development projects in the Indian state of Arunachal Pradesh, which China continues to claim as part of its own territory. Also, the suggestion by the Chinese to the US Pacific fleet commander last year that the Indian Ocean should be recognized as a Chinese sphere of influence has raised hackles in New Delhi. China's lack of support for the US-India civilian nuclear energy cooperation pact, which it tried to block at the Nuclear Suppliers Group (NSG), and its pro-Pakistan position on anti-India terrorist groups operating on Pakistani soil, including the orchestrators of the November 2008 Mumbai attacks, have further strained ties.

Sino-Indian frictions are growing, and the potential for conflict remains high. Alarm is rising in India because of frequent and strident Chinese claims about the Line of Actual Control in Arunachal Pradesh and Sikkim, where Indians have complained of a dramatic rise in Chinese intrusions into Indian territory over the last few years, most along the border in Arunachal Pradesh, which China refers to as "Southern Tibet". China has recently upped the ante on the border issue. It has been regularly protesting against the Indian prime minister's visit to Arunachal Pradesh, asserting its claims over the territory. What has caught most observers of Sino-Indian ties by surprise, however, is the vehemence with which Beijing has contested recent Indian administrative and political actions in the state, even denying visas to Indian citizens of Arunachal Pradesh.

The recent rounds of boundary negotiations have been a disappointing failure, with a growing perception in India that China is less willing to adhere to earlier political understandings about how to address the boundary dispute. Even the rhetoric has degenerated to such an extent that a Chinese analyst connected to China's Ministry of National Defence claimed in an article last year that China could "dismember the so-called 'Indian Union' with one little move" into as many as 30 states.

Pakistan, of course, has always been a crucial foreign policy asset for China, but with India's rise and US-India rapprochement, its role in China's grand strategy is bound to grow even further.

Not surprisingly, recent revelations about China's shift away from a three-decades' old cautious approach on Jammu and Kashmir, its increasing military presence in Pakistan, planned infrastructure linking Xinjiang and Gwadar, issuing stapled visas to residents of Jammu and Kashmir and supplying nuclear reactors to Pakistan, all confirm a new intensity behind China's old strategy of using Pakistan to secure its interests in the region.

India's Formidable Challenge

While it has not yet achieved the economic and political profile that China enjoys regionally and globally, India is increasingly bracketed with China as a rising or emerging power- or even a global superpower. Indian elites who have been obsessed with Pakistan for more than 60 years suddenly have found a new object of fascination. India's main security concern now is not the increasingly decrepit state of Pakistan but an ever more assertive China, a shift that is widely viewed inside India as one that can facilitate better strategic planning.

India's defeat at Chinese hands in 1962 shaped the Indian elite's perceptions of China, and they are unlikely to alter them anytime soon.

China is thus viewed by India as a growing, aggressive nationalistic power whose ambitions are likely to reshape the contours of the regional and global balance of power with deleterious consequences for Indian interests. Indian policymakers, however, continue to believe that Beijing is not a short-term threat to India but needs to be watched over the long-term. However, Indian defence officials are increasingly warning in rather blunt terms about the disparity between the two Asian powers. The Indian naval chief has warned that India neither has "the capability nor the intention to match China force for force" in military terms, while the former Indian air chief has suggested that China posed more of a threat to India than Pakistan.

China's recent hardening toward India could well be a function of its own internal vulnerabilities, but that is hardly a consolation to Indian policymakers who have to respond to an Indian public that increasingly wants the country to assert itself in the region and beyond. India is rather belatedly gearing up to respond with its own diplomatic and military overtures, setting the stage for a Sino-Indian strategic rivalry. Both India and China have a vested interest in stabilizing their relationship by seeking out issues on which their interests converge, but pursuing mutually desirable interests does not inevitably produce satisfactory solutions to strategic problems. A troubled history coupled with the structural uncertainties engendered by their simultaneous rise is propelling the two Asian giants into a trajectory that they might find rather difficult to navigate in the coming years. Sino-Indian ties have entered turbulent times, and they are likely to remain there for the foreseeable future.

The Indian and Chinese Experience

One of the cruel ironies of today's world is that India which is applauded as the world's largest democracy has the largest number of poor and destitute in any country, and China which has achieved, a steady rise in people's living standards and has also acquired the status of a world power has failed to develop democratic institutions and practices. It is also interesting to note that despite the absence of liberal democratic freedoms the West has a deep fascination with China which is reflected not only in the tourist inflow to China but also in the flow of foreign investment and government good will. Operation of democratic institutions such as free and fair elections, existence of competitive politics and dissent do not particularly attract either Western tourists or Western capital to India. On the contrary the geopolitics of South Asia has been governed by the US and other Western countries as compared by India's pre-eminent position and therefore they have followed by an large a policy of containment of India vis-a-vis its neighbours. The functioning democratic system of India has had little effect on their policy. The experience of India and China have put the theory of democracy to a severe test. Two old questions need to be asked again about democracy. In addition, two new questions have to be raised. Do formal political institutions and practices constitute democracy or does it involve appropriate socio-economic conditions which enable citizens to exercise their political rights. On this issue India scores poorly with nearly forty per cent of its people below what is statistically called a "poverty line". China has asserted that it is engaged in creating better living conditions for its people after overthrowing semicolonial and semifeudal domination. Today, however, this dichotomy between economic and political conditions of democracy is seriously questioned. Their mutual dependence is emphasised. Therefore both India and China have to achieve yet more conditions of democracy.

The other familiar question relates to equality and freedom. Western liberal democratic theory asserts the priority of freedom over equality even though the radical stream in liberalism stresses that gross inequalities are detrimental to the exercise of freedom. On this criterion pre-Reform China scored higher marks than India. Social inequalities were reduced in China to a very large extent with the abolition of landlordism and formation of cooperatives and Communes and also takeover of the bourgeoisie owned industries by the state. The wage system was directed towards promoting equality and limiting income differences within the six point grade system. In India too there were a number of measures taken in the early decades following independence to curb monopoly in industry, abolish zamindari system and carry out land reforms. In both the countries the stress on equality declined in the 1980s and almost disappeared in the 1990s. In the past decade or so equality has been a low priority in both China and India. The "equalitarianism", "theory of eating from the iron rice bowl" and such ideas of the Cultural Revolution were severely criticised by the Chinese reformers as being obstacles to the development of the productive forces. The perspective of the present day leadership in China is to "allow some people to get rich first" so that the general level of growth is raised steadily. In India the introduction of the Structural Adjustment Programme promoted the ideology of profit and the egalitarian programmes of social transformation took the back seat.

The two new issues arise from the great democratic upsurges of the past few decades, namely the social movements such as the women's movements, the environmental movement, the autonomy movement and the human rights movements. One question posed by them is to concretise freedom as freedom from multiple forms of domination so that freedom to realise the potentialities of the human being is advanced. Patriarchal domination continues substantially in all the countries of the world as evident from the deliberations at the Fourth World Congress of Women in Beijing and as documents in the 1995 *Human Development Report*. China and India have only marginal difference among them. As to ethnic self-determination there has not yet been a scientific measurement. But both the countries have fairly centralised regimes and both have regions manifesting popular discontent. The caste hierarchy and disabilities in India are targets of public attention and social action. There is no comparable social problem in China though new forms of social stratification have emerged in the recent years.

The other issue is response of the modern state to these expanding democratic demands. All ruling elites would like to have an appearance of being popular and responsive to the demands of the various unprivileged groups. And they engage in innumerable measures of legitimation to create a climate of acceptability among the people. Thus the modern state is coercive, responsive and legitimative at the same time. For this purpose it has developed sophisticated systems of management of society, complex methods of propaganda and innovative techniques of manipulation. Today the technology of repression and the vast networks of communication allow the formal democracy to continue while the citizens remain helpless. There is a new authoritarianism in the modern societies including those of the West which make the basic notion of democracy nominal. The tragedy is that while failing on the scores of either political or socio-economic freedom both India and China have fast accumulated the resources of modern authoritarianism. These tools include modern capitalist preoccupation with consumerism promoted through advertisement. Sensate entertainment that commefcialises culture in the global scale on the one hand and building up security forces of all kinds to suppress democratic movements on the other. It is this process which is strengthened by the forces of capitalist globalization. The alliance of Western capitalists and the native elites has intervened to assimilate the rest of the third world into the Western model of capitalist political economy. The alternatives which the socialist revolutions and the anticolonial struggles had presented have been defeated in course of the battles of the recent decades. The socialist experiments adopted the same economic goals as capitalist systems and failed to promote socialist democracy. The anticolonial struggles such as India's which centred on the comprehensive concept of *Swaraj* failed to institutionalise after Independence.

The result was the crisis of the state and crisis of development in the third world to tackle which the elites leaned on the West. Thus today on the one hand there is an expanding demand for multidimensional freedom while on the other hand there is a an advancing tide of global hegemony by the capitalist West. The experiments in India and China are caught in this historical conjuncture. With these comparative notes let us look at the democratic prospects in China.

SINO-INDIAN RELATIONS: COMPETITION OR COOPERATION?

The Sino-Indian relationship is maturing into one of the most important bilateral relationships in world politics and their continuing economic growth are projecting them to influential positions within the global market. According to the United

States National Intelligence Council Report on emerging global trends, by 2015, international community will have to confront the military, political and economic dimensions of the rise of China and India. How these two countries manage their relationship will have a tremendous impact on peace and stability in the regional and, increasingly, global context.

Against the backdrop of an international environment in constant flux, the two Asian powers find themselves locked into what Barry Buzan has called the 'security complex' within which they are expected to manage their rivalry and develop ties of cooperation (Buzan, 1991: 2009). The principal factor defining a complex, according to Buzan, is usually a high level of threat/ fear which is felt mutually among two or more major states. Historical evidence shows that although China has been a major security concern for India, the Chinese were less wary of India and concentrated more on the pattern of superpower rivalry existing between the United States and the former Soviet Union during the Cold War.

After 48 years of cold peace, mistrust and hostility since the Sino-Indian border clashes in 1962, the demands of realpolitik and pragmatism in policy-making are transforming one of Asia's most important relationships-bilateral ties between India and China. China and India, the two largest developing countries in the world, have a commonality of history, culture, economy and social characteristics, despite certain irreconcilable differences. Each is concentrating its resources to expedite internal economic development, carries out an independent foreign policy and strives for a peaceful international environment. China is a big power in East Asia while India is a big power in South Asia. Each enjoys advantages and influence in their respective regions. In spite of sharing a glorious civilizational past and having never fought a single war until their emergence as modern states, security competition between India and China is inevitable as their economies grow. However, the positive note is that this security competition does not have to be conflictual. The contemporary picture in China-India relations today is that both nations are engaged in attempting to put the past behind and forge new relationships based on the emerging global strategic realities. Trade and economic ties have grown exponentially in the last five years and leaders of both the countries have expressed determination to find solutions to the China-India boundary dispute which have distorted relations in the past.

The key factors which shaped the domestic as well as foreign policies of both the countries in post-Cold War period have been their respective perceptions of the changing contours of world politics; consensus on several issues like developing a fair, equitable, international political and economic order, the expanding role for the United Nations, and support of global disarmament, including efforts to prevent the weaponization of outer space. China's foreign policy emphasizes military security and national sovereignty, economic prosperity and social welfare (Parlez, 2002). Therefore, it has focused on establishing working relationship with as many states as possible, especially its neighbours assuring them that China intends to establish a peaceful regional environment conducive to economic development. Economic interest, therefore, is a significant motivation behind expanding the network of diplomatic relations. China has understood that India cannot be prevented from being a dominant player in the Indian subcontinent and from creating space for its larger role in Asia. This may be one of the reasons for China's positive attitude to solve several contentious issues and for apparently understanding the nuclear doctrine of India, the minimum nuclear deterrence and other security related issues. In the same period, India has also modified its foreign policy for promoting a peaceful environment in order to consolidate its economic foundation. It has realized that armed conflict will be economically disastrous and politically unwise.

The economic development of China and India needs America's cooperation and support. At the same time, America needs the huge markets of the two big Asian countries. The United States could be a positive factor for Sino-India relationships, if it tries to promote regional stability in South Asia and help China and India's economic modernization. It could, as well, cast itself in a negative role when it plays the 'India card' in its dealings with China; or plays the 'China card' in developing its relations with India. As both China and India have come to be important players in regional and global decision-making and given their rising economies which have come to be characterized as "soft power"(Rajamony, 2002), it remains to be seen how the United States accommodate the future actions and policies of these two nation-states within the sphere of its own national interests.

The end of the Cold War gave a new dimension to Sino-Indian relationship when the peace process was expedited with Chinese Premier Li Peng's visit to India, in 1991. The Indian Prime Minister P.V. Narasimha Rao visited China in 1993 when the Peace and Tranquillity Agreement was signed which was helpful towards reaching a solution to the Sino-Indian border dispute. In particular, the border dispute was addressed through a series of meetings of the China-India Joint Working Group (JWG), which began its first meeting in July 1989 (Sidhu and Yuan, 2003: 24). Following the Agreement, regular meetings were held between the soldiers on both sides, a hotline link between the two countries was set up, an agreement to maintain peace and security on both sides of the LAC was signed. Sino-Indian rapprochement was further solidified by President Jiang Zemin's visit to New Delhi in late 1996 (Shirk, 2004: 81). During his visit an accord was signed for partial demilitarization of the disputed border of 4,500 km shared by both the countries. New institutional links were established among not only the military but also members of the academic community, political parties and the media personnel. After the 1990s, the narrow track of cooperation gradually broadened. Between 1997 and 2007, bilateral trade increased from 1.6 to 38.7 billion USD. Figures from the China Statistical Yearbook and Indian Ministry of Tourism reveal that bilateral visits had grown ten fold to more than half a million by 2007. A review of the archives of the Indian and Chinese Ministry of Foreign Affairs also showed that the improving relations were reflected by the average annual number of ministerial exchanges that increased from two in the

1990s to four in the years afterwards, as well as the cumulated number of bilateral agreements that augmented from five in 1990 to 81 in 2006, and the cumulated number of Track I & II dialogues which in the same period has grown from two to twelve (Holslag, 2009).

The changing reality of India-China ties is clearly reflected in economic issues increasingly becoming the most vital component of official discourse and academic enquiry both in the Western countries, as well as, in India and China. As a result of this growing interest amongst experts and officials of both these countries, India-China economic engagement has since come to be recognized as one of the most reliable CBM (confidence-building measure) in the trajectory of India-China political rapprochement. It is only in the last few years that the two powers, overcoming their colonial and Cold War legacies, have begun to emphasize on their mutual linkages and on the advantages of mutual benefit and mutual accommodation. Especially, with China's continuous rise during the last three decades, Beijing's focus has moved from being a strong economic power to a reliable neighbour by building links between its 'multidimensional' economy and its immediate periphery (Singh, 2005). This perhaps partly explains the recent upsurge in China-India economic ties. From this perspective, their relations can today be described as shifting from politics-driven-economics to economics-driven-politics which explains the urge of their respective political leadership to establish a strong strategic partnership. It is possible to identify vital similarities in the reform process especially in the strengths of their political leaders, like the present Indian Prime Minister Manmohan Singh's vision to continue with the structural adjustment policy in the Indian economy and the Chinese leader Hu Jintao's determination to continue with global engagement of China.

Looking at their bilateral economic engagement for last few years, the recent initiatives in opening the disputed border for trade purposes and working together towards evolving a China-India Free Trade Area (FTA) remain some unique examples (Singh, 2005). These steps have already begun to show positive results in terms of reduction in force deployment and peace on their borders and revival of several cottage industries amongst their overlapping border communities which augurs well for the future of Sino-Indian relations.

In particular both countries' new generation of corporate magnets started to explore investment options. Since 2002, Indian software and information companies such as TCS, Infosys, Wipro and Satyam set up branches in China (Mukherjee and Bakshi, 2005). Zensar Technologies for instance, established a Global Development Centre in Hangzhou and trained 1,000 Chinese software project managers in India. In 2005, the influential Indian Tata holding reported to have increased its turnover in China to 200 million USD. Indian enterprises have located attractive investment opportunities in China, in areas such as pharmaceuticals, auto components, light engineering goods, automotives, financial services, besides, IT software and training. However, the process of sharing information on market, legal environment, trade policies, investment opportunities between the relevant government departments and trade bodies needs to be institutionalized (Ministry of External Affairs, India, 2005).

A deeply-embedded process of economic integration has to be based not only on both sides appreciating each other's strengths but also being able to appreciate each other's limitations.

There is definitely need, therefore, for all confidence-building strategies to continuously make appraisal of the nature and composition of their bilateral trade and commerce and to explore fresh investment opportunities (Singh, 2005). At the Joint Communiqué of the Ninth Meeting of Foreign Ministers of India, Russia & China held on October 27, 2009 at Bangalore, India, the Ministers agreed that dialogue in areas such as global economic governance architecture, climate change, trade policy and development cooperation through interaction between research institutes, exchange of experts/specialists, training of instructors/specialists and holding joint conferences and seminars should continue to promote global peace and prosperity (Ministry of External Affairs, India, 2009).

Since the early 1980s China and India embarked on what can be broadly described as the path of "cooperative security" (Sidhu and Yuan, 2003: 115). The concept of cooperative security derives from the liberal traditionalist paradigm offering a new approach to managing security dilemmas that states face in regional and global contexts. This approach is founded on two essential arguments. First, threats to security are no longer solely military. They are increasingly diverse and multidimensional ranging from economic underdevelopment and trade imbalances, irregular migration of people and uncontrolled population growth, human rights abuses and drug trafficking, conflict over access to natural resources and environmental degradation and the most effective being the threat of terrorist attacks from unidentified elements in society. Second, the management of these emerging security issues require multilateral efforts through the processes of discussion, negotiation and cooperation between both the governmental (Track I approach) and non-governmental (Track II approach) actors.

Chinese perspectives have evolved since the end of the Cold War, as Beijing gradually accepted some of the key element of cooperative security. These include unilateral disarmament measures such as the reduction of 1.5 million personnel from the PLA (People's Liberation Army) between 1985 and 2000; participation in multilateral cooperative security dialogues such as the ASEAN Regional Forum and CBM (Confidence Building Measure) negotiations with India and Russia (Yuan, 2000). However, at the same time, Beijing has increased defence spending, acquired advanced Russian weaponry and modernized its nuclear forces (Lilley and Shambaugh, 1999). India's approach to cooperative security measures and CBMs vis-à-vis China has been guided by the need to counter the diplomatic pressure exerted by the United States and the other Western powers (Chari, 1999, pp. 89-133). The Indian political leadership has been hesitant to apply CBMs and has been minimalist in embracing its scope and objectives. From the Indian perspective, CBMs are mostly conflict-avoidance measures and are predominantly declaratory in nature (Krepon, 1998).

A stable Sino-Indian relationship requires the effective management of the delicate China-India-Pakistan triangle. New Delhi remains suspicious of the Sino-Pakistani relationship and their resilient security ties, because of the Chinese decision to continue supplies of military equipment to Pakistan reinforcing the possibility of strategic encirclement of India (Tellis, 1997). While China's continuing support of Pakistan is partly motivated to contain India, it is also aimed at maintaining a stable relationship with an important Islamic country and a nuclear weapons state. By this, China would be able to retain its influence over the Islamic unrest in its own territory, especially in Xinjiang (Chung, 2002). India continues to regard Pakistan as the principal external factor in its relations with China while, China is attentive to the India-US strategic partnership and its implications for its relations with India on the other hand. Despite the remarkable improvements in bilateral relations in recent years, serious differences remain. These include the unresolved boundary issue, Tibet, and the Sino-Pakistan nexus. The boundary issue involves more than 125,000 square kilometres in disputed territories. Many seem to believe that Obama's recent visit to India is the indicator of the forging of a strong alliance against China. Both China and India being more than 3,000 years old as nations and with more than 2,000 years of recorded contacts between them do not necessarily need to tread that path. Both have respected and trusted each other from the ancient times. Chinese society believes in maintaining order, given Confucianism's influence and the majority Hindus of India is influenced by the concept of 'Basudaiva Kutumbakam' (universal brotherhood). Therefore, it is also imperative to look at the concepts and notions that shape the societal perceptions in these two countries, as the government and its policies are nothing but the reflection of the society.

It is acceptable, that as two neighbours, India and China will have their differences and they will give vent to their dissatisfaction and at times may pose to threaten each other to appease a small segment of their nationalist population, it is however unlikely that either one of them would enter into a serious strategic alliance against the other. As Professor

Chellaney continues to re-iterate (Chellaney, 2009) that if relations with China need to improve, India must have an honest and open debate on its diplomatic and military options. Zeng Jianhua, Director of Asian, African and Latin American Affairs at the Chinese People's Institute of Foreign Affairs (CPIFA) has also emphasized the need for non-governmental exchanges particularly in the cultural and media sectors, identify ways to deal with trade frictions and to explore avenues for enhancement of bilateral ties between China and India (Shen, 2010). The evolving Indo-China relationship can be described as "competition on some levels and co-operation on others," (Bagchi, 2010) wherein some discomfort, ambivalence and hedging will always remain, despite the level of engagement.

Conclusion

Diplomatic meetings between the leaders of India, China and the United States in recent years have drawn worldwide attention. Although critics said that the visits were more symbolic in nature, few would question their far-reaching impact on reshaping the bilateral relationships between America and the two rising global powerhouses: China and India.

Therefore, it can be concluded that the United States remains a major factor in the evolving India-China-U.S. triangle and both India and China seeks to maximise the benefits from this bilateral relationship with the United States in the context of the present international political system. On the other hand, Washington's engagement of the world's two most populous nations, each experiencing strong economic growth and a raised profile on the international stage, is strategically significant. As the U.S. Government's National Intelligence Council pointed out earlier in 2005 in its report 'Mapping the Global Future', "the likely emergence of China and India as new major global players will transform the geopolitical landscape in the early

21st century" (US National Intelligence Council [online]). The Report predicting a rising Asia by 2020 points out that "China will continue to strengthen its military through developing and acquiring modern weapons, including advanced fighter aircraft, sophisticated submarines, and increasing numbers of ballistic missiles. China will overtake Russia and others as the second largest defence spender after the United States over the next two decades and will be, by any measure, a first-rate military power". With regards to India, the Report outlines that "as India's economy grows governments in Southeast Asia— Malaysia, Singapore, Thailand, and other countries—may move closer to India to help build a potential geopolitical counterweight to China. At the same time, India will seek to strengthen its ties with countries in the region without excluding China."

A new, dynamic pattern of interaction has, thus, begun between the United States and Asia's two largest continental powers. The task for all three is, therefore, to manage ties as a virtuous circle rather than a competitive triangle (Inderfurth and Shambaugh, 2005). Inderfurth and Shambaugh in their article continue to argue that there are some geopolitical

thinkers in each capital who seek to use improved bilateral relations against the third party. Some in Beijing and New Delhi see strengthened Sino-Indian ties as a constraint on American hegemony. Others in Washington and New Delhi are suspicious of China and seek to build U.S.-India relations (particularly military ties) as a strategic counterweight to growing Chinese power. While the U.S.-India and China-India relationships steadily improve, Sino-American relations seem to be entering another strained and turbulent phase in their long, chequered relationship. A new wave of anti-China acrimony is currently gripping Washington, especially in the Congress, fuelled by assertions about China's military build-up, threatened posture towards Taiwan, unfair trading practices, product pirating, human rights violations and attempted buyouts of U.S. companies. Despite these concerns, there is no turning back from the growing interdependence of the three countries, including in the vital area of energy supplies. Managing these expanding relations will increasingly be a key challenge for Washington, Beijing and New Delhi.

Given the geopolitical situation in the region and America's continuous predominance in regional security, an inevitable question, and indeed a shared concern, for Beijing and New Delhi is that how the two bilateral relationships will affect each other. In other words, will the recent development in the US-India relations help to promote or undermine the US-China relations and vice versa? It is hard to imagine that the trilateral US-India-China relationship would evolve into the kind of 'strategic triangle' that was witnessed in the 1970s and 1980s between the US, China, and the former Soviet Union (Jing, 2009). The present US-China, US-India and India-China relationships are not, and will not likely be, defined by an irreconcilable, ideology-based confrontation that had existed between the United States, China and the former Soviet Union. Despite differences between their political systems, cultures, levels of economic development, and policymaking processes, the drivers of the three pairs of bilateral relationship are strategic interests rather than ideological faith, and the leaders in Washington, Beijing and New Delhi are realistic and pragmatic in their decision making.

Moreover, the growing economic integration, and hence interdependence, has made the zero-sum game between the three countries pointless. An aggressive bilateral relationship-be it the US-China, US-India or India-China against the third power would be damaging to all parties concerned. The major characteristic of this emerging strategic triangle lies in that it is still in an evolutionary phase and has not assumed a strong and mature form similar to the Sino-Soviet-U.S. strategic triangle during the Cold War. The evolving strategic triangle is also not sufficiently strong since the dominant issues in bilateral relations between two states do not directly relate to the third state (Garver, 2002). And finally, the relationship is asymmetrical as the US and Chinese apprehensions about the possible alignment of the other with India are stronger than India's apprehensions about a potential US-China alignment. It remains to be seen how these three powers manoeuvre their positions in the triangular framework addressing the security challenges of their times.

CHINA AND INDIA : THE 'EMERGING GIANTS' AND GROWTH

The economic performance of China and India is critical. This holds the key to global progress. China and India have been relatively 'closed' economies with limited dependence on trade. But they have been opening up. This is particularly so in the case of China.

Trade as a % of GDP has been 32% in China compared to 25% in India. This should be seen against a backdrop of relatively open East and South Asian economies: Malaysia (206%), Korea (Republic) (72%), Thailand (82 %), Pakistan (36%) and Bangladesh (35%). India's import duties as a % of imports, a key measure of openness, have also been declining in China and India. But it is lower in China compared to India: 3% in the former and 24% in the latter.

Foreign Direct Investment (FDI) can enable access to resources and increase productivity. There are two types: one by the transnationals from industrialized countries and the other by overseas Chinese and Non Resident Indians. In China overseas Chinese have been primarily responsible for Chinese FDI while India's FDI has been channeled through the Transnationals. Net flows of FDI as a % of GDP in China have been 12% in contrast to India's 0.61%.

Both countries have been growing fast over the last 25 years: China by 21 fold and India by 8 fold. The growth rate in China has been over 9% per annum making it possibly the fastest growing world economy while India's, too, has been impressive with over 8% per annum. The % living below the poverty line (1 $ a day) has also been appreciably reduced in both though it is more impressive in China compared to India: 12% in the former and 26% in the latter.

The major effect of China's and India's economic advance is evidenced by their contribution to global output: China's and

India's share being 20% and 7% respectively in 2004. Both, moreover, have rising demand for energy, raw materials and commodities. This has a positive impact on increasing the exports of developing countries, improving their terms of trade, and initiating shifts in their pattern of trade and investment.

Liberalisation policies have enhanced the economic prowess of both nations. China, moreover, as a recent member of the World Trade Organization (2001), could firmly influence global trade negotiations, possibly joining forces with India, and champion the rights of poor nations. They could establish a 'level playing field' in world trade. Indeed the combined efforts of China and India could ensure that the Uruguay Round (1986-93) to accelerate trade liberalization can be successful. They could pressurize the developed nations to fulfil their promise of opening up their markets to developing country agricultural and non agricultural exports.

Liberalisation emerged much earlier in China, in 1978, while it was initiated in India in 1991 though initial steps were taken in the 1980's. Pre-reform or pre-liberalisation forces laid the basis on which such measures were evolved. China's policies unfolded in the context of bold economic policies in the East Asia region between 1960-1990 emphasizing agricultural development, primary education, macroeconomic stability, firm public policies to support markets, and regional dynamism. China's liberalization has been embodied in market based thrusts in agriculture, industry and services, state owned enterprises, and deregulation of product prices. These have been backed by measures to induce labour mobility, and formation of Special Economic Zones.

On the domestic front, in the pre reform era in China, the savings level was high with significant capital formation (30%) and investment in infrastructure, irrigation and land development. Literacy and primary health care, too, have been impressive with virtual elimination of landlessness. It has also shed surplus labour-a move which has been inhibited in India possibly due to strong trade unions to safeguard the interest of workers. On the external front China's integration with the world economy, as mentioned earlier, has been advanced through its trade and FDI policies. This has made a significant contribution to China's growth and productivity.

India's growth rates have been relatively low in the pre-liberalisation period-4%-5% per annum compared to East Asia's 7%-8% per annum. The level of savings, too, has been lower than in China and East Asia; the levels of literacy and health care, too, have been lower, coupled with the presence of significant landlessness, and marked poverty and inequality between and within regions, sectors and socio-economic groups.

Liberalisation was initiated in India in the 1980's with a shift in attitude towards the private sector. Its momentum was increased from 1991 onwards. The high growth rate (8% per annum) in the post liberalization period and the future targets (9%-10%) are necessary but not sufficient. The structure of the economy has to be transformed. In this respect, though the % contribution of agriculture to GDP has been reduced to about 25% it still absorbs over 60% of the employed, while manufacturing and services contribute 28% and 55 % respectively to GDP. Over 62% of India's growth over 1990-2003 has been in services but it has been employment inelastic. Hence, the pace of industrialization has to be reinforced.

Though poverty in India has been reduced to about 26% it is critical to widen participation by the poor in development programmes. This can ensure that high growth rates are sustained. This calls for the use of labour intensive techniques, investment in human and physical capital, and infrastructure, enhanced flexibility in labour laws, and supporting institutions to meet socio-economic goals. The state has to play an active role to fulfil such goals though market forces may guide policies. This could enable the poor to be lifted from poverty.

No doubt China has grown faster and sharply reduced the % of people below the poverty line compared to India. However, inter regional and inter group inequalities in China have increased. China and India need to persist with their integration with the international economy to sustain growth. This should encompass incorporating the poor in the process, particularly in India, and reducing regional and inter-group disparities in China. Such goals are intertwined with maintaining peace within the respective regions. This is exemplified in India by efforts to minimize conflicts with neighbouring Pakistan, curbing terrorism from within and outside the state, resolving historical border disputes between India and China, and meeting the needs of dissatisfied groups within the state. In China it is essential to respect human rights.

China-India co-operation

Enhanced economic cooperation between India and China could bolster their economic power in spite of differing positions on politics and international affairs. Thus, it emerges that the economic relationship between China and India has taken place against a backdrop of tensions.

This is exemplified by China's past political, military and economic support for Pakistan, and China's claim to Arunachal Pradesh which has been vehemently challenged by India. Leaving aside such differences China and India are seen as contributors rather than competitors to each other's development. This is welcomed by India which has adopted a 'Look East' policy to expand trade and investment links with East Asia and forge strong ties with regional institutions (eg. Association of South East Asian Nations, Asia Pacific Economic Cooperation).

The recent visit of the Chinese President Hu Jintao to Delhi is a significant move in initiating a platform on development, peace and stability in Asia and the world. This was underscored by the Chinese President. He perceived the relationship between China and India as being between 'old and close brothers' citing the vision of Rabindranath Tagore the Nobel Indian poet. The President's visit culminated in a pledge to double trade between the two nations to \$ 40 billion by 2010. This contrasts with \$ 250 million in the 1990's.

China and India have been competing for resources in Asia and Africa. China has been the winner in virtually all the sectors excepting technology. However, the two nations could devise policies to complement each other's need. Thus, India could meet China's growing appetite for raw materials (iron ore, steel and plastics) fuelling its massive manufacturing sector. China in turn could furnish manufacturing expertise and investment for Indian infrastructure. Indian critics of Chinese policies have expressed concern over the lack of transparency exemplified by their high level of subsidies. They are also anxious over the sharply increasing Indian imports from China of clothes, electronic goods and even fireworks. The Chinese have responded by highlighting India's blocking of their investments in ports and telecommunications. This has been justified by India on grounds of security. Overall, though, as the Chinese President reaffirmed, the relationship between China and India was "an opportunity and not a threat." This could pave the way for cooperation between China and India and enhance the nature and pace of globalization.

INDIA'S CHINA POLICY

Certain scholars believe that India's China policy has undergone three major phases of adjustment since the end of the Cold War: the pre-1998 phase policy of reconciliation; the 1998–2000 phase policy of hostility; and the 2000 to present phase policy of engagement. The second phase around the time of the 1998 nuclear tests featured harangues from the Indian government regarding the 'China threat' and a brief deadlock in Sino–Indian relations. The author, however, believes that two, rather than three, phases of adjustment are applicable to an explanation of the state of bilateral relations between China and India in the post-Cold War era. When considering India's overall strategic aims at the time of the 1998 nuclear tests and the implications and specific actions of its subsequent China policy, it is difficult to pinpoint two 180 degree-policy shifts in the course of just two years. Facts demonstrate that India named China as a threat at the time of the 1998 tests as a matter of expedience to acquiesce in the anti-China stance of certain parties in the United States and other Western nations; it was a ploy whose purpose was to divert attention from and rationalize the nuclear tests, thereby dispelling any notion of sanctions.

It should be borne in mind, however, that India's understanding of comprehensive national strength deepened after the Cold War, as did its leaders' belief that nuclear arms and credible nuclear deterrence were hallmarks of a superpower. Entering the nuclear club was consequently a stride towards achieving one of the sub-continent's greatest national aspirations. The Rao government, which pursued a China policy of reconciliation and engagement, had made preparations for nuclear tests but stopped short of carrying them out for fear of the potential burden on the newly recovered economy of international sanctions.

Prime Minister Vajpayee and other political leaders repeatedly and publicly expressed soon after the 1998 tests that India had no wish to hold China as an enemy or a threat, stating, to the contrary, their desire for reinforced friendly relations. At no point during this period did diplomatic engagement between India and China cease. Indian External Affairs Minister Jaswant Singh's visit to China in June 1999 demonstrated that the Sino–Indian relationship had recovered in the space of a year from any damage that the nuclear tests had inflicted upon it. That becoming a nuclear power while maintaining stable relations with China were post-Cold War India's strategic goals was also implied by the sub-continent's explicit moves towards repairing its relationship with China. The 1998 nuclear tests constituted no fundamental change to India's China policy and should, within the scope of Sino–Indian relations, be regarded as a minor episode. Moreover, the shift of India's China policy in 1988 was not prompted by any change of security concept; Prime Minister Rajiv Gandhi's trip to China that year was motivated by the fact of Sino–Soviet reconciliation. Changes in security concept explicitly propelled India's; post-Cold War China policy adjustments. This book, therefore, primarily examines developments and changes in India's China policy after the Cold War. It holds that a substantive change indeed occurred; specifically from one of hostility and antagonism during the Cold War (especially 1962–1988) to reconciliation and engagement thereafter. This policy change, however, was by no means instantaneous but characterized by gradual, phased development. Two, rather than three, phases of adjustment tally with changes in India's post-Cold War security concept.

India's China Policy from the End of the Cold War to 1998

Indian leaders believed after 1962 that hostilities between China and India were inevitable, and viewed China as a major enemy. Prime Minister Indira Gandhi considered Sino–Indian antagonism as going far beyond border disputes, and that China was pursuing the more 'complex' policy of pressing India on all fronts and, moreover, displacing the sub-continent by establishing its own dominant position in the Asian power hierarchy.

The goal of India's China policy during this period, therefore, was to ensure its supremacy over China in Asia and, in the event of armed conflict, to avoid repeating mistakes that had led to its defeat in the 1962 Sino–Indian conflict. India's policy at the time can be so summarized: strengthen military capability and deployment; seek aid from major powers, respectively, the United States, United Kingdom and USSR; and support Chinese separatist forces.

After the Cold War ended, however, changes in India's domestic and international situation brought tremendous challenges, and its position as regards China and its related policy goals showed clear adjustments. India considered China as a nation going through a reflective, 'inward looking' period and, as such, had no intention of attacking the sub-continent. In the short-term, therefore, it constituted no threat. The goal of India's new China policy was to maintain stability in Sino–Indian relations, ensure peaceful borders and create conditions suitable for India to gather its resources and restore economic and military strength. The specific policy adjustments were as follows.

Achieve Simultaneous Progress in Solving Border Disputes

For almost two decades after 1962, India made resolution of border disputes a pre-condition for normalizing relations with China.

Its insistence in this regard was the main reason for the longstanding chill in Sino–Indian relations. Although the two nations restored ambassadorial-level diplomatic relations in 1976, and in 1981 agreed to begin talks on the border issue, this principled standpoint did not change.

Upon meeting with visiting then-External Affairs Minister Vajpayee early in 1979, Comrade Deng Xiaoping proposed an agreement that would provide 'a package solution' for relevant border disputes. He said that if it were not possible completely to resolve border disputes at an early date, he would consider cooperation in other areas.

But it was not until 1988 during Rajiv Gandhi's trip to China that the Indian government accepted this suggestion and formally initiated the process of normalizing bilateral relations which the successive Indian governments pursued and implemented after the Cold War ended.

It is notable that during the time the two sides promoted negotiations on border issues they also exchanged high-level visits in which the two nations signed cooperative agreements in such areas as trade, technology, education and culture, and that cooperation between them grew ever greater in depth and breadth.

Shift Strategies on Border Talks

As India needed a peaceful, stable environment in which to concentrate on economic recovery, securing Sino–Indian borders was its primary goal in the early 1990s. Because of India's; pre-1988 insistence on not normalizing Sino–Indian relations until the border issues were settled, there were suspicions that the sub-continent was 'taking improvements in bilateral relations as a bargaining chip through which to force China to yield in border disputes'. India consequently insisted in the talks that began in 1981 on its own position as regards a segmented solution to the issue.

India's objective understanding of the complexity of the Sino–Indian border dispute after the Cold War and of realistic strategic considerations and needs prompted an adjusted strategy for these talks. This was manifest in its suggestion of a gradual solution to border disputes: the first step would be to stabilize the Line of Actual Control (LAC) situation and eliminate disagreements over its demarcation; the second to reach agreement on preserving peace and tranquillity along the LAC; and the third to take measures to establish mutual trust along the LAC.

This accomplished, the two nations could then address substantive problems in their border dispute. This tentative plan enabled India and China to approach a consistent position whereby the two sides worked to achieve a solution to Sino–Indian border disputes and create an atmosphere of reasonableness and peace.

The two nations made progress, signing in 1993 the Agreement on Maintenance of Peace and Tranquillity along the Line of Actual Control in the Sino– Indian Border Areas, and in 1996 the Agreement Between the Government of the Republic of India and the Government of the People's Republic of China on Confidence-Building Measures in the Military Field Along the Line of Actual Control in the India–China Border Areas.

India saw these two agreements as on the one hand ensuring the two sides could resolve border disputes peacefully without resorting to violence, and on the other that border disputes would not inhibit the development of their bilateral relations.

Tibetan Issue and do not Provoke China

Leaders of India's independence movement had at the time of the British Raj followed the British colonialist concept of

Tibet as a 'buffer region' between India and China. After winning independence, therefore, the Indian government supported from the very beginning the so-called 'Tibetan independence movement'. At around the time of the founding of the People's Republic of China, India seized the opportunity offered by China's political upheaval to promote the international standing of the local Tibetan government and thwart China's liberation of Tibet.

New Delhi continued unremittingly in its efforts to convince China's central government, even during the 1950s heyday of Sino–Indian amity, to give Tibet substantial autonomy and to reduce to the greatest extent possible the size of its garrison there. After the insurrection of 1959 the Indian government was more overt in its support of Tibet, giving asylum to fugitive rebels and propping up the so-called 'Tibetan Government in Exile' established by the Dalai Lama in 1960 in the Indian city of Dharamsala. India further incited and encouraged Tibetan independence activities after the Sino–Indian conflict of 1962.

In truth, Indian leaders considered their support for exiled Tibetans' separatist activities as an effective containment against China. But when Prime Minister Rajiv Gandhi visited China in 1988 he issued the statement: 'The Indian side reiterates the long-standing and consistent policy of the Government of India that Tibet is an autonomous region of China and that anti-China political activities by Tibetan elements are not permitted on Indian soil,' which implied India's change of approach from that of support for Tibetan independence. Indian leaders reiterated this pledge after the Cold War ended and imposed limits on Tibetan fugitives' anti-China political activities.

For instance, Indian officials would generally contact the Dalai Lama and leaders of the so-called Tibetan government in exile before a visit by Chinese leaders to India, requesting that they refrain from Tibetan protests, demonstrations or other anti-Chinese behaviour.

Yet, differences still exist between China and India on the issue of Tibetan autonomy. Although, proceeding from the requirement of preserving stable Sino–Indian relations, the post-Cold War Indian government has been low-key in its support of the Dalai Lama and other Tibetan fugitives, this does not signify a substantial change in its strategic treatment of the Tibetan issue.

Changes in India's China Policy from 1999 to Present

Achieving recovery, contending for the status of global power had been India's ambition for decades. The growth of the sub-continent's comprehensive strength and improvements in the international environment in the late 1990s presented to it a real possibility of realizing this ambition, as well as a number of other unprecedented strategic opportunities.

Against this backdrop, reconciliation with China and the unchanged overall direction of the relationship produced several new adjustments to the positions and goals of India's China policy. At this stage, India saw China neither as enemy nor friend, believing that cooperation could coexist with competition between the two nations.

India still considered China as constituting no threat in the short term, but began focusing on long-term trends in the balance of power. The emphasis of the goals of its new China policy are on ensuring that future Sino–Indian relations are of benefit to India by making China a positive factor in the process of its rise. Maintaining the stability of Sino–Indian relations remains fundamental. The new policy adjustments are as follows.

Expand Economic Cooperation with China

Trade between the two nations ceased after the 1962 Sino–Indian Border Conflict, and did not resume until 1977. The volume of trade between the two sides in the 1980s wavered at around roughly Us." million. But after the Cold War ended, Sino–Indian trade experienced a seemingly spontaneous phase of rapid development. The trade volume between China and India increased from $264 million in 1991 to $1.988 billion in 1999—a yearly average of 31.2%—or an increase factor of 6.5

over eight years. Indian leaders' concerns about India's economic recovery nonetheless maintained at this point the China policy focus on stabilizing political relations and establishing tranquil borders. Indian leaders' understanding of economic strength and security having becoming more profound since 1999, their enthusiasm for developing bilateral trade soared.

As China and India were the world's two most rapidly developing nations, Indian leaders could see the obvious potential for trade between them and that strengthening bilateral trade would be of great mutual benefit. Also that close economic ties could have a stabilizing influence on their political relationship. Statistics show that bilateral trade since 1999 has entered into a new period of growth.

The average yearly growth to 2006 was 44.4%—a rate which exceeded that of the preceeding period and which is being achieved on an ever-stronger numerical foundation. The volume of Sino–Indian trade reached US$24.8 billion in 2006, having increased by a factor of 11.5 over 1999 and one of 93 over 1991. China became India's second largest trading partner in 2006, and India China's tenth largest. It may be said that the role of Sino–Indian trade has grown from one unworthy of mention to a decisive aspect of the overall bilateral relationship.

9

One Belt, One Road: A New Roadmap for a Sinocentric World

In May 2015, the National Development and Reform Commission, the Ministry of Foreign Affairs, and the Ministry of Commerce of the People's Republic of China jointly issued a document entitled "Vision and Actions on Jointly Building Silk Road Economic Belt and 21st-Century Maritime Silk Road," a highly strategic declaration endorsed by the State Council. This document is the final synthesis of the leadership's initiatives to promote trade cooperation between Asia, Europe, and Africa. The coordination center of this new global network, known as the "One Belt, One Road" (*yi dai, yi lu*) (OBOR) strategy or "New Silk Road" initiative, is located in Beijing, but the strategy as such is presented as a universal framework for global development and not a "Chinese" blueprint for a future regional and global order. Nonetheless, although China's new leaders spared no effort to convince the countries along the New Silk Road that the PRC is neither pursuing an expansionist foreign strategy nor trying to become a regional hegemonic center, in many surrounding countries China's new, active positioning is perceived as a potential threat to the existing regional and global power constellations and the institutional backbones of the post-WW II international system.

Given the old and new security spirals in East Asia and the PRC's sharp response to perceived violations of Chinese national core interests by Japan and its Southeast Asian neighbors, the fifth generation's foreign strategy has widely been categorized by the label "new assertiveness." This classification subscribes to neo-realist scenarios, which predict an inevitable clash between rising powers and the old power centersa1also involving the latter's (regional) allies. The theory narrative of "new assertiveness" is, thus, perceived by Chinese observers as a strategic attempt to contain China's rise by sowing distrust and spreading feara1and, hence, countered by "Chinese" narratives that construct a positive China image and present the country's international engagement as a contribution to peace and development.

In fact, China's positioning in regional and global affairs is strongly interwoven with domestic developments. The OBOR initiative, which includes two components, i.e. the New Silk Road Economic Belt as well as the 21 st Century Maritime Silk Road, is embedded in a top-level design (*dingceng sheji*) and, thus, follows a centralized master plan that links national and global dimensions of the PRC's domestic needs. It is, first of all, a growth-focused initiative that seeks to build a coherent infrastructure of transportation networks that link the Chinese economy to regional and global raw material suppliers and markets. Given the negative spillover of the financial troubles in the United States and Europe, the OBOR initiative is one among several strategic attempts to stimulate the Chinese economy and to maintain the stability of China's (political-economic) system by diversifying the network of China's regional and global partners. Furthermore, at the domestic level, the New Silk Road strategy seeks to modernize China's remote western provincesa1which in economic terms are far behind China's coastal areas, the current gravitational centers of China's modern economy. The New Silk Road, hence, includes nodal points of the historical Silk Roada1all situated in China's less-developed, western, peripheral provinces. But the New Silk Road also links China's domestic industrial centers, e.g. the Yangzi region, to the outside world.

OBOR is a Chinese response to perceived growing dependence and vulnerability of China's domestic (economic) development to changes occurring in its external (regional and global) environmenta1a response that does not secure the status quo but initiates a general transformation of China's national role-conceptions and its world order images. Seen from the outside, the announcement of China's OBOR initiative has re-activated the old debate on Sinocentrism, the role- identity of China as *tianxia* (literally: all under heaven) as well as the tributary system as the operational code of the Chinese empire's external relations. A revival of *tianxia* is expected to establish China as the only economical and political center in the Asian region: If the New Silk Road does have a focal point centered on Beijing, the ordering rules and general patterns could be expected to somehow mirror "Chinese" normative views and principled beliefs. Furthermore, the establishment of a strongly intertwined regional network of trade and financial cooperation would also imply that the PRC will have to engage in maintaining regional security and to protect its new trading lanes by expanding the mandate of its armed forces. This step, however, might trigger additional security spirals in the Asian region.

The tantalizing question to assess the drivers and main concepts behind China's 2013 OBOR initiative is how China's national role and world order conceptions have been redefined. Chinese foreign policy is still based on the Five Principles of Peaceful Coexistence; the PRC does, as underlined in diplomatic statements, not seek to achieve hegemony nor aspire to a leadership role. These articulated national role-conceptions stand in sharp contrast to the "international" debate on China's "new assertiveness" and the assumption of a remaking of the legendary "Sinocentric" Asian order.

Chinese Theory Debates

With regard to China's role-status or role-identity as an actor in the global realm, the PRC's elites are currently debating ways to upgrade China's international role (and influence) without simultaneously evoking the impression of inducing a role change of China from being a cooperative observer to becoming a coordinating, globally acting new power center. According to official speeches, the PRC has a "split," though loosely intertwined, role-identity as a developing country and a great power. A 2014 expert debate on *Fenghuang* (Phoenix Hong Kong) directly targeted the question whether China would seek to become an empire and, if yes, what role this "new" China would play in world affairs. Likewise, recent academic publications document a transformation of China from the role-identity of a "global big country" (*quanqiu daguo*) towards the new role and status of a "global power" (*quanqiu qiangguo*).

To understand the causal logic behind China's national role-conceptions and to assess its recent positioning as a global power, one has to take a closer look at internal academic theory debates on world order and world history. Three critical junctures in world history have accompanied China's rise to new global power status: the end of the Cold War 1989/1991 which, at least from a Chinese perspective, paved the way for the formation of a multipolar world order in which China is one of the major power centers; 9/11 and the following efforts to jointly combat terrorism that facilitated issue-specific cooperation between the United States and China; and the global financial crisis of 2007/2008, which strikingly illustrated that (financial) power has already shifted towards the Global South and symbolically marked the beginning of more self-confident positioning of the PRC in global affairs.

While the end of the Cold War, at least from a Euro-Atlantic point of view, had resulted in the formation of a unipolar power structure with the United States at its center, the latest global crisis of 2007/2008 and the perceived US decline have resulted in a turn to nonpolar world models. Both modelsa1unipolarity as well as nonpolaritya1are structures that, according to Chinese criticism, reflect the main US interests and US self-ascribed identity as a center of world politics. While the unipolar model provides the basis for US preeminence in world politics, the second notion, nonpolarity, introduces a new plurality of non-state actors that, effectively, counterbalance the rise of new power centers in the Global South and still conceives of the United States as the leader of world politics, although no longer in its role as a hyperpower.

By contrast, China's "idealized" images of a future world order area1at least according to official diplomatic statementsa1still based on multipolarity. Initially, this concept was coined to distinguish China's approach to world politics both from US unipolarity and the EU's multilateral pattern. Multipolarity is still one of the basic principles of Chinese foreign policy. The concept had originally been attributed to Deng Xiaoping (and Huang Xian), but had officially first been inscribed into China's foreign strategy by Jiang Zemin at the 14th Party Congress (1992). Multipolarity, following the orthodox definition given by the Ministry of Foreign Affairs, is opposed to "hegemony" and "power politics," aims at the establishment of "a just and equitable new international political and economic order" and "contributes to world peace and development." The original model consisted of five poles (USA, Russia, Europe/EU, Japan, and China). In 2001, Hu Jintao postulated that multipolarity had become a silent consensus among the international community of states, and he linked multipolarization to the idea of "democratization" of the international system that would grant equal rights of participation to all state-actors regardless of their current developmental status or political constitution.

The concept of "democratization of international relations" has been used since the late 1990s. In 2002, the 16th Party Congress integrated this notion into official foreign policy. The concept symbolizes a strategic reply to the strategy of democratization through constructive engagement. The model of a "democratization of international relations" openly criticizes the "dual standard" of democracy: Although the Western community of states is officially favoring democratic principles, the international system is, following the Chinese interpretation, identified as non-democratic and Western powers are hence accused of behaving as hegemonic power centers that monopolize the right to define and shape the rules of the game in international politics.

In political practice, the PRC seems to have acknowledged that the post-Cold War system is structured as "one superpower, many great powers."Instead of voting for a replacement of the still predominantly unipolar system, the PRC has proposed to construct a "harmonious world" (hejie shijie), which would transcend the polar structure of the international system.

WORLDVIEWS OF THE XI-LI ADMINISTRATION

China's fifth generation of political leaders, responding to the outcome of the global financial crisis, has started to reinterpret global power constellations and to adapt its visionary concept accordingly. These new worldviews reflect China's view of self and other as well as the images of other key players in the international system and of their world views. Shortly after taking up the position of general secretary in November 2012, Xi began using the term "Chinese Dream" (*Zhongguo meng*). To some observers this new notion might look like a re-making of the formula "a rich country, a strong army" (*fuguo, qiangbing*), which served as the ideological orientation for the Chinese self-strengthening movement that gained momentum in the decades following the Chinese empire's defeat by the West (and later also by Japan, in 1894a11895). A high-ranking colonel from the People's Liberation Army (PLA), Liu Mingfu, reactivated the use of this slogan with his well-received book *The Chinese Dream* published in 2010. So far, however, the notiona1as used by Xi Jinpinga1has remained rather opaque, and, thus, serves as a catch-all phrase that allows different groups within Chinese societya1namely the nationalist-assertive and the liberal-reformist onesa1to project their own ideas onto Xi's new slogan.

Xi's "Chinese Dream" is presented as a development model for China and the world and shows clear parallels to the twin concepts of "harmonious society" (*hexie shehui*) and "harmonious world." The former paradigm emerged at the 16th Party Congress (2002) as a follow-up to the earlier propagated "well-off society" (*xiaokang shehui*), and was continuously repeated in declarations made by the Hu-Wen government. In 2004 the

6th Plenum of the 16th Central Committee passed a resolution on some major questions surrounding the construction of a "harmonious society," defining the concept as a Chinese mode of good governance. While first used at the Asian-Africa Summit (April 2005), the concept of harmony was officially presented as a new guiding principle for global politics at the summit held to mark the 60th anniversary of the founding of the United Nations (September 2005). It replaced China's earlier concept of a "better world," formulated by Jiang Zemin during his speech at the 50th anniversary meeting of the United Nations. The "Chinese Dream" idea now combines the domestic and global dimensions of "harmony," and simultaneously addresses two audiences: the various actor groups within Chinese society and members of the international community.

Although this could be read as the transfer of the American Dream to the Chinese context, there remains one core difference between these two. While both describe the idea that everyone can make his own destiny by working hard to attain his goals, the "Chinese Dream" is not territorially bound. Even though it is deeply rooted in the Chinese context, the notion is also presented as a possible future scenario for the Asian region and world society. This clearly shows that China has taken the road towards becoming a global power. Previously reluctant to engage in issues of global governance, it is moving towards active participation in regional and global norm-building and the (re-)negotiation of the conceptual underpinnings of the existing world order. Domestic foreign policy discourse has in recent years been dedicated to developing frameworks of analysis and guidelines for political action that should allow China to effectively pursue its national interests through international cooperation and further integration into international trade.

Whereas the "harmonious world" paradigm had been criticized as an attempt to substitute for international norms and standards ordering principles derived from China's domestic governance concept, the idea of a common "dream" of wealth and power is obviously quite appealing to other rising powers and regional players from the Global South. Xi referred to this shared dream during his first trip abroad to Russia and South Africa.

Reinvention of the Tianxia and Revival of a Sinocentric Asia?

China's dream is first of all a dream of re-emergence to great power status and centre position. The way to achieve this goal, as Chinese politicians always underline, is a peaceful one and does not repeat the great tragedy of European power politics. The dream is linked to the reconstruction of "old" ordering principles rooted in Chinese history and philosophy.

Until the Opium Wars (First Opium War: 1839a11842), the "inter-national" order established by the Chinese empire was based on the idea of "all under heaven" (*tianxia*), the concept of China as the centre of the civilized world, with its external exchanges based on the tributary system. This traditional structural element established a hierarchy in the Chinese emperor's relations with other states and tribes. Depending on their geographical proximity to the Chinese empire and the degree to which they had assimilated and internalized "Chinese" norms and values, these actors were arranged in concentric circles around the power centre personified by the son of heaven. But the term *tianxia* signifies far more than just "empire": It merges the concept of the "state" and the "civilized world" into one.

A similar equation between "world" and "state-empire" has been documented for the *Imperium Romanum*. But despite all apparent similarities between the *tianxia* and the *orbis terrarium* regarding their claims to represent the "whole world," Chinese writings on the history of international relations stress that China and Rome chose different ways of constructing and sustaining their empires. Whereas the Roman Empire heavily relied on military expansionism and direct control over the conquered territories, the Chinese narrative conceives of the *tianxia* as a soft-power approach, based on the symbolic recognition of the charismatic authority of the Chinese emperor as prerequisite to engage in the exchange of goods. The Chinese empire did not collect taxes from its vassal states, but engaged in symbolic trade relations, which, in English language literature, has been classified as tributary relations. This stands in line with the proclaimed self- image of China as a peaceful and benevolent power in regional and world affairs.

Following the outbreak of the financial crisis, some Chinese scholars have started to undertake a selective reinterpretation of the *tianxia* and the Westphalian system. Their research begins from the assumption of a general incompatibility between "Chinese" and "Western" ordering principles.

The Westphalian order is linked with negative attributes: the international system is anarchic; nation-states compete against each other in zero-sum games; and wars and conflicts result from the absence of an ethical code of conduct. In contrast to this dark scenario the *tianxia* is depicted as a hierarchical but stable alternative blueprint for the 21st century, opposed to the "Western" concept of empire.

According to Zhao Tingyang, the *tianxia* concept might serve as a model for "world governance" as opposed to the failed concepts of international or global governance defined by the Westphalian order. His critics remark that this argumenta1the failure of the "Western" concept of global order and the moral superiority of the *tianxia*a1lacks empirical foundation and applies a dual standard to the evaluation of "Western" and "Chinese" IR concepts.His supporters, however, try to integrate Zhao's *tianxia* into global IR theorizing. They argue that Zhao's writings, which upgrade the *tianxia* from a regional institutional framework to an abstract global model, overcome the shortcomings of theory approaches that continue to rely on a state-centric construction of the international order.

In diplomatic practice, however, the PRC does not employ the *tianxia* concept, but rather refers to the idea of the "harmonious world" introduced by Hu Jintao in 2005. In contrast to Zhao's global model, this requires the existence and persistence of independent nation-states that remain the main actors in world politics. Rather than transferring sovereignty to a superior, common world government beyond the borders of the old nation-states, the "harmonious world" assumes the peaceful coexistence of divergent, multiple civilizations.

ONE BELT, ONE ROAD

The Silk Road Economic Belt and the 21st-century Maritime Silk Road, otherwise called The Belt and Road (shortened B&R), One Belt, One Road(abbreviated OBOR) or the Belt and Road Initiative is an advancement technique and structure, proposed by Chinese president Xi Jinping that spotlights on availability and collaboration among nations basically between thePeople's Republic of China and whatever is left of Eurasia, which comprises of two principle parts, the area based "Silk Road Economic Belt" (SREB) and oceangoing "Sea Silk Road" (MSR).

The procedure underlines China's push to play a greater part in worldwide issues, and its need to fare China's generation limit in territories of overproduction, for example, steel fabricating. It was uncovered in September and October 2013 in declarations uncovering the SREB and MSR, individually. It was likewise advanced byPremier Li Keqiang amid the State visit in Asia and Europe.

Infrastructure networks

The coverage area of the initiative is primarily Asia and Europe, encompassing around 60 countries. Oceania and East Africa are also included. Anticipated cumulative investment over an indefinite timescale is variously put at US$4 trillion or US$8 trillion. One Belt, One Road has been contrasted with the two US-centric trading arrangements, the Trans-Pacific Partnership and the Transatlantic Trade and Investment Partnership.

Silk Road Economic Belt

When Chinese leader Xi Jinping visited Central Asia and Southeast Asia in September and October 2013, he raised the initiative of jointly building the Silk Road Economic Belt and the 21st-Century Maritime Silk Road. Essentially, the 'belt' includes countries situated on the original Silk Road through Central Asia, West Asia, the Middle East, and Europe. The initiative calls for the integration of the region into a cohesive economic area through building infrastructure, increasing cultural exchanges, and broadening trade.

Apart from this zone, which is largely analogous to the historical Silk Road, another area that is said to be included in the extension of this 'belt' is South Asia and Southeast Asia. Many of the countries that are part of this belt are also members of the China-led Asian Infrastructure Investment Bank (AIIB). North, central and south belts are proposed. North belt goes through Central Asia, Russia to Europe. Central belt goes through Central Asia, West Asia to the Persian Gulf and the Mediterranean. South belt starts from China to Southeast Asia, South Asia, the Indian Ocean. Central belt is spoken down due to complex religion problems and separation movement along the belt.

Maritime Silk Road

The Maritime Silk Road, also known as the "21st Century Maritime Silk Road" is a complementary initiative aimed at investing and fostering collaboration in Southeast Asia, Oceania, and North Africa, through several contiguous bodies of water – the South China Sea, the South Pacific Ocean, and the wider Indian Ocean area.

The Maritime Silk Road initiative was first proposed by Xi Jinping during a speech to the Indonesian Parliament in October 2013. Like its sister initiative the Silk Road Economic Belt, most countries in this area have joined the China-led Asian Infrastructure Investment Bank.

East Africa

This region of Africa (In particular Zanzibar) will form part of the MSR after improvement of local ports and construction of a modern standard-gauge rail link between Nairobi and Kampala.

Closely related networks

The China Pakistan Economic Corridor (CPEC) and the Bangladesh-China-India-Myanmar (BCIM) Economic Corridor are officially classified as "closely related to the Belt and Road Initiative".

In coverage by the media, this distinction is disregarded and the networks are counted as components of the initiative. The CPEC in particular is often regarded as the link between China's maritime and overland silk road, with the port of Gwadar forming the crux of the CPEC project.

Financial institutions

AIIB

The Asian Infrastructure Investment Bank, first proposed by China in October 2013, is a development bank dedicated to lending for projects regarding infrastructure.

As of 2015, China announced that over one trillion yuan ($160 billion US) of infrastructure projects were in planning or construction. On 29 June 2015, the Articles of Agreement of the Asian Infrastructure Investment Bank (AIIB), the legal framework was signed in Beijing.

The proposed multilateral bank has an authorized capital of $100 billion, 75% of which will come from Asian and Oceanian countries. China will be the single largest stakeholder, holding 26% of voting rights. The bank plans to start operation by year end.

Silk Road Fund

In November 2014, Xi Jinping announced plans to create a 40 billion USD development fund, which will be distinguished from the banks created for the initiative. As a fund its role will be to invest in businesses rather than lend money for projects. The Karot Hydropower Station in Pakistan is the first investment project of the Silk Road Fund, and is not part of the much larger CPEC investment.

Oversight

The Leading Group for Advancing the Development of One Belt One Road was formed sometime in late 2014, and its leadership line-up publicized on February 1, 2015. This steering committee reports directly into the State Council of the People's Republic of China and is composed of several political heavyweights, evidence of the importance of the program to the government. Vice-Premier Zhang Gaoli, who is also a member of the 7-man Politburo Standing Committee, was named leader of the group, with Wang Huning, Wang Yang, Yang Jing, and Yang Jiechi being named deputy leaders.

In March 2014, Chinese Premier Li Keqiang called for accelerating the "One Belt One Road" initiative along with the Bangladesh-China-India-Myanmar Economic Corridor and the China-Pakistan Economic Corridor in his government work report presented to the annual meeting of the country's legislature.

Role of Hong Kong

On the eve of his 2016 policy address, Hong Kong chief executive CY Leung's announced his intention of setting up a Maritime Authority aimed at strengthening Hong Kong's maritime logistics in line with Beijing's economic policy. Leung mentioned the "one belt, one road" no fewer than 48 times during the policy address, but the amount of small detail presented in addition to the macro-economic measures related to "one belt, one road" which commentators considered to be irrelevant to Hong Kong people because it skirted over matters of importance to them.

Leung's apparent overemphasis was seen as a sycophantic promotion of Xi Jinping's concept, and was widely lampooned. The anchor ofTVMost, Dong Fong-sing, satirised it using a Chinese homonym – "one covered, one exposed" instead of "one belt, one road"– in a photograph of him half-wearing a brassiere in which one of his nipples was exposed. An op-ed in *Wen Wei Po* said CY Leung was "horrendously scandalised" by the picture, which was considered obscene.

CHINA'S ONE BELT AND ONE ROAD STRATEGY AND SILK ROAD

Since India does not have the assets today to set up contending systems, it might be advantageous to take an interest in those parts of the OBOR which may enhance Indian network to significant markets and asset supplies

The surely understood geopolitical scholar Halford Mackinder proposed in 1904 that the inward zone of Eurasia – described by inside or polar waste and impervious via ocean power – was bound to be the "Turn Area" of world legislative issues. It was his view that the tenet over the heart of the world's most noteworthy landmass would turn into the premise for global control, inferable from the prevalence of rail over boats as far as time and reach. Russia and China, in the event that they met up, he anticipated, could defeat the sea world.

The course of the First World War led him in later years to modify his initial perspective. In looking at the shape of the post-World War II order, he foresaw a world geopolitically balanced between a combination of the North Atlantic, or what he termed as Midland Ocean, and the Asian heartland powers. In effect, he conceded that geopolitical dominance required both a continental as well as a maritime dimension. Another important geopolitical theorist, Alfred Mahan, also had a Eurasian centred global perspective, but his emphasis was on maritime power mediating between a two-fold global framework – a Western and an Oriental system. Against this backdrop, what we may currently be witnessing is a carving out by China of a continental-maritime geo-strategic realm constituted by its initiative labeled 'One Belt and One Road', also known as the Belt-Road Initiative and the abbreviation OBOR.

The belt manifests the continental dimension of this geo-strategic realm. It consists of a network of rail routes, overland highways, oil and gas pipelines and other infrastructural projects, stretching from Xian in Central China, through Central Asia and Russia, with one artery crossing Kazakhstan and the other through Mongolia but both linking up with the trans-Siberian railway and going on to Moscow, Rotterdam and Venice.

The road is the maritime dimension and consists of a network of ports and other coastal infrastructure from China's eastern seaboard stretching across South East Asia, South Asia, the Gulf, East Africa and the Mediterranean, forming a loop terminating at Piraeus (Greece), Venice (Italy) and Rotterdam (Netherlands) in Europe and Mombasa (Kenya) in Africa.

Both the Road and the Belt include regional loops and branches which extend the reach of the emerging transportation networks but also serve to tie the Road to the Belt at critical points. Thus the China-Pakistan Economic Corridor is significant precisely because the port of Gwadar is one of the points where the Road and the Belt intersect. Of interest to India is the branch constituted by the BCIM corridor, which proposes to connect Yunnan in southern China with Myanmar, Bangladesh and eastern India.

More than just routes

The OBOR is not only about putting in place physical infrastructure, although this is an indispensable component of the initiative. The 'Vision and Actions on Jointly Building the Silk Road Economic Belt and 21st-Century Maritime Silk Road' document – announced by the China National Resource and Development Commission and the Ministry of Foreign Affairs in March this year – sets out the overall rationale behind the initiative.

According to Zhang Gaoli, Vice Premier and head of the high level group charged with piloting the project , its objectives are:

- Enhancing policy coordination across the Asian continent;
- Trade liberalisation;
- financial integration; and
- Connectivity including people to people links.

The document describes OBOR as "a systematic project which should be jointly built through consultation to meet the interests of all and effort should be made to integrate the development strategies of the countries along the Belt and the Road".

Thus the initiative is seen as an instrument to create a contiguous land and maritime zone where countries pursue convergent economic policies, underpinned by both physical infrastructure and supported by trade and financial flows. The inclusion of people to people links is a recognition that soft power will play an important role in creating a congenial political environment for the sustained roll-out of the ambitious initiative.

The document further states, "The initiative to jointly build the Belt and the Road enhancing the trend towards a multi-polar world, economic globalisation, cultural diversity and greater IT application, is designed to uphold the global free trade regime and the open world economy in the spirit of open regionalism".

Thus the OBOR may also be seen as China's response to the more exclusive mega-economic blocks in the making, the Trans-Pacific Partnership (TPP) in Asia and the Transatlantic Trade and Investment Partnership or T-TIP, both of which are led by the United States. The Road, for example, is explicitly oriented towards South East Asia, while Europe is the destination of the Belt. The OBOR, therefore, represents an alternative and supposedly more inclusive economic architecture led by China, competing with that promoted by the United States. The document says:

"The Belt and the Road run through the continents of Asia, Europe and Africa, connecting the vibrant East Asia economic circle at one end and developed European economic circle at the other, and encompassing countries with huge potential for economic development."

It should be apparent from these Chinese pronouncements that China sees the twin-dimensional initiative as a long-term project to secure its geo-strategic realm, which has both a continental and a maritime dimension. It is not just an economic initiative. It has obvious political and security implications. In any case, China's strategists do not draw lines separating economic and security objectives. Each dimension reinforces the other, even though the economic dimension may sometimes mask the security imperative.

A key road map for the Chinese economy too

Having spelt out its vision and a broad plan of action, China is now focusing on the deployment of the next phase, identifying "key directions, key countries and key projects".

It may be worth mentioning at this point another major Chinese strategic plan labeled as "Made in China 2025" which seeks to transform the country from a "world factory to a world manufacturing power, complete with innovative products and manufacturing processes". Made in China 2025 fits in neatly with the OBOR initiative. Li Teng, the CEO of Bank of China International claimed recently that OBOR "will push China to transform from low-end commodity export to high-end commodity exports, capital and technology exports".

The OBOR is therefore part of an economic strategy that will enable China to deal with the problem of massive overcapacity in its industry. The infrastructure to implement OBOR will require vast amount of construction materials and capital equipment, sectors where China has vast unused capacity.

There will also be an incentive to export skilled and semi-skilled labour employed in these sectors, also rendered surplus by a slowing Chinese economy. Furthermore, such infrastructural investment will require significant financial flows. The OBOR initiative is underpinned by the Chinese led Asian Infrastructure Investment Bank (capital of $100 billion), the BRICS New Development Bank (capital of $50 billion but may rise to $100 billion) and a proposed Shanghai Cooperation Organisation Financing Institution.

A dedicated Silk Road Fund of $40 billion has also been established to finance projects under the initiative. Part of the China-Pakistan Economic Corridor project comprising of roads, railways and Gwadar port totalling $11 billion will be financed from this Fund. The Chinese business paper, *Caixin*, reports that China will draw upon its substantial foreign exchange reserves to inject $62 billion of capital into the state-owned "policy banks" in support of the OBOR initiative. Half of the amount will go to the China Development Bank and $30 billion to the China Exim Bank. The residual amount will be available to the Agricultural Development Bank of China. Therefore, a significant stream of finance is available to fund projects under the OBOR.

One important motivation behind OBOR is to accelerate the development of the country's relatively poorer western and southern provinces. It has been reported that a sum of $20 billion is available for infrastructure and cross-border projects in the provinces which will be linked to the 'Belt' component of the initiative, in particular Sichuan, Gansu and Qinghai on China's western flank and Yunnan on the southern flank. Thus Chongqing in Sichuan is being established as the starting point of one of the branches of a rail freight corridor, linking it with the German city of Duisburg. Another freight corridor will link Beijing with the port city of Hamburg, while a third corridor is proposed linking Wuhan with an as yet unidentified terminus in Europe. It is apparent that China has managed to secure the participation of Russia in the Eurasian component of the initiative, overcoming the earlier hesitations in Moscow about China muscling Russia aside in what the latter regards as its "near neighbourhood". China has attempted to fold the OBOR into the Russian-led Eurasia Economic Union, which currently groups together Russia, Armenia, Belarus, Kazakhstan and Kyrgyzstan as well as into the Shanghai Cooperation Organisation. A Russian statement has welcomed the initiative, claiming that Siberia, Kazakhstan, Central Asia and the western provinces of China "are the natural centre of Eurasia". At the last SCO summit, Chinese President Xi Jinping said that his country would push for the completion of 4,000 kms of railways and 10,000 kms of highways within the region and that $16 billion of the Silk Road Fund would be dedicated to projects in Central Asia.

There are two significant energy projects linking Russia and China. One is the much publicised $400 million "Power of Siberia" pipeline and the other is the Altai gas pipeline connecting west Siberia to China. However, it is reported that both these projects may be delayed due to shortage of funds promised by China.

Why Europe matters for China

An important aspect of OBOR which has not been much in focus so far is the European end of the Belt and the Road, which is integral to securing China's influence both on the eastern and western flanks of Eurasia. There are carefully selected nodal points along the land corridor and terminal points along the maritime corridor. For example, Hungary has been chosen as a key logistics hub on the trans-Siberian link. It may serve as a distribution point for Chinese exports to Europe and an aggregating point for imports from Europe.

China has taken advantage of the Greek economic crisis to establish itself at the strategic port of Piraeus. The Chinese Shipping Company, COSCO, has a 35-year concession to expand the port by adding two modern container terminals.

It is likely to bid for the 67% Greek government stake in the port, when it is fully privatised. Greek shipping tonnage is one of the largest in the world and most ships for Greek shipping lines are built in China, which has the world's largest ship building industry. Piraeus will thus serve as a major logistics hub for Chinese trade with Europe. China is planning a Land-Sea Express which will link Piraeus with points on the European mainland. A $2.5 billion project is envisaged to build a key high speed rail link from Piraeus into Western Europe.

Another major European terminus is the Dutch port of Rotterdam, which is one of the most important cargo hubs for the entire continent. Like Gwadar in Pakistan, Rotterdam is the other point where the Belt and the Road on the land and maritime corridors come together. This, too, is projected as a major logistics centre for China-Europe trade.

The third terminal is Hamburg in Germany, although details of Chinese activities or investments there are not known yet. In addition, to Piraeus and Rotterdam, China has set up three major logistics and transport hubs, one at Wigan (Manchester) in the UK and two more at Schiphol airport, Amsterdam in the Netherlands. The latter will connect with the nearby port of Rotterdam.

Recently, during Premier Li Keqiang's visit to Brussels, China announced its readiness to invest in Europe's new infrastructure. It may contribute funds to the Juncker-sponsored Euro 315 billion European Fund for Strategic Investment. It should come as no surprise if China invests in those projects which are aligned to its OBOR objectives.

One should also add that the OBOR project also includes a Digital Silk Road and a Silk Road in Cyber Space. There is a proposal for a cooperative Internet Plus Plan which would link the OBOR countries to a super-fast broadband network.

China attaches great importance to promoting financial integration among countries along the OBOR. It seeks to do this both through the setting up of institutions (such as the AIIB and the NDB) and the deployment of substantial sums. In this context, the UK has become a key platform for the internationalisation of the renminbi, the creation of an off-shore yuan bond market and the spread of Chinese banking in Europe. Apart from the Wigan logistics hub referred to earlier, London has become China's preferred centre for the launch of yuan-denominated bonds.

China has invested in the redevelopment of real estate in the British capital and will guarantee $3 billion for the proposed nuclear power station in Hinckley. Several British banks have been favoured with licenses to operate in China. The British head start is leading to competitive courting by other European financial centres such as Frankfurt and Paris. Thus China sees Europe as helping it to put in place a sophisticated financial network which could underpin the ambitious physical networks that will bind Eurasia together.

This aspect is important because it could – and probably already has – weakened the trans-Atlantic alliance which has been a stable and predictable feature of geopolitics since the end of the Cold War. The British rush to join the AIIB followed by several other European powers, against US opposition, was a clear indication of this emerging trend. The longer it takes for the TTIP to be actualised, the greater the chances of China's Eurasian project succeeding.

What's in this for India?

While looking at the emerging geo-political landscape, Saul Bernhard Cohen, in his book*Geopolitics*, envisages the emergence of three strategic realms this century. One is the US-dominated maritime world of the North Atlantic and the North Pacific Basin; there is the second realm of Maritime Europe, organised around the European Union, and a Continental Asia geo-strategic realm covering the Eurasia landmass with Russia as the original core. But, as pointed out earlier, China has emerged as a separate Continental Maritime realm, shrinking the space for Russia in Central Asia and for the US in the North Pacific. There is an incipient effort to co-opt Russia on the one hand and Europe on the other to confine the US to the American hemisphere. The playing out of this story has major implications, because in case China succeeds with the global strategy underlying OBOR, India may well be consigned to the margins of both land and maritime Asia or become, by compulsion or by choice, a subordinate component of the Chinese-dominated network that is, in the words of Foreign Secretary S. Jaishankar, "hard-wiring" the new world.

Interestingly, Cohen foresaw a time when India, like China, could carve out a fourth geo-strategic realm also continental/maritime in nature. This it would do by dominating the eastern and western reaches of the Indian Ocean and the sub-continental landmass, south of Eurasia but linked to it. If this were indeed possible then India would have an opportunity to deal with the challenge of the Chinese geo-strategic realm on its doorstep with greater room for manoeuvre. I have argued before and do so again: If there is one country which has the potential to catch up with China and even overtake it, it is India. The current asymmetry is not riven in stone. What it will take India to achieve this long-term goal is well-known and I will not repeat it.

Currently, India has neither the resources nor the political and economic weight to put in place competitive and alternative connectivity networks on a global scale. Therefore, for the time being, it may be worthwhile to carefully evaluate those components of the OBOR which may, in fact, improve India's own connectivity to major markets and resource supplies and become participants in them just as we have chosen to do with the AIIB and the NDB.

For example, building a road/rail link to Central Asia through Iran using the port of Chahbahar could then use Chinese built routes to access both Central Asian and Russian destinations as well as Europe. It may be more important to deploy our limited resources to build an Indian Ocean network of ports, with connecting highways and rail routes such as exemplified by the planned Mekong-Ganga corridor and the Sittwe-Mizoram multi-modal transport corridor. There have been longstanding plans to develop the deep water port on Sri Lanka's eastern coast, Trincomalee, as a major energy and transport hub and yet, despite the warning message in the shape of Chinea building the Hambantota port in southern Sri Lanka and expanding the Colombo port, virtually no work has been undertaken since Indian Oil acquired the tank farm located at the port. The Andaman and Nicobar Islands lie at the very centre of the Bay of Bengal and could be developed to serve as a regional shipping hub for the littoral states and beyond. And yet, India continues to treat these islands as a distant outpost rather than leveraging their unique location at the very centre of one of the most strategic stretches of ocean space. There has been much talk about India launching a Spice Route, a Cotton Route and even a Mausam project tying the countries around the Indian Ocean bound together by the monsoon winds. Instead of spreading our limited resources thinly over these mostly rhetorical ripostes to China's OBOR, it may be more prudent to focus on limited but strategically key routes and ports along our adjacent seas and islands to safeguard our most important equities.

To recapitulate, the first priority would be developing our own Andaman and Nicobar Islands as a modern transport and shipping hub for the Bay of Bengal Basin. At the next level would be Chahbahar port to the west with road/rail links to Central Asia; Trincomalee port to the east, with shipping links to the Bay of Bengal littoral ports and beyond; the Mekong-Ganga corridor linking India's east coast with Indo-China; and the Kaladan multi-modal transport corridor in Myanmar's Rakhine province, including the port of Sittwe. The proposed BCIM corridor could then become part of this broader network. Once this primary circle has been secured one could move on to progressively expanding circles as resources become available. What is important to note is that in this 21st century strategy, security and economics go together. Creating a dense web of economic and trade relations itself becomes an assurance of security.

It is fair to say that China, in deploying the OBOR initiative, has demonstrated a level of ambition and imagination which is mostly absent in India's national discourse. It is time both scholars and practitioners started to think and act strategically on issues such as OBOR which will have a significant impact on India's vital interests.

HISTORICAL PARALLELS: THE OLD QUEST FOR STATUS AND IDENTITY

The utopian construction of the (regional and global) world from a Chinese perspective is not just a phenomenon of the 21st century, but has its historic roots in the late 19th and early 20th centuries, when s intellectual elites struggled to rebuild China's territorial integrity and its national sovereignty. Among these literati-scholars was Kang Youwei, who, opposed to most of his contemporaries, did not pledge an overthrow of the Confucian norms, but instead favored a constitutional monarchy based on a reformed and modernized Confucianism. In his *Datongshu*, Kang drafts an utopian world community without any frontiers or territoriesa1a global community beyond the nation-state, similar to a reformulation of the *tianxia*, this time not as a local, but as a universal, global order.

The ideational background of his utopian imaginary is to be found in the *Liji*, which contains a whole chapter on the ideal order of society (*Liyun*). The passage describes the decline of the old order and the subsequent transition from the era of the *datong* (great unity) to the *xiaokang* (well-off) society. The *Gongyang* Commentary on the *Liji*, on which Kang Youwei bases his utopia, argues that the development from *datong* to *xiaokang* is reversible. The return to the paradise lost, the old order, has ever been and continues to be a guiding principle in Chinese state philosophy. One of the most prominent examples is Sun Yatsen, the founding father of the Chinese Republic, who referred to the passage "tianxia wei gong" (in the sense: all under heaven form a communality) from the *Liji* to illustrate his vision of China's future state constitution.

Taking into account the historical circumstances under which Kang Youwei and Zhao Tingyang propagated their visionary models of a world order as derived from Chinese philosophy, it is more than obvious that, in both cases, these utopian models are part of an ongoing and unfinished state-building process. The *Datongshu* was written in the shadow of the national humiliation by external forces and the growing internal dispute over the right path to modernize China. Only after the abolition of the unequal treaties, forced upon the Chinese empire during the Opium Wars, did China regain its status as a sovereign state. But the quest for rebuilding its old power position continues and determines China's politics to date.

During the late 19th century, various streams of intellectual thought influenced the understanding of the "nation" and the "state," ranging from Marxism to anarchism and Social Darwinism. Quite a few influential afterthoughts on the ideal society and good governance criteria were authored by Kang Youwei's disciple Liang Qichao. The rejuvenation of the Chinese "nation" was one of Liang's central contributions to the Chinese intellectual debate on the modernization and reform of the Chinese empire (first dimension of the *tianxia* model). Even though the Westphalian concept of the sovereign nation-state has had a lasting effect on China's positioning in international politics, the self-image as a "civilizational state," displaying the legacy of China's imperial past, is still discernible in contemporary Chinese writings on international politics. According to Zhang Weiwei, who counts as one of China's most influential contemporary intellectual thinkers, a "civilizational state," in contrast to a nation-state, does not rely on military-based expansion. It does not copy any other state's or empire's development model, and the guidelines of its strategic behavior are derived from its owna1and distincta1cultural traditions and historical patterns.

The debate about a "Chinese" world order model finally reveals itself as a continuation of the late imperial intellectual debates on self-strengthening and reform. Furthermore, it is at the same time also a variation of the "China model" debate, which Chinese scholars trace back to the writings of Deng Xiaoping. The term "China model" stands for a pragmatic and flexible development approach that integrates market economic principles into the overarching frame of planned economy and stands for high-speed economic growth. It is often contrasted with the "Washington Consensus," a normative condition-based approach to national development, and presented as an alternative orientation model for the developing world.The OBOR initiative is not based on coercion, but uses financial, monetary incentives to generate diffuse support for the Chinese model.

A New Type of Great Power Relations and New Neighborhood Policy

Chinese political analysts generally measure the world and international power relations in terms of comprehensive national power (CNP). On this matrix, the United States is still ranked as the world's number one superpower. However, recent reflections about a potential power shift occurring have started to move the internal debates in a new direction. This power transition scenarioa1though generally backed as being the new "trend of the era," or in Chinese Marxist terminology as "mirroring the objective development laws of history"a1is a source of major concern for Chinese scholars involved in the shaping of China's official foreign strategy. From their perspective, the decline of the United States could throw the world into chaos if no other state steps in and up to fill the power vacuum left behind.

Chinese scholars are grappling with various scenarios and almost unanimously conclude that the future is most likely to be found in a multipolar order with one predominant player, the United States (thus reversing the order of China's formula "one superpower, many great powers"). Unipolar structuresa1in other words, ones centered on the United Statesa1and bipolar structuresa1such as the USa1USSR power antagonisma1are seen as being unstable and conflict-laden.

The likely future development of Chinaa1US relations is seen as a key determinant of Chinese foreign policy. The international debate speculates about a possible struggle for hegemony between the United States and China. To avoid the emergence of a regional or global security dilemma, Chinese scholars thus advocate the idea of a cooperative relationship being formed between these two powers. Already prior to being promoted to the highest levels of political power, Xi Jinping, in his function as the PRC's Vice President, visited the United States in February 2012 and proclaimed that a "new type of great power relations" was emerging. Later, both State Councilor Dai Bingguo and Hu Jintao, in his function as president, would use the same formulation at several meetings held between China and the United States. Simultaneously, the PRC has started to pay more attention to events in its close neighborhood: This "new" neighborhood policy, however, generally confirms China's commitment to the Five Principles of Peaceful Coexistence.

Conclusion

Perceptions of self and other as well as utopian visions of idealized world order, not quantifiable power shifts as such, are the main drivers behind states' positioning in the still changing post-crisis world order. Some observers have argued that China's rise in the wake of the global financial crisis might result in a substitution of existing principles and paradigms of international politics by "Chinese" norms. Others, again, assume that China's integration into the globalized world economy will socialize the country into the existing international order. Communitarian approaches, which seem more apt to cover these complex global realities, would predict a new synthesis of the normative beliefs propagated by the "West" and those of the "Asian" hemisphere.

Norm-making and norm-taking are causally interwoven with the distribution of power in the international system among major players involved. Soft power, status recognition, and access to participation in regional and global bargaining rounds are key determinants of a country's international positioning strategy. The PRC's demand to have equal access to norm-bargaining (*huayuquan*) is clear evidence of China's shift from the role of observer to active participant.

Chinese commentaries and background notes on the OBOR initiative, which combines regional and global dimensions of China's foreign strategy, outline that the New Silk Road project should not be taken as a Chinese Marshall Plan nor as a geopolitical calculation to establish China as a new hegemonic power center. The narratives formulated as conceptual backbones of China's OBOR initiative reiterate the rhetorical patterns of China's imaginary *tianxia* as an idealized model of a harmonious regional and global ordera1offering an alternative to the "Western" tradition of zero-sum power games and global order based on means of coercion. The regional and global network of trade and investment financed and coordinated by the OBOR initiative operates with the attractiveness of the unconditional financial support offered to all countries willing to join the "Chinese" network. This abstract master frame of the OBOR initiative shows direct analogies and parallels to the "Chinese" reconstruction of the *tianxia* model. However, the current debates on OBOR avoid linking it to the idea of hierarchy, which had been an integral element of the "historical" Sinocentric order. Having carefully studied the history of the rise and fall of great powers, China's elites have turned to a post-polar master frame of world order that is composed of a network built around various major nodal points, which can only function if cooperation prevails over conflict and containment. While (economic, financial, monetary) power might currently be shifting in favor of China, the PRC remains concerned that new threat perceptionsa1as manifested in the debates on China's "new assertiveness" or the remaking of a "Sinocentric order"a1could lead to containment measures that would threaten the implementation of China's national development interests. Therefore, China's OBOR initiative is presented as being in the interests of humankind as such; official statements have even started to operate with the term "community of shared destiny."

China's senior policy advisers recommend abstaining from pursuing too self-confident positioning as this would reactivate threat perceptions by others and fuel uncontrollable radical waves of nationalism at home. Cai Liang proposes to coin the PRC's new role-identity under the fifth generation as one of "constructive reformer" (*jianshexing de gaigezhe*), a formula that reverberates with the US strategy of "constructive engagement."

The Chinese outline of the OBOR initiative illustrates that confrontational leadership claims are seen as being potentially harmful to China's national development goals. Leadership, i.e. the act of taking over the role of a regional or global centre, can only be exerted, if other players accept this claim and behave as cooperative followers. Confronted with rising anti-Chinese resentment among China's regional neighbors the PRC's foreign strategy works based on the assumption that national core interests can best be implemented through cooperative networks in which China acts as a fierce advocate of certain group interests, i.e. those of developing countries or rising economies.

While the final result of China's network activities might be the re-emergence of China as a powerful economic and, in the long run, political center in the East Asian region and beyond, the formation of a new unipolar "Sinocentric" world order is rather unlikely to happen. First of all, power competition among the (East) Asian actors and the interference of external players, the United States and Russia, into regional politics lead to an implicit fragmentation of the regional order instead of integration. Secondly, power constellations are continuously changingaland given that China is facing unsolved domestic socio-economic imbalances and is severely vulnerable by shifts in its external environment, its power position is far from stable. Finally, claiming a centre position might imply that China would have to shoulder more responsibilities and to "pay" for maintaining the stability along the New Silk Road. A networked regional and global order, by contrast, would grant China participation in the configuration of global norms and standards, but would always come with an opting-out option. China's OBOR initiative, to quote the PRC's Minister of Foreign Affairs, should not be taken as a "solo," but as a contribution to a regional and global "symphony."

Bibliography

Ajey Lele: *Strategic Technologies for the Military : Breaking New Frontiers*, Sage, Delhi, 2009.

Allen Carlson, *Unifying China, Integrating with the World: Securing Chinese Sovereignty in the Reform Era,* Stanford: Stanford University Press, 2005.

Amitabh Sikdar: *India and China : Strategic Energy Management and Security*, Manas, Delhi, 2009.

Anil, K.C.: *Military and Democracy in South Asia : Challenges, Politics and Power*, Sumit Enterprises, Delhi, 2009.

Atar Singh Jadoan: *Military Geography of South East Asia*, Anmol, Delhi, 2001.

Bhat, T.P. : *India and China : Trade Complementarities and Competitiveness*, Bookwell, Delhi, 2008.

Chuh, Kandice and Karen Shimakawa. *Orientations: Mapping Studies in the Asian Diaspora.* Durham, NC: Duke University Press. 2001.

Conway, G. 1992. *Sustainable Rural Livelihoods: Practical Concepts for 21st Century.* Sussex: Institute of Development Studies.

Deepak, B R : *India and China : 1904-2004 : A Century of Peace and Conflict*, Manak, Delhi, 2005.

Diamond, Jared M. *Guns, Germs, and Steel: The Fates of Human Societies.* New York: W. W. Norton & Co. 1998.

Digumarti Bhaskara Rao: *Military Conversion : Impact on Science and Technology*, Discovery, Delhi, 2003.

Dixit, A.K. : *Military Wars and Rescue Techniques*, Cyber Tech Pub, Delhi, 2010.

Evelyn Goh, *Meeting the China Challenge: The U.S. in Southeast Asian Regional Security Strategies*, DC: East-West Center, 2005.

Friedman, G.: *The Future of War: Power, Technology and American World Dominance in the 21st Century*, N.Y., Random House, 1996.

Fu, Chunjiang, and Liping Yang. *Chinese History: Ancient China to 1911*. History Express. Singapore: Asiapac Books. 2006.

Gao, Mobo: *The Battle for China's Past: Mao and the Cultural Revolution,* London, Pluto Press, 2008.

Garraty, John Arthur, and Peter Gay. *The Columbia History of the World*. New York: Harper & Row. 1972.

Gautam, P.K. : *Environmental Security : New Challenges and Role of Military*, Shipra, Delhi, 2010.

Hansen, Valerie: *The Silk Road: A New History,* Oxford University Press; 2012.

Harrison, Selig: *China, Oil and Asia: Conflict Ahead*. New York: Columbia University Press, 1992.

Heathcote, T. A.: *Indian Ocean – The Garrison of British Imperial India, 1822–1922*. David & Charles. Newton Abbot, Devon. 1974.

Huntington, S.P.: *The China Modernisation Military and the State,* N.Y., Vintage Books, 1964.

Jackson, Major Donovan: *India's Navy*. Sampson Low. London, 1940.

Jagannath P. Panda: *China's Path to Power : Party, Military and the Politics of State Transition*, Pentagon, Delhi, 2010.

Johnston, Douglas: *The Theory and History of Ocean Boundary Making*. Kingston: McGill-Queen's University Press, 1988.

Jones, W.H.: *The Government and Politics of Indian Military*, London, Hutchinson, 1971.

Kuzmina, E. E.: *The Prehistory of the Silk Road*. University of Pennsylvania Press, Philadelphia. 2008.

Major Donovan: *Indian Ocean*. Sampson Low. London, 1940.

Marie Lecomte : *Hindu Kingship, Ethnic Revival, and Maoist Rebellion in Nepal*, Oxford University Press, Delhi, 2009.

Mary, W.: *Military Space Force: the Cultural Dimensions of Authority*, Cambridge, Belknap Press, 1985.

Namboodirim, P. : *Intervention in the Indian Ocean,* New Delhi: ABC Publishing House, 1982.

Neil Frank R.: *The Philippines and the South China Sea Islands: Overview and Documents*. Metro Manila: Foreign Service Institute, 1993.

Park Hee Kwon: *The Law of the Sea and Northeast Asia*. The Hague: Kluwer, 2000.

Peter Lambron Wilson : *Traditional Modes of Contemplation and Action*, University Press, Tehran, 1977.

Posen, B.R.: *The Sources of Indian Navy Doctrine*, Ithaca, 1984, Cornell Univ. Press.

Prabla, Dixit: *Communalism: A Struggle for Power*, New Delhi, Orient Longman, 1981.

Raj Kumar: *Weapons and Military Technology*, Sumit Enterprises, Delhi, 2009.

Randall Forsberg: *The Arms Production Dilemma: Contraction and Restraint in the World Combat Aircraft Industry,* Cambridge, Massachusetts: MIT Press, 1994.

Rhodes, Richard, *The Making of the Atomic Bomb*, New York: Simon and Schuster, 1988.

Rosen, P.: *Societies and Military Power: India and its Armies*, Ithaca, Cornell University Press, 1996.

Sam Bateman: *Maritime Change: Issues for Asia.* St. Leonards: Allen & Unwin, 1993.

Samuel P. Huntington: *The Soldier and the State : The Theory and Politics of Civil-Military Relations*, Natraj Pub, Delhi, 2005.

Samuels, Marwyn: *Contest for the South China Sea.* New York: Methuen, 1982.

Shaun Narine, *Explaining ASEAN: Regionalism in Southeast Asia*, Boulder, CO: Lynne Rienner Publishers, 2002.

Stephen Bates : *Calming the Waters. Initiatives for Asia Pacific Maritime Cooperation.* Canberra Papers on Strategy and Defence, 1996.

Thapa, Deepak : *Understanding the Maoist Movement of Nepal*, Centre for Social Research and Development, Delhi, 2003.

Thubron, C.: *The Silk Road to China,* Hamlyn, 1989.

Vice Admiral Mihir K. Roy: *War in the Indian Ocean.* New Delhi: Lancer Publishers. 1995.

Watson, William. *China Before the Han Dynasty.* New York: Praeger. 1962.

Wilborn, Thomas L.: *International Politics In Northeast Asia : The China-Japan-United States Strategic Triangle.* Carlisle Barracks, PA: Strategic Studies Institute, 1996.

Wishnick, Elizabeth: *Mending Fences: The Evolution of Moscow's China Policy from Brezhnev to Yeltsin.* Seattle: University of Washington Press, 2001.

Index

E

F

G

H

I

L

M

N

O

P

Q

R

S

T

◆◆◆